The Rule of Women in Early Modern Europe

The Rule of Women in Early Modern Europe

Edited by
ANNE J. CRUZ AND
MIHOKO SUZUKI

University of Illinois Press
URBANA AND CHICAGO

Manufactured in the United States of America
1 2 3 4 5 C P 5 4 3 2 1

This book is printed on acid-free paper.

Library of Congress Cataloging-in-Publication Data
The rule of women in early modern Europe / edited by Anne J. Cruz
and Mihoko Suzuki.
p. cm.
Papers from 2005 Medieval, Renaissance, and Baroque conference
held at University of Miami.
Includes bibliographical references and index.
ISBN 978-0-252-03416-9 (cloth : alk. paper) — ISBN 978-0-252-07616-9
(paper : alk. paper)
1. Queens—Europe—History—Congresses.
2. Queens—Europe—Biography—Congresses.
3. Monarchy—Europe—History—Congresses.
4. Women—Europe—History—Congresses.
5. Sex role—Europe—History—Congresses.
6. Women in politics—Europe—History—Congresses.
7. Europe—Kings and rulers—History—Congresses.
8. Europe—Politics and government—1492–1648—Congresses.
9. Europe—History—1492–1648—Biography—Congresses.
I. Cruz, Anne J., 1941– II. Suzuki, Mihoko, 1953–
D226.7.R85 2009
940.2092'2—dc22 2009010875

Contents

Acknowledgments vii

Introduction 1
Anne J. Cruz and Mihoko Suzuki

PART I: THE RULE OF WOMEN: THEORIES AND CONSTRUCTIONS

1. Notions of Late Medieval Queenship: Christine de Pizan's Isabeau of Bavaria 13
Tracy Adams

2. "Satisfaite de soy en soy mesme": The Politics of Self-Representation in Jeanne d'Albret's *Ample déclaration* 30
Mary C. Ekman

3. *Tanto monta:* The Catholic Monarchs' Nuptial Fiction and the Power of Isabel I of Castile 43
Barbara F. Weissberger

4. Sword and Wimple: Isabel Clara Eugenia and Power 64
Magdalena S. Sánchez

5. "Princeps non Principissa": Catherine of Brandenburg, Elected Prince of Transylvania (1629–30) 80
Éva Deák

PART II: SOVEREIGNTY AND REPRESENTATION

6. Juana of Austria: Patron of the Arts and Regent of Spain, 1554–59 103
Anne J. Cruz

7. Elizabeth I as Sister and "Loving Kinswoman" 123
Carole Levin

8. Fashioning Monarchy: Women, Dress, and Power at the Court of Elizabeth I, 1558–1603 142
Catherine L. Howey

9. Thrice Royal Queen: Katherine de Valois and the Tudor Monarchy in *Henry V* and *Englands Heroicall Epistles* 157
Sandra Logan

10. Warning Elizabeth with Catherine de' Medici's Example: Anne Dowriche's *French Historie* and the Politics of Counsel 174
Mihoko Suzuki

11. History, Power, and the Representation of Elizabeth I in *La Princesse de Clèves* 194
Elizabeth Ketner

Selected Bibliography 205

Index 217

Acknowledgments

We would like to thank everyone who made this volume possible: first and foremost, our contributors, as well as those who attended the 2005 Medieval, Renaissance, and Baroque conference on "The Rule of Women" at the University of Miami. Donna E. Shalala, president of the university, fittingly welcomed the participants. We also thank Joan Catapano at the University of Illinois Press for her early interest in our project and the support and help she provided us throughout the process. Michael Halleran, the Dean of Arts and Sciences at the University of Miami, generously granted us funds for indexing.

The Rule of Women in Early Modern Europe

Introduction

ANNE J. CRUZ AND MIHOKO SUZUKI

> If we grant that men deserve praise whenever they perform great deeds with the strength bestowed upon them, how much more should women be extolled—almost all of whom are endowed by nature with soft, frail bodies and sluggish minds—when they take on a manly spirit, show remarkable intelligence and bravery, and dare to execute deeds that would be extremely difficult even for men?
>
> —Boccaccio, *Famous Women*

> I could tell you countless other examples . . . we do not need to go any further to seek examples from history: you yourself saw in childhood the noble Queen Jeanne, widow of King Charles, the fourth of that name. As you recall her, remember this lady's good deeds to which her fame attests, as much in the noble arrangement of her court as in both customs and the maintenance of sovereign justice. Never has any prince been as renowned as this lady for having so upheld justice and preserved her land's prerogatives.
>
> —Christine de Pizan, *The Book of the City of Ladies*

This volume seeks to contribute to the growing scholarship on women's sovereignty in early modern Europe, building on the important studies on the topic that have appeared in the last decade. As Merry Wiesner-Hanks has pointed out, the early modern debate about the "nature and proper role of women . . . also became one about female rulers, sparked primarily by dynastic accidents in many countries that led to women serving as advisers to child kings or ruling in their own right."[1] Yet the greater part of feminist scholarship on women's rule during this period has heretofore focused on the most prominent sovereigns, such as Isabel of Castile and Elizabeth Tudor.[2] A pair of recent studies on Marguerite de Navarre focuses attention on a queen who was also an important author in a number of literary genres.[3] By juxtaposing essays on rulers in different countries, some lesser known, but whose sovereignty nevertheless deserves attention (Isabeau of Bavaria, Jeanne d'Albret,

Isabel Clara Eugenia, Juana of Portugal, and Catherine of Brandenburg) as well as examining the representation of foreign rulers (Catherine de' Medici in England, Elizabeth I in France), we seek to bring a transnational and transcultural perspective on a topic that has until now been largely studied through the lens of a single nation.[4]

Originating from classical and medieval treatises on the (male) nature of monarchy, accepted but evolving understandings of gender and politics spurred debates about women's ability to exercise the virile qualities necessary for good government such as virtue, valor, and intelligence. Contemporary historians took advantage of social anxieties concerning female rule to interrogate the concept of female sovereignty, alternately condemning and eulogizing women rulers for their female characteristics and their purportedly manly behavior. As an example, Boccaccio's *De mulieribus claris* (*On Famous Women*) reveals his ambivalence toward three women sovereigns who lived in postclassical times. Boccaccio seeks to endow exceptional women with the same fame enjoyed by men, in order to equal his "teacher" Petrarch's biography of famous men.[5] Yet unlike his praise for women of antiquity—and although they are duly celebrated for their astuteness, integrity, and "glorious rule"—the sovereigns' actions in his stories nevertheless fall short: Irene, empress of Constantinople, removes her son with "feminine cunning" to occupy the throne herself; Constance, empress of Rome and queen of Sicily, is famous because of her "monstrous" pregnancy with her only son; and Joanna, queen of Jerusalem and Sicily, is generous "in the manner of a king rather than of a woman."[6]

Nevertheless, Renaissance treatises on women's virtues were influenced positively by Boccaccio's narratives. In fact, Christine de Pizan's *The Book of the City of Ladies*, which was intended in part as a response to Boccaccio's catalogue of notorious women, gave an extensive account and numerous examples of female rulers throughout history. In particular, she emphasized examples from French history, such as Fredegonde, whom she praised for her "wise government" and Blanche of Castile, regent during the minority of Saint Louis, for governing France "so nobly and so prudently that it was never better ruled by any man."[7]

Although the arguments both for and against female rule would continue, early modern humanists supported women's education, especially for future monarchs. One of the earliest examples of a "mirror for princesses" is that of the Augustinian friar Martín de Córdoba for the adolescent princess Isabel of Castile. His brief treatise *Jardín de nobles doncellas* (*Garden of Noble Maidens*) intended to prepare Isabel for the Spanish throne, the right to which Isabel wrested from Juana, the daughter of her brother Enrique IV in 1469.

Both Peggy Liss and Barbara Weissberger have shown, however, that despite Córdoba's strong support of Isabel's accession, the treatise perpetuates the traditional view of woman's frailty and her necessary submission to a husband.[8] Similarly, Juan Luis Vives's treatise on female education, *De Institutione Feminae Christianae* (*The Instruction of a Christen Woman)* written for Mary Tudor, the daughter of Catherine of Aragon and the granddaughter of Isabel of Castile, remains, for some critics, ambivalent toward women's education, in that it condemns women's public roles.[9] Others who consider Vives an advocate for women's learning nevertheless agree that he subscribed to the contemporary view that women should not depart from their domestic functions.[10] Sir Thomas Elyot's *Defence of Good Women* (1540) and Agrippa of Nettesheim's *De nobilitate et praecellentia sexus foeminei* (1509), dedicated to Margaret of Austria and translated into English as *Of the Nobilitie and Excellencie of Womankynde* (1542), functioned as responses to Vives in affirming woman's capacity to rule.[11]

During the sixteenth century, the issue of women's sovereignty became difficult to elide, as queens assumed thrones across the continent, as well as in England and Scotland. Whether they acted as consorts, regents, or regnants, women's political roles were deliberated not only in didactic treatises, but in pamphlets, popular poetry, and drama. John Knox's *The First Blast of the Trumpet against the Monstrous Regiment of Women,* written in 1558, had as its main purpose the defense of Protestantism, threatened by the reign of four women: Catherine de' Medici, Marie de Lorraine, Mary Queen of Scots, and, in particular, Mary Tudor; he claimed that a woman would "pollute and prophane the royalle seate, the throne of iustice, which oght to be the throne of God."[12] John Aylmer, Lady Jane Gray's tutor, was unconvincing in his response to Knox, *An Harborowe for Faithful and Trewe Subjectes* (1559), because he defended Elizabeth's rule by stating that male counselors would control a female monarch's tendency to fall into excessive passion.[13]

The matter in question, however, was not whether women were unsuited to govern, despite Knox's contention that such an act "rebell[ed] against God," since, at mid-century, Spain, England, Scotland, France, Navarre, and the Netherlands were all under female rule. Rather, the issue pressed by most male authors was that women's rule should be predicated on the imitation of and submission to that of men. The discourses that circulated on this topic, both popular and learned, were intended, for the most part, to allay male anxieties about female sovereignty by exhorting women to behave "as women" even while lauding them for acting in a virile manner. To counter this negative opinion, which limited their performance and compelled them to submit to their fathers, husbands, or brothers, women rulers tirelessly promulgated their own empowerment through propaganda from their chroniclers and by means of symbolic imagery such as portraiture, entries, and devices.

In order to investigate the various political, discursive, and symbolic measures employed to negotiate and support female sovereignty in early modern Europe, the essays in this collection focus on women rulers in France, England, Spain, and Hungary as exemplars of women who came to power and maintained their positions in spite of open or covert political opposition. Boccaccio concludes that he writes about so few women because "so small is the number of those who are outstanding."[14] Unlike his *Famous Women,* our collection of essays on women rulers is not limited solely by actual number, but by space. While several of the essays deal with the two most well-known women rulers in early modern Europe, Isabel of Castile and Elizabeth I of England, others select as their subjects women who held power as princesses, regents, and governors. They seek to analyze specific processes through which these female sovereigns seemingly adhered to contemporary beliefs about women's rule, yet also responded, explicitly and implicitly, to the many attacks brought against them because of their gender. Some of our contributors examine the ambiguity in the terminology of sovereignty (i.e., whether the titles "prince" and "duke" can be held by women); others redefine the concept of "rule" beyond the exclusively political to include a woman's agency in governing her own will and body.

The collection is composed of two parts, "The Rule of Women: Theories and Constructions," and "Sovereignty and Representation." The first addresses the numerous discursive and symbolic strategies by which contemporary writers and frequently the sovereigns themselves attempted to justify and even exalt their rule. The second part investigates the material and affective methods through which women rulers established their sovereignty as they dealt with members of their court and family, and examines the representation of female sovereignty in theater and political writings to serve as a cautionary message to other women rulers.

The first essay, "Notions of Late Medieval Queenship: Christine de Pizan's Isabeau de Bavaria" by Tracy Adams, analyzes the protofeminist work of Christine de Pizan as a strong endorsement of queenship. Through a careful reexamination of contemporary documents, Adams persuasively demonstrates that Isabeau's negative reputation as queen arose only after her death and could not have been the basis of Christine's writings addressed to her. Rather, Adams argues that these writings were meant to be read aloud by the public as "mirrors of magistrates" to promote the idea of a powerful woman ruler as an effective mediator for peace. The placement of Christine's writings in a specific historical context enhances our understanding of both her political theory concerning women's rule and the role of women in late medieval France when the monarchical system was under siege.

The act of self-defense on the part of the sovereigns required great rhetorical skill to maintain the balance between submission and subversion. In "'Satisfaite de soy en soy mesme': The Politics of Self-Representation in Jeanne d'Albret's *Ample déclaration*," Mary C. Ekman examines the "memoir" of d'Albret, daughter of Marguerite de Navarre and mother of Henri IV, and an important leader of the Huguenots. By publishing the work shortly after writing it, d'Albret intended it as a political self-justification, through which she asserts her loyalty to her subjects, her fellow Protestants, her family, and the king of France. She thus explains her rebellion against the monarch as motivated by her loyalty to him. Deploying literary and rhetorical devices while presenting her account as unvarnished and truthful, d'Albret constructs herself as an agent with multiple subject positions effectively negotiating the politics of the Reformation.

Although Jeanne d'Albret's memoirs conformed to a long-standing tradition of writings that defended and validated women's political actions, many women rulers left only letters to relatives in which they expressed their opinions on policy. These forms of communication were frequently insufficient to develop and sustain close ties with political allies. Female sovereigns moved within concentric circles of power: from the court, to the immediate urban surroundings, past the city walls, and beyond the borders of their reign. The more separated and distant they were from their subjects, the more they were compelled to maintain their image and represent themselves through visual and material means. Barbara F. Weissberger's essay, "*Tanto monta:* The Catholic Monarchs' Nuptial Fiction and the Power of Isabel I of Castile," addresses the complex system of public imagery created by Isabel to negotiate resistance to female rule. Focusing on the devices of the royal couple, the yoke and arrows, with the motto "*tanto monta,*" the essay states that the royal devices were circulated by the monarchs to ensure the perception of their joint monarchy. Displayed on architecture, coins, and domestic items such as tapestries and book covers, the conjoined devices substantiated the monarchs' unity. Yet the two rulers were far from equal, since Isabel reigned over the largest and richest kingdom in Spain. Her appropriation of the masculine symbolism initially carried by the yoke and arrows, Weissberger suggests, stands as much for her defiance of gender roles as for her acceptance of the unifying power of the symbols. That these symbols continued to be used by Franco's fascist regime confirms Isabel's influence over political propaganda well into the twentieth century.

Isabel of Castile's appropriation of the masculine symbolism initially held by the yoke and arrows is emulated by her great-granddaughter's use of the sword and wimple. Philip II's daughter, Isabel Clara Eugenia, was named after an empress, a queen, and a princess—her great-grandmother, Isabel of Castile; her grandmother, the Empress Isabel of Portugal; and her mother, Isabel de Valois, daughter of Henri II of France. Despite her beauty and her status as daughter of the world's most powerful monarch, Isabel Clara Eugenia remained unmarried until her father planned her wedding to Albert of Austria so both could serve as cosovereigns of the Netherlands. Magdalena S. Sánchez's essay, "Sword and Wimple: Isabel Clara Eugenia and Power," suggests that her joint rule of the Low Countries with Archduke Albert was carried out indirectly, leaving the major issues of government to him. After Albert's death in 1621, she agreed to remain in the less important position of governor. Yet Sánchez notes that through a series of symbolic ceremonies and acts, Isabel Clara Eugenia took precedence as sovereign over Albert, following the example of Isabel of Castile. Sánchez shows that as her status evolved from coruler to governor, Isabel Clara Eugenia assumed a more direct role in government. Throughout her lengthy rule in the Netherlands, she effectively negotiated her traditional role as wife even as she exercised her influence and power as sovereign.

Although most studies of early modern Europe have paid scant attention to Central Europe, female rule extended beyond the Western Continental nation-states and Britain. Éva Deák gives a rare and important account of the theory and practice of women's sovereignty in early modern Hungary in "'Princeps non Principissa': Catherine of Brandenburg, Elected Prince of Transylvania (1629–30)." Although she ruled for only a year after her husband's death, and was compelled to abdicate in favor of her husband's brother, Catherine was designated as her husband's successor and duly elected by the diet. Her brief sovereignty highlights the contradictory beliefs concerning women's ability to rule: sister of the elector George William, she was highly educated as a "princely woman" and her marriage contract established a large court of her own as well as her succession. Although the Ottoman sultan accepted her election, her rule was limited by the governor and the council, and she was considered unfit to rule because of her gender during the country's military crisis.

The second part of the collection, "Sovereignty and Representation," centers on the practice of political power by women and the ways that practice was often held up as an example to other sovereigns. The essays by Anne J. Cruz, Catherine L. Howey, and Carole Levin argue that women rulers held strong feelings for their relatives and friends, creating familial bonds through their care and gifts. Yet they often expected complete loyalty in return, and as in the case of Elizabeth I's execution of Mary Stuart, they were capable of abandoning familial relations for political motives. Their success in the public realm came at the price of grave personal losses caused by their accession to power.

Anne J. Cruz's essay, "Juana of Austria: Patron of the Arts and Regent of Spain, 1554–59," begins by calling attention to Juana's filial obedience on leaving her only son in Portugal to serve as regent of Spain. On her arrival from Portugal, however, she served as surrogate mother to her brother Philip II's children and his young wives, enlivening the Philippine court with her patronage of the arts. Although she gave up her own right to rule as queen mother in Portugal, during her regency in Spain, she rebelled against the mandates of her father and her brother and proved to be an adept ruler despite their attempts to control her and insidious attacks led by her religious adversaries.

Carole Levin's "Elizabeth I as Sister and 'Loving Kinswoman'" examines the relationships Elizabeth had with her siblings, Mary and Edward. While Elizabeth often used the rhetoric of family to emphasize her good will toward fellow monarchs, her relationships with her actual siblings were fraught and ambivalent due to their competing claims for power. In her letters to Edward, Elizabeth addressed a younger brother who was at the same time her sovereign. When Mary ascended to the throne, she treated her younger sister with great affection, but she soon repudiated their kinship: she eventually accused Elizabeth of participating in a rebellion against her and imprisoned her in the Tower. Elizabeth enjoyed less complicated and more positive relationships with her cousins (who may have been her half siblings), such as Catherine Carey, who became her close friend, and Henry Carey, whom she ennobled and promoted.

In "Fashioning Monarchy: Women, Dress, and Power at the Court of Elizabeth I, 1558–1603," Catherine L. Howey calls attention to the importance of gift exchange as a way for Elizabeth to assert sovereignty on the one hand, and on the other for her subjects to affirm and consolidate political loyalty. Howey examines Elizabeth's gifts to her courtiers upon her coronation, the New Year's exchange of gifts between the queen and her subjects—which were carefully recorded—and exchanges between the queen and foreign sovereigns and ambassadors as tools of statecraft. Assessing the political role of the gentlewomen of the queen's privy chamber in directing the gifts to be given and managing the gifts received, she concludes that through the system of gift exchange, women actively participated in the network that supported Elizabeth's sovereignty.

Female sovereigns were often forced to remain under the protection, if not domination, of their male relatives, and their status was often questioned and diminished in plays that emphasized male protagonists. In "Thrice

Royal Queen: Katherine de Valois and the Tudor Monarchy in *Henry V* and *Englands Heroicall Epistles,*" Sandra Logan calls attention to the contradiction between Katherine de Valois's multiple roles vis-à-vis the monarchy—as daughter, sister, wife, widow, and mother—which gave her access to considerable political power, and her erasure from English genealogical and historical representations in order to assert the "Englishness" of the royal succession. To this end, Logan examines her complex representations as a young princess—who functions as a pawn between her vanquished father and the victorious English king—in Shakespeare's *Henry V* and as a widow wooing Owen Tudor, her union with whom established the Tudor line in Michael Drayton's *Englands Heroicall Epistles.*

While male writers such as Shakespeare may have diminished the importance of queens, women writers such as Anne Dowriche and Madame de Lafayette acknowledged their power, although they did not always celebrate it. They nevertheless saw the rule of women as an opportunity, not only to critique the sovereign's behavior, but to use her history as an admonishment to others. Mihoko Suzuki suggests, in "Warning Elizabeth with Catherine de' Medici's Example: Anne Dowriche's *French Historie* and the Politics of Counsel," that Dowriche's work functions as a political intervention, specifically concerning Elizabeth's relation to the Catholic French monarchy and to Protestant forces, both foreign and domestic. By representing Catherine de' Medici as a Machiavellian ruler who was instrumental in launching the St. Bartholomew's Day Massacre, Dowriche ostensibly calls attention to the contrast between Catherine and Elizabeth; yet the inescapable similarities can be read as an implicit critique of Elizabeth (who was allied with the French) and an exhortation to separate herself from duplicitous and tyrannical Catholic monarchs. As a member of a family of Members of Parliament, Dowriche seeks to counsel Elizabeth on policy and statecraft, although she carefully uses indirection to avoid the dire fate of those who spoke and wrote too directly.

Elizabeth Ketner's "History, Power, and the Representation of Elizabeth I in *La Princesse de Clèves*" sheds new light on the political meanings of Madame de Lafayette's novel concerning the court of Henri II. The allusive references to Elizabeth Tudor present her as an analogue and foil to Mademoiselle de Clèves, in that they both renounce love and marriage to protect their autonomy. At the same time, Ketner demonstrates that Elizabeth's execution of Mary Stuart exemplifies the dangers of absolutism. Thus, this figure of an English queen from the past enables Lafayette to critique the tyrannical rule of the contemporary French king Louis XIV, who closely scrutinized all writings published during his reign.

In 1995, Pauline Stafford called for a "gender-aware discussion" of "the link between the exercise of women's power and its presentation."[15] The essays in our collection focus on the often contradictory relationship between the theory and practice of women's sovereignty: as corulers, both Isabel of Castile and Isabel Clara Eugenia were publicly subordinate to their husbands, yet they effectively called attention to their political power through various kinds of symbolism. Called by her father Charles V to serve as regent of Spain, Juana of Austria was obligated to abandon her position as queen mother in Portugal. Although, in France, Salic law proscribed women's rule, female sovereigns such as Jeanne d'Albret and Catherine de' Medici became powerful rulers.[16] By contrast, in the case of Catherine of Brandenburg, a duly elected regent was unable to exercise effective sovereignty and was forced to resign. Even a legitimately recognized and publicly supported queen such as Elizabeth Tudor found herself compelled to execute Mary Stuart to protect her sovereignty and was accused, implicitly, if not explicitly, of being a tyrant, not only by male subjects but also by female writers in both England and France. While previous studies of women rulers have tended to emphasize positive aspects of female sovereignty even when acknowledging the constraints under which they ruled, these essays seek to explore further the often complex and vexed situation of the woman ruler in early modern Europe.

Notes

1. Merry Wiesner-Hanks, "Women's Authority in the State and Household in Early Modern Europe," in *Women Who Ruled: Queens, Goddesses, Amazons in Renaissance and Baroque Art,* ed. Annette Dixon (London: Merrell; Ann Arbor: University of Michigan Museum of Art, 2002), 29–30.

2. On Elizabeth, see Carole Levin, *The Heart and Stomach of a King: Elizabeth I and the Politics of Sex and Power* (Philadelphia: University of Pennsylvania Press, 1994); Susan Frye, *Elizabeth I: The Competition for Representation* (New York: Oxford University Press, 1996); John Watkins, *Representing Elizabeth in Stuart England: Literature, History, Sovereignty* (Cambridge: Cambridge University Press, 2002). On Isabel, see Barbara F. Weissberger, *Isabel Rules: Constructing Queenship, Wielding Power* (Minneapolis: University of Minnesota Press, 2004); Peggy Liss, *Isabel the Queen: Life and Times,* rev. ed. (Philadelphia: University of Pennsylvania Press, 2004).

3. Barbara Stephenson, *The Power and Patronage of Marguerite de Navarre* (Aldershot, UK: Ashgate, 2004); Patricia Francis Cholakian and Rouben C. Cholakian, *Marguerite de Navarre: Mother of the Renaissance* (New York: Columbia University Press, 2005).

4. With the exception of Louise Olga Fradenburg's *Women and Sovereignty* (Edinburgh: Edinburgh University Press, 1992) and Theresa M. Vann's *Queens, Regents and Potentates* (Cambridge, UK: Academia, 1992)—the former focusing on the medieval and early modern periods, and the latter on the medieval period—even the most recent essay collections of female sovereignty during this period tend to focus on a single nation. See, for example,

Carole Levin, Jo Eldridge Carney, and Debra Barrett-Graves, eds., *"High and Mighty Queens" of Early Modern England: Realities and Representations* (New York: Palgrave, 2003); Clare McManus, ed., *The Courts of the Stuart Queens* (New York: Palgrave, 2003); Theresa Earenfight, ed., *Queenship and Political Power in Medieval and Early Modern Spain* (Aldershot, UK: Ashgate, 2005). The subject of the essays in Barbara Garlick, Suzanne Dixon, and Pauline Allen, eds., *Stereotypes of Women in Power: Historical Perspectives and Revisionist Views* (Westport, Conn.: Greenwood, 1992), range from ancient Egypt to late twentieth-century Australia, focusing on, in the title of the conclusion, "The Enduring Theme: Domineering Dowagers and Scheming Concubines." A collection on a time frame later than ours is Clarissa Campbell Orr's *Queenship in Europe 1660–1815: The Role of the Consort* (Cambridge: Cambridge University Press, 2004).

5. Giovanni Boccaccio, *Famous Women,* ed. and trans. Virginia Brown. The I Tatti Renaissance Library (Cambridge, Mass.: Harvard University Press, 2001), 9. Francesco Petrarca, *De viris illustribus,* ed. Guido Martellotti (Florence: G. G. Sansoni, 1964).

6. Boccaccio, *Famous Women,* 443, 455, 471.

7. Christine de Pizan, *The Book of the City of Ladies,* trans. Earl Jeffrey Richards, rev. ed. (New York: Persea, 1998), 33–34.

8. Liss, *Isabel the Queen,* 56; Weissberger, *Isabel Rules,* 32.

9. Constance Jordan, *Renaissance Feminism: Literary Texts and Political Models* (Ithaca, N.Y.: Cornell University Press, 1990), 117–19. See the recent editions of Juan Luis Vives, *The Education of a Christian Woman: A Sixteenth-Century Manual,* trans. Charles Fantazzi (Chicago: University of Chicago Press, 2000); *The Instruction of a Christen Woman,* eds. Virginia Walcott Beauchamp, Elizabeth H. Hageman, and Margaret Mikesell (Urbana: University of Illinois Press, 2002).

10. Timothy Elston, "Transformation or Continuity? Sixteenth-Century Education and the Legacy of Catherine of Aragon, Mary I, and Juan Luis Vives," in Levin et al., eds., *"High and Mighty Queens,"* 11–26.

11. Jordan, *Renaissance Feminism,* 119–26. For a modern edition of Agrippa, see *Declamation on the Nobility and Preeminence of the Female Sex,* ed. Albert Rabil, Jr. (Chicago: University of Chicago Press, 1996).

12. John Knox, *The First Blast of the Trumpet Against the Monstruous Regiment of Women* (1558; Amsterdam: Orbis Terrarum; New York: Da Capo Press, 1972), 47v.

13. See Ann McLaren, *Political Culture in the Reign of Elizabeth I: Queen and Commonwealth 1558–1585* (Cambridge: Cambridge University Press, 1999), chap. 2, for an analysis of the exchange between Knox and Aylmer that finds more similarities than differences between the two.

14. Boccaccio, *Famous Women,* 473.

15. Pauline Stafford, "More than a Man, or Less than a Woman? Woman Rulers in Early Modern Europe," *Gender and History* 7, no. 3 (1995): 490.

16. See Éliane Viennot, *La France, les femmes et le pouvoir: L'invention de la loi salique (Ve–XIe siècle)* (Paris: Perrin, 2006), who points out that the original laws of the Salian Franks did not in fact exclude women from ruling. She then goes on to examine the effect of this fabricated prohibition on French society and culture from the fifth through the sixteenth centuries.

PART I

The Rule of Women

Theories and Constructions

1. Notions of Late Medieval Queenship

Christine de Pizan's Isabeau of Bavaria

TRACY ADAMS

Isabeau of Bavaria, queen of mad King Charles VI of France at the turn of the calamitous fourteenth century, had two lives: although esteemed by her contemporaries, she has long been depicted in modern popular and scholarly histories as a scandalous figure who carried on multiple affairs, including one with her brother-in-law, Louis of Orleans, who pronounced her own son Dauphin Charles a bastard in the Treaty of Troyes in 1420, and who was cupidinous, slothful, obese, and recklessly negligent of her children.

Over the past two decades, some historians have revised the queen's black legend, tracing its origins to the English, who, after the Treaty of Arras of 1435 reconciling the French and the Burgundians, sought a new justification for Henry VI's claim to the French throne. But legends die hard. Many scholars working in tangential areas, such as the Hundred Years War, Joan of Arc, Charles VII, queenship, and Christine de Pizan, either perpetuate the myths about Isabeau or, if they recognize them to be false, assume that they circulated already during the queen's lifetime.[1] The tenacity of the black legend haunting this unfortunate queen can be attributed partly to the fact that her rehabilitation offers no obvious return. Although as a representative of royal power her support was sought by the factions competing for power in the vacuum created by the king's insanity, she seems to have been regarded as an easily deflected inconvenience by both, and the sudden death of her son, Dauphin Louis of Guyenne, whom she was grooming for kingship, at the age of eighteen in 1415, terminated her life's work to a large extent. Considered unimportant, her story has most often functioned as a sort of digression in larger analyses where it is not central to the work's overall purpose.

Yet, as I will suggest here, even though the queen's story is only peripheral to the major events of the early fifteenth century, her black legend has caused distortion. In this chapter, I would like to consider its effects upon Christine de Pizan scholarship, arguing that it has obscured a major purpose of that poet's defense of women. In a number of her works, Christine promotes a significant role for women in political life, creating a model for the conciliatory but clever mediator/regent capable of holding warring factions together. Given the brutal struggle for power between the king's male relatives, the dukes of Orleans and Burgundy, that was taking place when Christine wrote and the presence of a queen well known for her peace-making ability, it seems clear that the poet's defenses of women were meant to promote Isabeau as a safeguard against the ambitions of the unruly dukes. However, a negative image of Isabeau entered Christine scholarship via the French historians upon whom the first Christine scholars relied, and, once embedded in the historical narrative of Christine's life, the queen became a sort of metonymy for court life, seen as frivolous and corrupt.[2] The misperception about the queen's reputation among her contemporaries has prevented Christine's defense of women from being historically contextualized and its relevance to the political events of the day from being recognized.

Isabeau of Bavaria

Before considering Christine's Isabeau in more detail, I will briefly recount the events of the queen's life relevant to the reading of Christine's writings on women that I am proposing. Elisabeth von Wittelsbach, as she was known in her native Bavaria, was born in 1370 to Stephan, later Duke Stephan III, of Bavaria (1337–1413), and Thaddea Visconti, daughter of Bernabo Visconti, Lord of Milan. The Valois sought her as a bride for Charles VI in 1385 to counterbalance the marriage between Anne of Bohemia, of the House of Luxembourg, traditional ally of the Valois, and Richard II of England. Archrival of the Luxembourgs for control of the office of Holy Roman Emperor, the House of Wittelsbach became the Valois's ally through the marriage.

The first seven years of Isabeau's marriage, during which she bore the first five of her twelve children, appear to have been calm and happy. However, her life changed forever on an August morning in 1392 when her husband, en route to Brittany where he intended to carry out a military expedition against the duke of Brittany, suffered his first known episode of the insanity that would lead to terrible strife and eventually to the civil war between the Armagnacs and the Burgundians. Although he recovered from this first attack within a few days, inspiring hope that the incident would be isolated, this was not to be. Over the years, the episodes occurred with increasing frequency and lasted longer, lingering for months at a time.

The king's incapacity occasioned a struggle for control of the government between Charles's uncle, Philip, Duke of Burgundy, and his younger brother, Louis, Duke of Orleans. Early on, Philip monopolized the government, painting an image of his nephew as immature, debauched, and spendthrift, but as Louis matured, the young man became increasingly powerful and challenged his uncle with growing intensity.[3] From 1392 to 1402, Isabeau, whose continued childbearing undoubtedly impeded her entrance into politics during this period (she bore another five children), played little visible role in the conflict, although she generally followed Philip of Burgundy, whose goals coincided with those of her family on the major matters of the day: the interrelated problems of the political situation in Italy, the Great Schism, and the struggle between the Wittelsbachs and the Luxembourgs for the imperial crown.

The rivalry between the dukes created warring factions and raised the fear that one of the dukes, prevailing over the other, would assume total control over the king. During his lucid moments, Charles responded to the threat by creating ordinances aimed at lessening the possibility that any one individual could amass sufficient power to impose a form of *tutelle* upon him or his heir, in the case of his death. His earliest strategy for avoiding such a seizure of power was to create ordinances to distribute influence between a council of tutors and a regent in the event of his death. In January 1393, he named Isabeau coguardian of the royal children. She would share the task with the dukes of Burgundy, Berry, Bourbon, and her brother, Louis of Bavaria.[4] At the same time, in a second ordinance, he awarded regency to Louis of Orleans.[5] In this arrangement, Charles clearly followed the lead of his father, Charles V, who had also separated the two functions of *tutelle* and regency, with the intent of balancing power by dividing it among different people.[6] However, the arrangement exacerbated the strife it was designed to calm, for while the regency ordinance said nothing about governance during the king's periods of indisposition, Louis used it to proclaim himself ruler during the king's absences, a claim that Philip denied.[7]

Charles next tried to diminish the rivalry by assigning Isabeau to arbitrate between the dukes during his absences. He did this first in an ordinance of March 1402.[8] In July of the same year, he augmented her authority with an ordinance that reauthorized her to mediate between the unruly relatives and furthermore authorized her to preside over the royal council during his periods of debility.[9] This theoretically imposed equality upon the two dukes as leading members of the council, while installing Isabeau as impartial president over both. However, the struggle continued. In April 1403, Charles tried yet another strategy, passing ordinances stipulating that all decisions during the king's absences be made by majority rule of the council.[10] Isabeau remained president of the council, with the difference that responsibility for decisions was now shared equally by all members.

However, more significant for Isabeau, the ordinances dealt with anxiety surrounding the regency in a new way by abolishing it altogether: if the king died, there would be no official regent. Instead, the kingdom would be safeguarded by a body of counselors governing in the name of the minor king, as opposed to a regent governing in his own name until the king came of age. Presumably, a corporation would be unable to usurp the throne but an individual might do so. As for Isabeau, the ordinances of 1403 in effect elevated the potential power of the Queen Mother. Because there would no longer be a male regent occupying the highest office in the land, the Queen Mother, who would be part of the governing counselors, would be able to wield tremendous influence through her son.

Philip's death in 1404 might have spelled the end of conflict. However, the new Duke of Burgundy, John the Fearless, quickly appeared on the scene, determined to take up his father's position. Supported by the Parisians and the university, who believed him to be a reformer, his demands were treated as attempts at usurpation by Louis and the council. Philip and Louis had been equals, each of the two men possessing a legitimate claim to power in the absence of a competent king. Son of King John the Good and brother of King Charles V, Philip's credentials were identical to those of Louis, who was also the son of and brother to a king. John the Fearless, in contrast, mere cousin of the king, was not entitled to a position equal to that of Louis. With Philip's death, Isabeau, according to a common modern perception, abandoned the House of Burgundy for the House of Orleans. This reading cannot be accepted. Isabeau, like Louis and the council, viewed John as overstepping his rank, and her reaction was to block the Duke of Burgundy from setting Louis aside to assume the regency. She spells out her own position in a treaty with John, stipulating that she will defend John, but only as far as appropriate within their family hierarchy, where Louis's interests must precede John's.[11] John did not retreat. Rather, he continued Philip's program of demanding money from the royal treasury all the while publicly denouncing the mismanagement of government funds under Louis. On November 23, 1407, the struggle between the dukes culminated in the assassination of the Duke of Orleans by John's order, a catastrophic event that set in motion a cycle of violence and revenge the effects of which would be felt for nearly one hundred years.

The story of Isabeau's political career between the assassination of Louis and her entry into the Treaty of Troyes, which made Henry V of England the heir of Charles VI, depriving the king's son (later Charles VII) of the throne, is a complex and fascinating one. However, my argument concerning Isabeau's place in Christine's defense of women requires only that the queen's story be traced up to the assassination and that special note be taken that Charles VI's ordinances abolishing the role of regent would give a great deal of power to the Queen Mother if the king died leaving a minor son. I will conclude this section by noting that after the Treaty of Troyes, Isabeau moved to English-controlled Paris and seems to have exerted no further influence over public affairs. Charles died in 1422 after which Isabeau's public life appears to have come to an end. The queen died in Paris in 1435.

The Queen's Black Legend

Christine de Pizan scholarship routinely assumes that Paris of the early fifteenth century buzzed with the rumor of an affair between the queen and her brother-in-law, Louis of Orleans. Isabeau and Louis entered into a political alliance after the death of Philip and the subsequent ascension of John the Fearless. However, while at least one contemporary chronicler, the Religieux of St. Denis, now identified as Michel Pintoin, complains of the pair's greed, no mention of an affair between the two exists from the period. The rumor is first mentioned shortly before the queen's death. According to the *Chronique de Charles VII, roi de France* of Jean Chartier, named royal historiographer in 1437, the English shortened Isabeau's life by diminishing her estate.[12] However, she had one more cause for sorrow, continues Jean: the English had spread a rumor that her son Charles was not the son of Charles VI.[13]

What motivated the rumor? In 1435, Philip the Good, son of John the Fearless, rejected his English allies and recognized Charles VII as king of France with the Treaty of Arras.[14] The Treaty of Troyes obviated by this accord, the English were forced to invent a new justification for their claim to the throne of France. Although no evidence, at least official, indicates that the English believed Charles VII to be a bastard, the fact that claims to the English throne—most notably that of Edward, son of Henry VI—were countered with the charge that the claimant was illegitimate suggests that a similar strategy might have been employed to harm Charles VII.[15]

Before Chartier's chronicle, the *Pastoralet,* an allegorical account from a Burgundian perspective of the conflict between the Burgundians and the Armagnacs, hinted at an affair between Isabeau and Louis. Composed between 1422 and 1425, it was intended to justify Louis's murder.[16] The allegory presents the pair as lovers in the figures of Belligere and Tristifer, a shepherdess and a shepherd.[17] Pastoral allegory was a common vehicle for political satire in the fourteenth and fifteenth centuries. The affair in the *Pastoralet* is merely an allegorized version of the pair's well-known political association, not proof that rumors linked the two romantically. Charles VI, Florentin in the story, approaches the allegorical counterpart of John the Fearless, Lëonet, and asks him to assassinate Tristifer, because he has become aware of the affair between him and Belligere. Lëonet agrees.[18] This element of the allegory, however, has never been read literally. Nor should the love affair; amorous shepherds and shepherdesses were part of the pastoral genre.

The rumor was taken up by Brantôme, who includes it in a chapter on Louis XII, king of France and grandson of Louis of Orleans.[19] Brantôme wryly contrasts Louis XII with his "gallant" grandfather. Louis spent most of the night he was assassinated with his sister-in-law, Brantôme reports. Although he does not know whether the story is true or false, he continues, the English king said that Charles VII was the offspring of an adulterous affair. Still, Brantôme is not in general critical of the queen. Later, in a section defending female regency, he remarks simply that Isabeau "eust la regence de son fils, son mary Charles VI, estant alteré de son bon sens, par l'advis de son conseil."[20]

The rumor took on a life of its own, however. The correspondence of Michael Huber, language teacher and translator of Bavarian origins living in Paris in 1764, reveals that the black legend of Isabeau was fully formed in France by that time. Referring to Isabeau's critics, Huber complains that his heroine has been terribly defamed by them; they all agree that she was a monster.[21] Huber notes that the bias of the queen's critics is clear. Although he intended to write an objective history of the queen, based on the primary sources to which he had access in Paris, he seems to have abandoned the task, for no such history exists.

The Marquis de Sade was responsible for the next important treatment of the rumor.[22] Still, even he, in his entertaining account of Isabeau's life, admits that no mention of the queen's shocking behavior can be found in contemporary chronicles. Indeed, he scolds fifteenth-century chroniclers for failing to report the story of the adulterous queen, a story he claims to have found in two "confessions" formerly held in Dijon, subsequently (and conveniently) destroyed by Revolutionaries. However, the truths (*vérités*) contained within these confessions are so obvious, the marquis continues, that they do not even require the proof that he provides.[23]

Yet it is important to note that a sober and dignified image of the queen was transmitted by sixteenth- and seventeenth-century *légiste*-historians of the kings of France, whose purpose was to support the kings' interests. In a pamphlet defending the age of majority as fourteen, Jean du Tillet, supporter of Catherine de Médicis, dismisses the arguments of those who would install the king of Navarre as a regent over the young King Francis II. In determining what French legal tradition had set as the age of majority, only trustworthy historical witness—charters, in other words—should be consulted, he writes. The false stories promulgated in chronicles should be treated with caution. Du Tillet specifically cites as unreliable the Religieux of St. Denis, the major source for the notion that Isabeau bore a bad reputation during her own day. About Isabeau, du Tillet mentions only that she was badly treated by the English king, remarking, "Cette royne fut petitement entretenue de l'estat de sa maison par les Anglois, es mains desquels elle estoit, & porta fort patiemment ses afflictions" (This queen was kept in poor estate in her house by the English, in whose hands she was, and bore her afflictions very patiently).[24]

However, this sober strand of history was subsumed in the nineteenth century by the magnificently outrageous stories of an adulterous, luxurious, meddlesome, scheming, and spendthrift queen perpetuated by nineteenth-century historians such as Michelet, and, later in the century, Auguste Vallet de Viriville, and, especially, Marcel Thibault, who, even as he claims to be regarding the evidence surrounding the queen objectively, incorporates her story into a larger narrative of French nationalism.[25] For Thibault, Isabeau's usefulness as a figure against which to construct the French character appears to have been more compelling than the obligations of historical objectivity.

Already believing that Isabeau was infamous for her adultery in her own time, modern scholarship has discovered evidence in three principal sources that cannot in fact be seen as such when read without the bias of hindsight. Two of the sources are contained in the same chapter of the chronicle of the Burgundian-biased Religieux of St. Denis, which records the complaints of the Parisians about the mismanagement of the realm by Louis and Isabeau during the king's illness.[26] Outrage at their greed was tremendous, Pintoin writes.[27] According to him, the Parisians deplored the couple's devotion to luxury and their seeking after material as opposed to spiritual delight (*deliciis corporeis).* Yet, the complaints do not include illicit sexual activity and certainly not with each other; moreover, Pintoin received his information on Louis and Isabeau from Burgundian sources, which casts doubt on their validity.[28] The second source follows closely upon Pintoin's recording of public outrage at the pair's greed. No one dared criticize the royalty publicly, Pintoin writes, until an Augustinian monk named Jacques Legrand excoriated Isabeau's courtiers: "In tua curia domina Venus solium occupans, ipsi eciam obsequntur ebrietas et commessacio, que noctes vertunt in diem, continuantes choreas dissolutas. Hee maledicte et infernales pedissece, curiam assidue ambientes, mores viresque enervant plurium" (Lady Venus occupies the throne in your court: certainly drunkenness and debauchery follow her, turning night into day, with continual dissolute dancing. Oh, the cursed and infernal lackeys, who constantly inhabit your court, greatly sap morals and strength.)[29] The criticism, however, is aimed at the government (the *curia*) rather than at the queen's personal household, an entirely different entity. Moreover, it gradually becomes clear that the complaint concerns the French defeat at the hands of the English. Soldiers of Venus rather than Mars, the French army is castigated for wasting the taxes raised to support them. The third source is a propagandistic Burgundian poem called the "Songe Véritable," recorded in a pamphlet from 1406. Once again, Isabeau is criticized for greed. However, as Rachel Gibbons points out, because the poem does not mention an affair, far from providing evidence of an illicit relationship, it offers valuable evidence for the queen's defense.[30] Furthermore, compared with the members of the royal council criticized in the poem, Louis of Orleans, the king's uncle, Jean of Berry, and the king's *grand maître d'hôtel,* Jean de Montaigu, Isabeau is only mildly criticized. The criticism is short and imprecise compared with that of the others, which castigate their subjects for various crimes; the composer of the works seems to have been able to find nothing specific for which to criticize Isabeau.

Some historians have also adduced the Treaty of Troyes, which disinherited Charles VII in favor of Henry V of England, as proof of Isabeau's promiscuity, believing that the document designates her son as illegitimate. This misconception arises from the treaty's reference to Charles as the "*soi-disant*" (so-called) dauphin of the Viennois. Some historians construed *soi-disant* as a veiled reference to Charles's uncertain paternity. In fact, *soi-disant* was a standard insult, challenging the bearer of a title's fitness for the title, and was employed in letters between Charles of Orleans and John the Fearless.[31]

Christine de Pizan's Isabeau

The popular but untenable view of the debauched Isabeau found its way into scholarship on Christine de Pizan, where the relationship between the poet and the queen was cast as one of outraged moralist castigating a wastrel queen, neglectful of her obligations to her people. References to the queen's supposed affair with Louis of Orleans and Christine's imagined disapproval abound in Christine scholarship. "The duke was a notorious philanderer, and by the summer of 1405 his extramarital relations with the queen were causing a public scandal. The same summer a scandal broke out among the ladies of the queen's court, resulting in the dismissal of some of them. Christine was not merely a moralist but a keen observer of the society that surrounded her," writes one scholar.[32] An entire hypothetical social narrative has been constructed wherein scholars have found traces of the queen in Christine's early "courtly" writings, construing the poet's observations about the woes of love as veiled criticisms aimed at the supposedly promiscuous Isabeau, even though piety seems to have been one of the real Isabeau's most prominent characteristics.[33] For example, Isabeau's imagined infidelity with her brother-in-law has been read into *Le Livre du duc des vrais amans:* "The name of Isabeau of Bavaria has not fared well in accounts of French history, for a number of reasons. One of those is her alleged infidelity to the king, perhaps encouraged by Charles VI's bouts of insanity, the first of which occurred in 1392. The advice given especially to the 'high-ranking princesses,' whose every gesture is noted by all around them, as Sebille writes, may well have had some relevance to Isabeau's situation."[34] Along with references to Isabeau's scandalous behavior, comments about her presumed cupidity are common.[35]

These misperceptions about Isabeau's reputation during her lifetime have caused Christine's championing of the queen in a series of works dating from the last years of the fourteenth century and the first five years of the fifteenth to be overlooked. Although the place in political life that Christine envisioned for women has long been studied, her writings on women as mediators and regents have never been placed in their political context. When perceptions of the queen are corrected, these writings appear to promote Isabeau, as opposed to the king's male relatives, as head of the government during the king's absences.

One of Christine's earliest works, "L'Epître au dieu d'amours," composed in 1399, explores in detail the kind of resistance Isabeau must have faced when she was first appointed president of the king's royal council during his absences and offers a hint as to why the poet took up her pen to bolster the queen's authority. The poem recounts the danger posed by envious *médiseurs,* slanderers at court, as it elaborates the problem of courtly divisiveness. Complaining of slander in general, it evokes the renowned Burgundian "propaganda machine," directed by Philip of Burgundy (and later by his son John the Fearless), against the reputation of Louis of Orleans. However, the poem focuses on the slander of women in particular, which is significant, because it was during these years that Isabeau was first beginning to be called upon to mediate between Philip and Louis during the king's absences, although the position of mediator was not officially awarded her by royal ordinance until 1402. Cupid, narrator of "L'Epître au dieu d'amours," through his invocation of the Virgin Mary, makes an impassioned plea in favor of the queen as the proper replacement for her husband during his periods of indisposition. The Virgin's exalted position next to her son, subordinate and yet crowned, reminds readers of the queen's greatest advantages.[36] The association of queens with the Virgin Mary, heavenly mediator, was commonplace from the late twelfth century on (and an association that Christine exploits again in "Une Epistre a la Royne de France" and the *Livre de la cité des dames*). Cupid also highlights women's gentleness, once again a promotion of Isabeau at the expense of the warlike dukes. Unlike men, women are "not inclined towards making war, / Or murdering, or fashioning the torch / To set the blaze."[37]

It cannot be a coincidence that soon after penning this poem, Christine dedicated the collected letters of the *Querelle de la Rose,* containing the poet's own vigorous defense of the feminine character against the misogynistic discourse promulgated in the *Roman de la Rose,* to the queen. Christine offers the work to the "Tres Noble Excellence," who delights in hearing well-expressed stories of virtuous things ("se delicte a oïr lire dittiéz de choses vertueuses et bien dictes").[38] Christine goes on to depict herself as less clever and eloquent than the clerics who denigrate women, but insists upon the truthfulness of her defense of women. By dedicating the work to Isabeau, Christine draws the queen into the group of righteous women slandered by misogynistic discourse, constructing her as both a victim of that discourse and a defender of women.

In "Une Epistre a la Royne de France" of October 5, 1405, Christine explicitly identifies the queen's political role as mediator, asking her to intervene in a confrontation that was threatening to break into civil war. This letter has given many modern readers the impression that Christine believed Isabeau to be indifferent to the struggles surrounding her.[39] However, placed back into its historical context, Christine's letter suggests that Isabeau is unaware of the support of her people, not of her duty to mediate. The queen is surrounded by counselors who tell her only what they want her to know; therefore, she does not realize that her people are asking her to intervene, writes Christine. Far from a criticism of the queen, this is a warning to the unruly dukes that the people support their queen, although technically her authority to arbitrate was limited. In other words, the ordinance of 1402 designating Isabeau mediator between the dukes was valid only when the king was indisposed. When he was sane, they were to go to the queen who would call upon other princes of the blood for aid.[40] The king was lucid from August 26 through September 23 or 25, 1405, that is, during nearly the entire period of the crisis to which "Une Epistre" refers.[41] Thus, Isabeau was ineligible to act as mediator by the king's order during the time of the crisis.

The king relapsed during the last week of September, which meant that as of this date Isabeau became once again the official mediator. However, as the fact that the king felt the need to reiterate the position he had assigned his wife attests, Isabeau faced heavy resistance. For this reason, a little more than two weeks after the king's relapse, on October 12, the royal council reconfirmed Isabeau's power to mediate between the dukes, which she then proceeded to do.[42]

However, just before, Christine penned her famous letter. This letter, of course, was not addressed to Isabeau alone. The question of the audiences for Christine's political writings is vexed, but given the "aural" state of the early fifteenth-century court, it is certain that the audience of a given political writing would not have been restricted to its addressee. Political writings, rather, were read aloud and discussed.[43] It was not that Isabeau had no interest in mediating, but that she lacked the authority to act on her own uninvited. Christine's purpose is not to convince Isabeau that she should act, but to gather support for the mediation she was about to carry out, focusing the support of her readers upon the queen, which she does by reminding them of the historical precedent for queenly intervention. For the letter goes on to cite the epitome of illustrious precursors in mediation, the Virgin Mary, along with Esther and Bathsheba. In comparing Isabeau's potential role to these and other illustrious mediators and affirming that the good and wise queen is the comforter and advocate of her people ("conffortarresse, et advocate des ses subjiez et de son pueple"), Christine raises her above all other mediators.[44]

Furthermore, Christine's epistle argues for a type of coregency, in contrast with what the poet views as a usurpation of the king's power by the unruly dukes. Fleshing out the potential power implied by the ordinance of 1403 abolishing regency, Christine cites Blanche of Castile and describes how the queen held the baby Louis in her arms, and, then, extending him toward the quarrelling barons, reproved them for behaving in a way that the little king would never approve when he reached the age of discretion.[45] Isabeau, like Blanche, can only be a coregent; she poses no danger. Throughout the letter, Christine deliberately foregrounds the queen's mediating position, emphasizing that she thereby represents no threat to the king and that she is therefore able to represent the totality of the French community.[46] Isabeau is different from the dukes, Christine argues, who menace the king in their struggle for political control and who persist in trying to carry out their own agendas despite their claims to represent the good of the people.

Christine makes a similar argument for female regency in *Le Livre de la cité des dames,* which was most likely also composed sometime during 1405. In this work, she celebrates female regency with her *exempla* of women, past and contemporary, who ruled with or in place of their husbands, fathers, or sons: Fredegunde, Semiramis, Zenobia, Artemisia, Lilia, Berenice, Dido, Opis, Lavinia, Clotilde, Blanche, and contemporary princesses of France, along with the Virgin Mary. The work comes to a close with the installation of the Virgin Mary as the leader of the *Cité des dames.* Justice introduces Mary to the ladies as "celle qui est non pas seulement leur royne mais qui a administracion et seigneurie sur toutes puissances creés apres un seul filz" (she who is not only their queen, but who has administration and dominion, after her only son). In a series of important articles, E. Jeffrey Richards has argued that Christine employs the imagery of Mariology to construct an intricate and erudite argument for coregency. According to Richards, the *Cité des dames* implicitly presents the Virgin as model of feminine power by creating a parallel between the *regalitas* of the queen of Heaven and the *regalitas* of the queen of France.[47] Although the *Cité des dames* praises women for their various achievements—literary, artistic, moral, spiritual—it begins and ends with regents. In the fraught climate of 1405, a book promoting female regency could only have been interpreted as an argument in favor of the queen.

Isabeau does not figure in the list of Christine's wise female rulers in this work, giving rise to the comment that the reason for the queen's absence is that she was not a "wise" female ruler.[48] However, Isabeau is not part of the list because the ladies of book 1, chapter 3 of the *Cité des dames* are all widows who governed France after the deaths of their husbands. Charles was living when Christine composed this book. On the other hand, Isabeau does appear in book 2, along with the good and generous princesses of France. Christine praises Isabeau "en laquelle n'a riam de cruaulté, extorcion ne quelconques mal vice, mais tout bonne amour et benignité vers ses subgés" (in whom is nothing of cruelty, extortion, or any evil vice, but only good love and beneficence toward her subjects).[49] The odd negative construction of the phrase has been interpreted as faint praise. I would suggest that rather than criticism by understatement, the logic behind Christine's construction is that it stresses the contrast between Isabeau and the warring dukes. They are cruel; they are extortionists; they are filled with vice. She is *not.* The list of female rulers of book 1 reminds readers that women are capable of assuming power. Isabeau, Christine implies, can and should rule for the king while the dukes should be kept from power.

Conclusion

To date, no close examination of Isabeau based upon contemporary evidence has been advanced to support the unflattering image of the queen that many scholars have claimed to discover reflected in Christine's work. In reality, the queen's position was paradoxical. Isabeau is perceived by modern scholars to be powerful, in that she had access to power. Yet, as president of the royal council during the king's absences, she had little power to make decisions on her own and no way of enforcing her decisions. She was less powerful than the enemy dukes, who sat continually on the council and between whom the other council members divided their loyalty. Thus, even though in theory she could call up the king's army, the king's men who contributed men-at-arms were loyal to one or the other of the dukes, who, furthermore, possessed their own men-at-arms. In other words, Isabeau was called upon to rule during the king's absences, but effectively prevented from doing so.

This is the Isabeau whom Christine attempts to bolster in her works, an Isabeau paralyzed within an untenable situation. Writers of the fifteenth century worked to clarify the meaning of royalty, as Larry Scanlon has noted, which was not "some fully formed and uncontested institution."[50] On the contrary, it was a partial and developing political ideology, and it thus required the support of writers to articulate itself. As Lynn Staley observes, this input was important: "This category of literature [mirror for princes] . . . gave a poet a means of addressing what became an increasingly broad reading audience of those who were concerned with the elements of government."[51] Christine's early fifteenth-century defenses of women address the problem of how to maintain the kingship in the face of Charles's mental illness, and her answer to the problem is that the public rally round Isabeau, the monarchy's only hope of survival. The "entrée du poète dans le champ politique" during the last decade of the fourteenth century has been studied, as well as the implications of this new position of the poet as political advisor.[52] Yet, the type of political activity that I am attributing here to Christine de Pizan has not been explored by scholars of political writings at the court of Charles VI, although it has been well studied for the English courts. Poets did more than attempt to change their leaders' behavior; through the dialogues set up among themselves, the royalty, and the public, they sought to effect change by training the public how to view figures and institutions. Power at the Valois court was still a highly personal issue, exercised through physical contact. In this context, Christine's defenses of women would have served to instruct their listeners in how to imagine the queen's role and apprised them of her personal fitness for it.

However, the paradoxical position of the mediator queen as Christine analyses it has been transformed within Christine studies into the assumption that the queen was indifferent to the struggles surrounding her, preferring to immerse herself in frivolous and licentious activity. It is ironic that in foregrounding Isabeau's difficult position, Christine only helped to prepare her subsequent vilification. Marginal in many senses—she was a queen, a foreigner, and a woman—Isabeau today continues to be blamed for the ills resulting from the disastrous struggle for power between Charles's relatives.

As I hope to have shown, however, even though Christine deliberately and fruitfully deploys the imagery of the paradoxical position of mediator-queen in a number of her writings, it is never for the purpose of taking Isabeau to task for frivolity or inaction. The sinful body of a debauched queen is not the object of Christine's investigations, but rather the social structures that require her participation while at the same time refusing to heed her advice. The perception that Christine was strictly a moral philosopher and defender of women but that she had nothing to offer the field of political history has been revised by scholarship demonstrating the practical cast of many of her works.[53] During the early fifteenth century, the very institution of the monarchy was threatened by the violent struggle for control of the French government. This situation necessitated new discourses on how to incorporate a dysfunctional ruler into an ideology of the kingship, and it was necessary to concentrate public support behind the correct substitute for royal power if the monarchy was to remain intact at all. Thus, Christine's defense of female participation in government is wholly practical, wholly related to historical circumstance. For too long Isabeau's unjustified negative reputation has prevented scholars from considering precisely why Christine took up her pen to defend women in the first years of the fifteenth century.

Notes

1. See Heidrun Kimm, *Isabeau de Baviere, reine de France 1370–1435. Beitrag zur Geschichte einer bayerischen Herzogstochter und des französischen Königshauses* (Munich: Stadtarchiv, 1969); Yann Grandeau, "Le Dauphin Jean, duc de Touraine, fils de Charles VI, 1398–1417," *Bulletin philologique et historique ACNSS 93, Comité des travaux historiques* 2 (Tours, 1968, 1971), 665–728, and "Les Enfants de Charles VI: essai sur la vie privée des princes et des princesses de la maison de France à la fin du moyen age," *Bulletin philologique et historique* (Paris: Bibliothèque Nationale, 1969), 809–32; Theodor Straub, "Isabeau de Bavière, Legende und Wirklichkeit," *Zeitschrift für Bayerische Landesgeschichte* 44 (1981): 131–55; R. C. Famiglietti, *Royal Intrigue at the Court of Charles VI* (New York: AMS Press, 1986), and *Tales of the Marriage Bed from Medieval France (1300–1500)* (Providence, R.I.: Picardy Press, 1992); Rachel C. Gibbons, *The Active Queenship of Isabeau of Bavaria, 1392–1417* (PhD dissertation, University of Reading, 1997), and "Isabeau of Bavaria, Queen of France (1385–1422): The Creation of an Historical Villainess," *Transactions of the Royal Historical Society* series 6.6 (1996a): 51–73. Some examples of the perpetuation of her black legend include Richard Vaughn, *John the Fearless: The Growth of Burgundian Power* (London: Longmans, 1966), 30; Jean Favier, *La Guerre de Cent Ans* (Paris: Fayard, 1980), 40; and Favier's entry for Isabeau in the *Dictionnaire de la France Médiévale* (Paris: Fayard, 1993).

2. The black legend entered Christine de Pizan studies through the pioneering work of Charity Cannon Willard, primarily in *Christine de Pizan: Her Life and Works* (New York: Persea, 1984). Maureen Quilligan drew attention to the fact that historians recognize that Isabeau was not believed to have been promiscuous during her own time in *The Allegory of Female Authority: Christine de Pizan's* Cité des Dames (Ithaca, N.Y.: Cornell University Press, 1991), 246–47. Still, the myth continues to crop up in Christine studies.

3. For details on the Burgundian vilification of Louis, see Michael Nordberg, "Sources Bourguignonnes des accusations portées contre la mémoire de Louis d'Orléans," *Annales de Bourgogne* 31 (1959), 81–98.

4. *Ordonnances des rois de France de la troisième race,* ed. Denis-Francois Lecousse, 21 vols. (Paris: L'Imprimerie nationale, 1723–1849), 7: 530–35.

5. *Ordonnances,* 7: 535–38.

6. Ibid., 7: 518–22.

7. See Enguerrand de Monstrelet, *La Chronique d'Enguerran de Monstrelet,* ed. L. Douet D'Arcq, 6 vols. (Paris: Mme ve. J. Renouard, 1857–62), vol. 1, where Louis reminds delegates from the University of Paris that he is son and brother of a king, who has also been given control ("*baillé*") of the realm when the king is unable to function (121).

8. See L. Douët-d'Arcq, *Choix de pieces inédites relatives au règne de Charles VI,* 2 vols. (Paris: Renouard, 1863), 1: 227–39.

9. Ibid., 1: 240–43.

10. *Ordonnances,* 8: 581–83.

11. See Famiglietti, *Royal Intrigue,* 40: "To these ends, she would use all her power against everyone except the king, her children, and all those to whom by 'reason and honesty' she was more obliged because they were more closely related to her than John was." These included the duke of Orleans, her brother-in-law; the king's uncles, the dukes of Berry and Bourbon, and her brother, Louis of Bavaria.

12. Jean Chartier, *Chronique de Charles VII, Roi de France,* ed. and intro. Vallet de Viriville, 3 vols. (Paris: P. Jannet, 1858), 1: 209.

13. *Chronique de Charles VII,* 1: 209–10.

14. On the "affair" see Famiglietti, 42–45, and Rachel Gibbons, "Creation of an Historical Villainess," 62–67.

15. See Craig Taylor, "Sir John Fortescue and the French Polemical Treatises of the Hundred Years War," *English Historical Review* 114 (1999): 113–14.

16. *Le Pastoralet,* ed. and intro. Joel Blanchard (Paris: Presse Universitaire de France, 1983).

17. For the probable date of composition, see Blanchard's introduction, 26–27.

18. *Le Pastoralet,* 91, lines 2059–60.

19. Pierre de Bourdeille Brantôme, *Œuvres complètes de Branthôme,* (1858–95), ed. Prosper Mérimée and Louis La Cour de la Pijardière, 13 vols. (Paris: P. Jannet; Nendeln: Liechtenstein; Kraus reprint, 1977), 3: 80–81.

20. Ibid., 11: 219.

21. Quoted in Straub, "Isabeau de Bavière," 132–33.

22. Because the marquis's work was not published until 1953, it influenced modern historians more than historians of the nineteenth century.

23. Marquis de Sade, *Histoire secrète d'Isabelle de Bavière,* ed. Gilbert Lely (Paris: Gallimard, 1953), 26.

24. Jean du Tillet, *Les Mémoires et recherches de Jean du Tillet* (A Rouen: pour Philippe de Tours 1578), 125–26.

25. See, for example, Marcel Thibault, *Isabeau de Bavière: Reine de France. La Jeunesse (1370–1405)* (Paris: Perrin et Cie, 1903), 315, who considers all Isabeau's actions to have been in the service of the grandeur of the House of Bavaria.

26. For Pintoin's well-known Burgundian bias, see Nordberg, "Sources Bourguignonnes des accusations."

27. *Chronique du Religieux de Saint-Denys contenant le règne de Charles VI, de 1380–1422,* ed. and trans. M. L. Bellaguet, 6 vols. (Paris: Crapelet, 1844; rpt., *Editions du Comité des travaux historiques et scientifiques,* 1994), 3: 266.

28. For further discussion, see Nordberg, "Sources Bourguignonnes des accusations."

29. *Religieux de St. Denis,* 3: 268.

30. Gibbons, "Creation of an Historical Villainess," 66–67.

31. Pintoin uses the expression to refer to the fact that Charles VII has been disinherited; hence, he is the "so-called" dauphin.

32. Charity Cannon Willard, ed., *The Writings of Christine de Pizan* (New York: Persea, 1994), 39.

33. See Rachel Gibbons, "The Piety of Isabeau of Bavaria" *Courts, Counties and the Capital in the Later Middle Ages,* ed. Diana Dunn (Stroud, UK: Sutton Publishing, 1996), 205–224.

34. *The Book of the Duke of True Lovers,* trans. and intro. Thelma S. Fenster (New York: Persea Books, 1991), 31.

35. For example, see Rosalind Brown-Grant, *Christine de Pizan and the Moral Defence of Women: Reading beyond Gender* (Cambridge and New York: Cambridge University Press, 1999), 104, and Roberta Krueger, "*'Chascune selon son estat'*: Women's Education and Social Class in the Conduct Books of Christine de Pizan and Anne de France," *Papers on French Seventeenth Century Literature* 46 (1997), 27.

36. Christine de Pizan, *Poems of Cupid, God of Love,* ed. Thelma Fenster and Mary Carpenter Erler (Leiden: Brill, 1990), lines 572–90.

37. "Ne sont a ce, n'a user de batailles, / N'a gent tuer, në a faire fouailles / Pour bouter feu" (lines 659–61).

38. *Le Débat sur le "Roman de la Rose,"* ed. Eric Hicks (Paris: Champion, 1977), 5.

39. *The Epistle of the Prison of Human Life With an Epistle to the Queen of France and Lament on the Evils of the Civil War,* ed. and trans. Josette Wisman (New York: Garland, 1984).

40. Douët d'Arcq, *Choix de pieces inédites relatives,* 1: 234.

41. Bernard Guenée, *La Folie de Charles VI, Roi Bien-Aimé* (Paris: Perrin, 2004), 206–8.

42. On the king's relapse, see Guenée, *La Folie de Charles VI,* 206–7. For a description of Isabeau's mediating activity, see the *Religieux de St. Denis* for October 16, 1405, 3: 345.

43. See Joyce Coleman, *Public Reading and the Reading Public in Late Medieval England and France* (Cambridge and New York: Cambridge University Press, 1996), chap. 5, "Aural History."

44. "Epistre," 78.

45. Ibid., 81.

46. Christine de Pizan, *Le Livre des trois vertus,* ed. Charity Cannon Willard (Paris, Champion, 1989).

47. E. Jeffrey Richards, "Les Enjeux du culte mariale chez Christine de Pizan," *Actes du 7e congrès international sur Christine de Pizan,* ed. Anne Paupert (Paris: Champion, forthcoming); "Justice in the Summa of St. Thomas Aquinas, in Late Medieval Marian Devotional Writings and in the Works of Christine de Pizan," *Christine de Pizan, Une femme de science, une femme de lettres,* ed. Juliette Dor, Marie-Elisabeth Henneau, and Bernard Ribémont (Paris: Champion, 2008): 95–114; "Political Thought as Improvisation: Female Regency and Mariology in late Medieval French Thought," *Virtue, Liberty, and Toleration: Political Ideas of European Women, 1400–1800,* ed. Jacqueline Broad and Karen Green (Berlin/New York: Springer, 2007), 1–22.

48. Julia Walker, "Re-Politicizing the Book of the Three Virtues," *Au champ des escriptures: actes du colloque international sur Christine de Pizan,* ed. Eric Hicks, Diego Gonzalez, and Philippe Simon (Paris: Champion, 2000), 543.

49. Christine de Pizan, *La Città delle Dame,* ed. Patrizia Caraffi and Earl Jeffrey Richards (Milan: Luni Editrice, 1997), 422.

50. Larry Scanlon, "The King's Two Voices: Narrative and Power in Hoccleve's *Regiment of Princes,*" *Literary Practice and Social Change in Britain, 1380–1530,* ed. Lee Patterson (Berkeley, Los Angeles: University of California Press, 1990), 217.

51. Lynn Staley, "Gower, Richard II, Henry of Derby, and the Business of Making Culture," *Speculum* 75 (2000), 71.

52. Joël Blanchard, "L'Entrée du poète dans le champ politique au XVe siècle," *Annales: Histoire, Sciences Sociales* 41 (1986), 44.

53. See Claude Gauvard, "Christine de Pizan et ses contemporains: L'engagement politique des écrivains dans le royaume de France aux XIVe et XVe siècles," *Une femme de lettres au moyen âge: études autour de Christine de Pizan,* ed. Liliane Dulac and Bernard Ribémont (Orléans: Paradigme, 1995), 105–28.

2. "Satisfaite de soy en soy mesme"

The Politics of Self-Representation in Jeanne d'Albret's Ample déclaration

MARY C. EKMAN

In the first sentence of her autobiographical *Ample déclaration sur la jonction de ses armes à celles des Réformés* of 1568 (*Ample Declaration on the Joining of Her Arms to Those of the Reformers*), Jeanne d'Albret writes: "J'ay toujours estimé que, si la personne n'est satisfaite de soy en soy mesme, le contentement que les autres en peuvent avoir ne luy est que demy sentiment du repos de sa conscience." (I have always deemed that if a person is not satisfied with herself in herself, the satisfaction that others may have of her is only a half feeling of contentment in her conscience.)[1]

A surprising instance of self-assertion for the period, it is made even more so because it opens a text penned by a woman. We must remember that this is well before Montaigne audaciously claims in his address to the reader, "Je suis moi-même la matière de mon livre." (I am myself the substance of my book.)[2]

It may not actually be so unusual given the circumstances. Jeanne d'Albret (1528–72) was the daughter of Henri d'Albret and Marguerite de Navarre, the sister of François I. In 1541, her first marriage to the Duc de Clèves was contracted against her wishes to solidify ties with the Habsburgs in the hopes of recovering the Spanish part of Navarre. Though a young girl of only twelve, she showed a strong sense of will by protesting vehemently against the marriage and had to be physically carried to the altar. When it was no longer politically necessary, François I had the marriage annulled on the grounds that it had not been consummated. Her second marriage was also contracted for political reasons, this time to create ties with the Bourbons of France; her father agreed to it, again in an attempt to reunify Navarre. Her second husband, Antoine de Bourbon, was first prince of the blood (i.e., he was in line for the French throne if the French king had no direct male heirs) until his death in 1562, when that distinction passed to their son, Henri III de Navarre, who was to become king of France as Henri IV. At her father's death in 1555, Jeanne d'Albret became sovereign in Béarn and the part of Navarre north of the Pyrénées (called Basse Navarre, or lower Navarre), though in Foix, Guyenne, and Albret, among other places, she was subject to the French monarchy. Her husband was named king consort. As queen of Navarre and Viscountess of Béarn, she was in a political position far greater than the size of her lands would indicate. Precariously perched between the two great powers of France and Spain, Béarn and lower Navarre were important geographically because they included two of the main passages through the Pyrénées: any movement of France against Spain or Spain against France would have had to go through her territory. D'Albret's efforts to keep Béarn independent and free from domination occupied a great deal of her life's work.

In addition to her important political position, Jeanne d'Albret was one of the staunchest and most important leaders of the Reformation in France. It is well known that her mother, Marguerite de Navarre, was a sympathizer and protector of such reformers as Lefèvre d'Etaples, Gérard Roussel, Clément Marot, and Jean Calvin, though she never converted. D'Albret's humanistic education was overseen by her mother and undoubtedly influenced by men such as these; she converted publicly along with her husband in 1560. He did not remain in the Huguenot camp, however, but wavered back and forth depending on political expediency, always looking to reunify Navarre and extend his political reach. Tension between husband and wife exploded during the Colloquy of Poissy in 1561. She arrived there with Theodore Beza and openly practiced Protestantism. The Spanish ambassador remarked on it and Catherine de' Medici called for Antoine to repudiate his wife or put her in a convent; Antoine's firm adherence to Catholicism after this date was due to a belief that Philip II of Spain would return Navarre or exchange that claim for other lands if he promoted the Catholic cause. Antoine was on the point of imprisoning his wife when she fled to Vendôme and then Gascony where she foiled Montluc and his soldiers, who had been sent to capture her, and was able to find safe passage to Pau, the capital of Béarn, where she would be safe. These events profoundly influenced d'Albret's firm resolution to establish "the true religion" in the lands where she was sovereign. In Béarn, d'Albret allowed the practice of the reformed religion and had the Bible translated into Basque, the language of most of the people in her lands. In 1566, she even prohibited Catholicism and confiscated church lands. She had been a pacifying force during the first war of religion but became increasingly engaged in the second and, finally, was a head organizer in the third. Her husband's brother, Louis de Bourbon, the prince de Condé was her ally and the chief military officer of the Huguenots until his death in 1569. From the time of her conversion, Jeanne d'Albret was the highest-ranking Huguenot until her death in 1572 from natural causes (tuberculosis or pneumonia), just a short time before the wedding she had helped arrange of her son to Marguerite de Valois, which led, as we know, to the St. Bartholomew's Day Massacre.

The political position of her family placed her in direct conflict with the Guise family, the ultra-Catholics who would eventually found the Catholic League. The house of Guise was a ducal family from Lorraine that had entered French service under François I. The Huguenots and the Guise family were direct rivals for power in France, especially during the period after the death of François I. When Mary Queen of Scots, who was a member of the Guise family, married François II in 1558, she had her two uncles, François, the Duc de Guise, and Charles, the cardinal de Lorraine, appointed to high political positions. As in England, the intertwined struggle over religion and power is at the heart of politics in this period.

While the writing of memoirs in the period necessarily participates in what Stephen Greenblatt calls "the generation of identities,"[3] examination of the identities generated in memoirs and the discursive means employed to do so remains a fruitful field of inquiry. Although scholars of the Reformation generally recognize the important participation of women in the movement, they often imply that the possibility of that involvement is due to the fact that only religion offered women a suitable venue for agency in the public realm. Likewise, scholarship on women's autobiographical writing of the early modern period frequently asserts that expression of the female spiritual self was virtually the sole means for women's self-representation.[4] As my analysis shows, d'Albret's self-representation belies these notions. As Mack P. Holt asserts, the binary so often established between politics and religion is a false one:[5] indeed, the two are not separable. In writing and publishing the *Ample déclaration,* d'Albret insists on several aspects of sovereignty that would hold for both herself and for the French monarchy. However, her insistence on divine right disrupts the binary of sovereign and subject, for she is both subject within France and sovereign in her own territories. Her *Ample déclaration* is a prime example of how Protestant assertion of the individual is a threat to the nascent national entity of France.

Others have signaled the development and proliferation of memoirs in France beginning in the sixteenth century,[6] though as yet, there has been no study linking the genre to the Reformation. Neither has there been a systematic analysis of the earliest memoirs by women. Recent work on self-inscription in the early modern period either continues the focus on canonical works such as Montaigne's *Essais* or, especially for the genre of memoirs, largely concentrates on later texts.[7] Historians often use memoirs produced during the wars of religion as primary source material (Brantôme, Bordenave, de l'Estoile, de Thou, Montluc, among others) and literary scholars have made efforts to establish a critical apparatus with which to approach these texts. The opposition between history and fiction is too often replicated, however, even in the latest scholarship. As Marc Fumaroli has illustrated, memoirs are a type of writing found at the intersection of prose genres. Most often addressed to a superior, the earliest texts recount military exploits.[8] In all cases, the author of memoirs, nearly always noble and male, writes from the privileged perspective of personal experience, an emerging ideal of the early modern period.

The self-confidence evident in the first sentence of the *Ample déclaration* cited earlier is apparent throughout the text, which diverges from the self-justification or disculpatory discourse of other memoirs of the period. Jeanne d'Albret does not inscribe herself in a confessional mode as others do, but offers a forthright account of her political stance and indicts the house of Guise. This does not mean that self-justification is not one of the primary goals of the *Ample déclaration*. Indeed, d'Albret had reason to wish to justify and explain her actions on several fronts. Some would see her flight as a direct confrontation with the French monarchy, and others would see this escape to the Protestant stronghold of La Rochelle as an abandonment of her people. In this narrative, she demonstrates the complexity of her situation and represents her flight as the inevitable culmination of a series of events.

Jeanne d'Albret wrote the *Ample déclaration* in October or November after her flight to La Rochelle to join rebel forces in 1568. This first-person account of her actions is often referred to as her memoirs. Analysis of this text shows that d'Albret constructs herself as simultaneously loyal to her subjects, her fellow believers, her family, and the king of France. The form of rulership in Béarn was similar to that in France and Spain in that it was ostensibly hereditary, but different in that the sovereign needed to be ratified by a vote from the Estates General. At the death of d'Albret's father in 1555, her husband, Antoine, called the Estates General of Béarn and attempted to have himself ratified as the sovereign in Béarn in her absence. This request was refused, and they awaited d'Albret's arrival before ratifying their sovereignty together. Antoine was named lieutenant general of France by Catherine de' Medici in 1561. When Antoine died in 1562 from battle wounds while he was fighting on the Catholic side during the siege of Rouen, d'Albret became sole ruler of Béarn and Navarre, though Catherine de' Medici had d'Albret's son, Henri III of Navarre, immediately named governor of Guyenne, thereby reducing d'Albret's power there. She continually argued for her right to freely rule in her lands even as the Guise family pushed Catherine de' Medici to confiscate all of her territories in the name of peace. D'Albret's decision to air her issues in a public forum is thus an important one for establishing her legitimacy as a ruler and influencing public opinion about her participation in the reform.

In *Economy and Society,* Max Weber outlines three forms of legitimation of authority: traditional, charismatic, and rational-legal. Traditional authority is that which comes from established tradition, such as inheritance, what Weber calls "the eternal authority of yesterday" and identifies it as the authority of monarchies.[9] Charismatic authority comes from the strength of individual personality. Legal domination, also called legal-rational authority, stems from the office rather than the office holder. In this text, Jeanne d'Albret enacts all three forms of authority and asserts that she owes fealty to "none but God" in the lands where she is sovereign. Derrida's concept of sovereignty is useful in this analysis as well. For Derrida, sovereignty emanates from the indivisibility of power: from an absolute power and the right to exceptionality.[10] D'Albret writes and publishes the *Ample déclaration* before the establishment of the absolute monarchy in France and shortly preceding Jean Bodin's publication of *Les six livres de la République* (*The Six Books of the Republic*) in which he is the first to elaborate a theory of necessary monarchic absolutism in his chapter "De la souveraineté" (On sovereignty).[11] It is precisely because of the Protestant threat to French monarchical power that Bodin was compelled to write this work. Indeed, as is evident in this text, d'Albret disrupts the power structure of sovereign and subject by interrogating the legitimacy of the French monarchy, first in its denial of justice to her as a subject and second in its denial of her sovereign rights in the lands she held outside of French control. In her self-inscription, she makes the dual assertion of her moral rectitude and her sovereign authority. In insisting on her individual conscience, she constructs a sophisticated argument for her own power and independence and also for the Reformers' cause.

Although Claudie Martin-Ulrich implies that the *Ample déclaration* is intended solely for the royal family, analysis of the text shows that there really is no specific implied reader.[12] It was published in 1570 in La Rochelle as a part of a collection of Huguenot texts titled *L'Histoire de nostre temps.*[13] Biographies of Jeanne d'Albret also allude to a prior publication of the text alone as a political pamphlet in 1568, the same year it was authored.[14] One can surmise, then, that it was not written as a simple appeal to Charles IX, the then king of France and his entourage, but also as a political justification, meant for a larger readership.

Many memoir writers of the period claim that they were asked by a particular person to record the important events in which they had participated, or address their account to their children, but d'Albret simply states that she has not been able to fully explain herself elsewhere and that she wanted to clarify her position by writing her book:

> parce que, par quelques lettres que j'ay escrites au Roy, Monseigneur, à la Royne sa mère, à Monseigneur son frère, et Monsieur le cardinal de Bourbon, mon beau-frère, et depuis à la Royne d'Angleterre, je n'ay touché que bien sommairement les choses que je desire plus amplement faire entendre à un chacun, j'ay mis la main à la plume pour amplifier ce dont j'ay desclaré le principal subject en mes susdites lettres, touchant les occasions qui m'ont fait abondonner mes pays souverains. (1)

> [because, in writing several letters to my lord the king, to the queen, his mother, to my lord his brother, and sir the cardinal of Bourbon, my brother-in-law, and since to the queen of England, I only touched summarily on the things that I desire more fully to have understood by all, I put my hand to the pen to amplify that which I declared to be the principal subject of my above-mentioned letters, regarding the occasions that made me abandon my sovereign lands.]

One might imagine that d'Albret is using what were short private letters as a pretext to more fully explain her position in a public document, but this is not the case. These letters were printed shortly after they were written and circulated widely. At the time that she was writing both the missives and her *Ample déclaration,* Charles IX had her lands confiscated claiming that d'Albret and her son were being held against their will by the Duc de Condé in La Rochelle, and that he was "protecting" them for her while the matter was being resolved. She undoubtedly wrote both the letters and the more extended narrative with a view to rationalizing her position and airing her issues with the French monarchy in a highly public manner. The fact that both were published nearly immediately after they were written supports this assertion.

She outlines three very specific points that she wishes to make in her narrative that she had not fully delineated in her letters: "par ce que mon intention est de desclarer plus particulièrement les dictes occasions, que j'ay seulement tracées par mes lettres mentionnées cy-dessus, qui sont la Religion, le service du Roy, Monseigneur, et le devoir au sang" (1) (because my intention is to declare more particularly the said occasions, that I only outlined in my above-mentioned letters, which are the Religion, service to my lord the king, and the duty to blood). Although it may seem surprising for her to assert that her flight and resistance are in line with her loyalty to the king, this position was typical of the nobility in general and of Protestant strategy in particular. Arlette Jouanna's historical study of nobiliary revolt against the monarchy very aptly describes the understanding nobles had in sixteenth-century France concerning the rights and responsibilities of the monarchy.[15] On numerous occasions, nobles used similar arguments to justify rebellion against the actions of the king, claiming that their loyalty to the crown was the very reason for their deviation from expected behavior. This is just such a case.

D'Albret reminds the reader of her public and highly publicized religious conversion and refers to her well-known perseverance and unwavering commitment to the new faith as a demonstration of her character:

> Depuis ce temps-là, par sa mesme grace, il m'y a faict persévérer, de sorte que je me suis toujours employée à l'avancement d'icelle [de la Religion]. Et mesme, du temps du feu Roy, mon mary, lequel, s'estant retiré de ce premier zèle qu'il en avoit, me fut une dure espine, je ne diray pas au pied, mais au coeur, chacun sçait (et me sied mieux de le taire que d'en dire davantage) que les faveurs ou rigueurs ne m'ont faict aller ne d'un costé ne d'autre. J'ay tousjours, par la grâce de Dieu, suivi le droit chemin. (3–4)

> [Since that time, by his same grace, he made me persevere in it, such that I have always worked for the advancement of it [the Religion]. And even, in the time of the late king, my husband, who, having withdrawn from the first zeal that he had had for it, was for me a tough thorn, I won't say in the foot, but in the heart, all know (and it is better for me to keep it to myself than to say more) that the favors or rigors did not cause me to go to one side or the other. I have always, by the grace of God, followed the straight path.]

She alludes here to past troubles with her husband, Antoine de Bourbon, who before his death had vacillated from one side to another following the political winds. He had tried to force her to abjure Protestantism along with him and resorted to violence against her, forcing her to go to Mass, barring her from her religious practices, and taking her son away from her (3, n. 3). Over and beyond comparing her own actions and firmness of belief favorably to her husband's dithering and reprehensible behavior, she inscribes herself as a discreet narrator in the disclaimer, "and it is better for me to keep it to myself than to say more." The parenthetical device here is more than just a transgression. D'Albret is writing for an audience well aware of her husband's deceit, his physical violence against her, his agreeing to her imprisonment, as well as his philandering (he had a bastard child in 1555, the same year as their accession to rulership). In not explicitly laying out these well-known facts, d'Albret reinforces the idea of herself as spiritually superior. Concurrently, in opening the parenthesis, she makes space for herself to speak her mind, because in the end, she has not kept her silence. With this deliberate mitigation or understatement, she has said exactly what she wanted to on the subject.

Of the many incidents that d'Albret narrates in the body of the text that together illustrate and reinforce her trifold claim of devotion to king, family, and faith and demonstrate that the Guise family, and particularly the cardinal de Lorraine are in the wrong, several episodes stand out. The first and earliest is an eight-page account of attempts on her husband's life by the ultra-Catholic Guise party. She emphasizes the storylike quality of her account and in so doing, casts her family as the heroes and the Guise family as the villains. To do so, she uses several literary devices. First, she sets up the story using intertextual references saying that the cardinal de Lorraine had cried crocodile tears and that his behavior is like that of the fox in the medieval tales. She also refers to Psalm 10, calling the cardinal and his brother, the Duc de Guise, false. To do so, she uses Marot's translation of the psalm into French: "D'un parler fainct, plein de déception; Le faux parjure est toujours embouché" (the King James version is: "Whose mouth is full of cursing and bitterness and deceit"). Mention of this psalm serves to reinforce her accusation of the Guises' dishonesty by associating them with the devil. The Psalms were quite popular among the Huguenots of this period and any of them reading this reference would have been familiar with the rest of it. Later in this psalm is a call for God to "brise le bras du méchant" (break the arm of the wicked), and thus a contrast is made between God as almighty power and nations on earth on which he visits destruction: "L'éternel est roi à toujours et à perpétuité; les nations sont exterminées de son pays" (The eternal is king forever and perpetually; nations are exterminated in his kingdom). It is no wonder that François I decided in 1542 to censure Marot's version of the Psalms by putting it on the index of banned books. Jeanne d'Albret also underscores the veracity of her account saying that if this had been fabricated, it would have needed a poet or an orator to tell it properly, but as it is true, she need only present it unadorned. The events she relates are fairly simple. After failed attempts at poisoning and shooting her husband, the Guises concocted a plot to have the king get in an argument with him so that they can stab Antoine on the pretext of defending the king. Because the king failed to cooperate with the plot as he had initially agreed, Antoine de Bourbon slipped away from their grasp.

The story is presented almost anecdotally, but one can find within it all of the themes that d'Albret develops in her text: Her husband's indecisiveness and naïveté compared with her own constancy, the Guises' deceit, and the munificence of the royal family. This latter is shown in the king's resistance during the actual attempt on Antoine's life as well as in the warning Catherine de' Medici gives before he goes to the meeting. In stating that Antoine owed the queen his life, d'Albret is enacting the ties of fealty by which the subject owes everything to the sovereign. Yet those ties bind both ways, and thus she reminds the sovereign that the lives of one's subjects also tie them to one's royal responsibility; indeed, reminders such as these permeate the entire text. I would argue that they are not just a message sent to the addressees of her previous letters, as others have pointed out, but also a message to the reading public of France regarding the responsibility of the sovereign. Here as elsewhere, d'Albret takes care to represent herself as an exemplum, the person whose actions are above reproach and thereby legitimates the idea of herself as a charismatic leader.

In another instance, d'Albret claims outright injury to her power and lists the wrongs done to her and her people: "le tort que l'on me feit pour mon comté de Foix et villes de Pamiez et Foix, qui avoyent esté en temps de paix pillées, saccagées et mangées de garnisons et commissaires, dont me fut déniée toute justice; et par là anéantis les privileges donnés par les rois à mes prédécesseurs" (the wrong that was done to me for the county of Foix and the towns of Pamiez and Foix, which had been in times of peace pillaged, sacked and the garrisons and stores emptied, for which all justice was denied; and thereby were annulled all the privileges granted by the kings to my predecessors) (38). Here again, this time in a very brief complaint, she invokes her rights, and the right to have these wrongs redressed, based on her personal and inherited ties to the French monarchy. She reminds her readers that her inherited rights and privileges have been violated, espousing traditional sovereignty—the second form of legitimation of authority outlined by Weber.

Almost halfway through the text, d'Albret repeats her claim of fidelity to both Protestantism and the king and states that she has three reasons for having joined the rebel cause (45). The first is the fact that the king has gone back on his word and signed an ordinance on September 25, 1568, making it illegal to profess publicly anything other than the Catholic religion, in direct contradiction to the rights allowed Protestants in the Pacification of Amboise of 1563. She once again places the blame on the Guise family. The second reason she gives is her claim that the Catholic party broke the Pacification by taking up arms against her subjects. In this explanation, she calls the Catholics the "true rebels" for taking up arms against the king's wishes and once again portrays her side as being in the right. The third cause she claims is keeping her freedom. Knowing that if she stays in her own lands or goes to the French court she will be taken prisoner, d'Albret affirms that those who wish to control her movements are in the wrong and that she will better be able to serve her cause and her king if she remains free. Here, she questions the sovereign authority of the French state, this time by questioning the legality of the king's actions against his Huguenot subjects. D'Albret uses Weber's third form of legitimation, the legal, to undermine the authority of the French monarchy and thereby asserts her own position as legal sovereign of Béarn and Navarre.

D'Albret closes her *Ample déclaration* in a way that resembles other memoirs of the period, though it is in its closing as stylistically different and surprising as the rest of her text: "Je prieray ceux qui liront cecy excuser le style d'une femme, qui a estimé le subject de son livre si excellent qu'il ny a eu besoin de belles paroles pour le farder; seulement de la vérité, laquelle elle y a si fidèlement observée, qu'au moins, si elle est dicte ignorante et imbécille, elle sera dicte veritable" (I entreat those who will read this to excuse the style of a woman who deemed the subject of her book so excellent that it didn't need beautiful words with which to paint it; only the truth, which she faithfully observed, and that at least, if she is said to be ignorant and imbecile, she will at least be said to be truthful) (120–21).Once again, she shows remarkable self-assurance. This closing passage contains the claims of truth and purposeful avoidance of rhetorical ornament characteristic of memoirs of the period. She also anticipates possible criticism, stating that she expects her words to be dismissed because of her gender. While she does not hesitate to make reference to herself as a woman at many moments throughout the text, as she does here, she never makes the moves that so often characterize women's autobiographical writing of the early modern period. She neither separates herself from her sex by claiming to have a masculine nature, nor does she elicit pity for her status as a "mere" woman. Admittedly, this boldness may come from her relatively high social station. The two other women to author memoirs in the sixteenth century were also of the high nobility.

In comparison, I will briefly discuss these two other examples. Charlotte Arbaleste de la Borde de Mornay (1548–1606) was born into a well-to-do Parisian family and converted to Protestantism along with her father in the 1560s. A survivor of the 1572 St. Bartholomew's Day Massacre, she fled to Sedan where she met and, in January 1576, married Philippe de Mornay, seigneur du Plessis-Marly, also a survivor of the massacre and a propagandist for the Huguenot cause. Her memoirs are addressed to her son, who was sixteen when she began writing in 1584.[16] She states that she is writing to help guide him through life, and her message is as much spiritual as anything else. Holding her husband's life up as an example for her son to follow, she also narrates her own participation in the Huguenot cause and her unwavering commitment to the Protestant faith. A hybrid between biography and autobiography, narration of this text is sometimes in the first-person singular and sometimes in the first-person plural. De Mornay stops writing at the death of her son in 1605, making him both the figurative and the literal addressee.

Marguerite de Valois, Jeanne d'Albret's daughter-in-law and eventual queen of France, authored memoirs that were only published after her death in 1628.[17] She recounts the important events of her life beginning with her birth, through her marriage and just after. Despite the prior publication of the texts by d'Albret and de Mornay, this work is often called the first example of memoirs written by a woman, because de Valois's text fulfills our expectations for an autobiography, which does not hold for either the d'Albret or the de Mornay memoirs. Neither narrates the birth and childhood of their authors, for example. Like the *Ample déclaration,* these works extensively treat Reformation politics, all three women having been involved on one side or the other. Neither de Mornay nor de Valois published her memoirs during her lifetime, however, and neither one is narrated and presented in such a purposeful, straightforward way.

In his *Queen Jeanne and the Promised Land,* David Bryson makes a distinction between d'Albret's memoirs and the letters she sent on her way to and once she had arrived in La Rochelle. Calling the letters her "living, 'real-time' declaration," he implies that the *Ample déclaration* is of lesser importance as her "published testimony."[18] I would argue that both the letters and the memoirs, having been published close to the time of their writing and having been meant to influence the course of events, should be viewed together as a discursive effort on the part of this queen to represent herself and her cause as just and loyal to the French monarchy, and also to assert her rights as sovereign in her own lands. Much debate has arisen over d'Albret's motivations for taking up the reform cause. Some scholars, including Bryson, portray her as a religious fanatic,[19] and others see her actions as politically motivated.[20] As I have shown, it would be a mistake to consider religion and politics to be mutually exclusive in this case.

In conclusion, I would like to return to the first sentence of the *Ample déclaration* because it really is extraordinary. Her self-assertion as a person "satisfaite de soi en soi-même" (satisfied with herself in herself) is not only different from other women's self-inscription of the period, but different from men's as well. In the end, I believe she makes this claim of self-satisfaction for two reasons. First, as we have seen, she is writing "sur le vif," as the events are unfolding and thus her writings are a part of those events. Second, she is asserting her right as ruler over her subjects and over her own self. The Calvinist emphasis on the relationship of the individual to God excludes terrestrial power in a way that threatens both the church and the king in France. Furthermore, if we see sovereignty as the Derridean ideal of individual freedom, then we can see this text as an assertion of sovereignty through d'Albret's declaration of individual conscience.[21] Her declaration of self-satisfaction then is much more than an insistence on the self as individual; the sovereign self that d'Albret generates in this text is clearly a "living, 'real-time'" agent in the politics of Reformation France.

Notes

1. Jeanne d'Albret, *Mémoires et poésies,* ed. A. de Ruble (Geneva: Slatkine Reprints, 1970), 1. Further references will appear parenthetically in the text.

2. Michel de Montaigne, *Les Essais,* eds. Jean Balsamo, Catherine Magnien-Simonin and Michel Magnien (Paris: Gallimard/Pléiade, 2007), Livre I, "Au lecteur" (1595).

3. Stephen Greenblatt, *Renaissance Self-Fashioning: From More to Shakespeare* (Chicago: University of Chicago Press, 1980), 1.

4. As in, for example, such works as Marguerite de Navarre's *Le Miroir de l'âme pécheresse,* published in 1531, or Teresa de Avila's *Historia de la vida,* completed in 1565 and first published in 1611.

5. Mack P. Holt, *The French Wars of Religion, 1562–1629,* 2nd ed. (Cambridge: Cambridge University Press, 2005).

6. See Jacques Hennequin and Noémi Hepp, eds., *Les Valeurs chez les mémorialistes Français du XVIIe siècle avant la Fronde* (Paris: Klincksieck, 1970); Marc Fumaroli, "Les Mémoires du XVIIe siècle: Au carrefour des genres en prose," *XVIIe siècle* 94–95 (1971): 7–38; and Nadine Kuptery-Tsur, *Se dire à la Renaissance* (Paris: J. Vrin, 1997).

7. See Nicholas Paige, *Being Interior: Autobiography and the Contradictions of Modernity in Seventeenth-Century France* (Philadelphia: University of Pennsylvania Press, 2001); Frédéric Charbonneau, *Les Silences de l'histoire: Les Mémoires français du XVIIe siècle* (Québec: Presses de l'Université de Laval, 2001); Elizabeth Goldsmith, *Publishing Women's Life Stories in France, 1647–1720* (Aldershot, UK: Ashgate, 2001); and Timothy Reiss, *Mirages of the Self: Patterns of Selfhood in Ancient and Early Modern Europe* (Stanford, Calif.: Stanford University Press, 2003).

8. Fumaroli, "Les mémoires du XVIIe siècle."

9. Max Weber, *Economy and Society: An Outline of Interpretive Sociology* (New York: Bedminster Press, 1968).

10. Jacques Derrida, *Voyous* (Paris: Galilée, 2002), 195–96.

11. Jean Bodin, *Les six livres de la République* (Lyon: Tournes, 1576).

12. Claudie Martin-Ulrich, "Catherine de Médicis et Jeanne d'Albret, la reine-mère et la reine conteuse," *Devenir Roi: Essais sur la literature addressée au Prince,* eds. Isabelle Cogitore and Francis Goyet (Grenoble, France: ELLUG, 2001), 223–33.

13. Anonymous, *L'Histoire de nostre temps contenant un receuil des choses mémorables passées et publiées pour le faict de la religion et estat de la France despuis l'edict de pacification du 23 jour de mars, jusqu'au présent* (La Rochelle: 1575), n.p.

14. See David Bryson, *Queen Jeanne and the Promised Land: Dynasty, Homeland, and Violence in Sixteenth-Century France* (Leiden, the Netherlands; Boston; Koln, Germany:

Brill, 1999) and Nancy Roelker, *Queen of Navarre: Jeanne d'Albret* (Cambridge, Mass.: Harvard University Press, 1968).

15. Arlette Jouanna, *Le Devoir de révolte: La Noblesse française et la gestation de l'Etat moderne (1559–1661)* (Paris: Fayard, 1989).

16. Charlotte Arbaleste de Mornay, *Mémoires de Madame de Mornay: édition revue sur les manuscrits, publiée avec les variantes et accompagnée de lettres inédites de mr et mme Du Plessis Mornay et de leurs enfants,* 2 vols. (Paris: Mme Ve Jules Renouard, 1868).

17. Marguerite de Valois, *Mémoires et autres écrits (1574–1614),* ed. Éliane Viennot (Paris: Champion, 1999).

18. Bryson, *Queen Jeanne,* 196.

19. This point of view can be found not only in the nineteenth century, for example, in M. Vauvilliers's *Histoire de Jeanne d'Albret Reine de Navarre,* 3 vols. (Paris: L. Janet et F. Guitel, 1818) and Alphonse de Ruble's introduction to his edition of d'Albret's *Mémoires et poésies* (Paris: Guillemin, 1893); it is also echoed more recently in Bryson.

20. See Roelker and Martin-Ulrich.

21. Derrida, *Voyous,* 216.

3. *Tanto monta*

The Catholic Monarchs' Nuptial Fiction and the Power of Isabel I of Castile

BARBARA F. WEISSBERGER

November 26, 2004, marked the five hundredth anniversary of the death of Isabel I of Castile, early modern Europe's first powerful queen regnant. For three decades, Isabel was sole proprietary ruler of Castile. She oversaw its union with the kingdom of Aragon and created the legal and administrative foundation for the future transformation of the two rival kingdoms into a nation-state. Notwithstanding these and other major accomplishments, modern historians have often had difficulty rendering unto Isabel what is Isabel's, separating her power from that of her husband Fernando of Aragon.[1] She is still too often construed as one-half of a monarchic couple, the quintessentially Catholic monarchs who shared and shared alike in the governance of their newly united kingdoms and such momentous decisions as the founding of the Inquisition, the expulsion of the Jews, and the financing of Columbus's voyages of exploration.[2]

In this chapter, I argue that Isabel was highly conscious of her singular power and that along with her husband, her court officials and writers, and her subjects, she fashioned a complex public image of her sovereignty, one that simultaneously affirmed and disguised her will-to-power and absolutist agenda. On one level, the self-fashioning that won Isabel the throne and subsequently furthered her political agenda is complicit with the medieval patriarchal sex/gender system that assigned wives at all levels a secondary status. At the same time, that complicity actually enabled her to overcome—or circumvent—the considerable resistance to female sovereignty both in Castile and Aragon.

The focus of my discussion of the complex interweaving of complicity and resistance in the fashioning of Isabelline power is a visual text: the conjoined royal devices of the yoke and arrows and the complementary motto “*Tanto monta*” (each as important as the other) that are the most enduring symbol of the monarchs’ joint reign. The Isabelline *flechas* and the *yugo* designating Fernando were frequently incorporated into the larger visual and symbolic field of the royal heraldic shield (fig. 3.1).[3] The shield or coat of arms is a complex, carefully balanced composition that gives priority to the Isabelline arms of Castile and León, placed in the upper-left quadrant, over the arms of Aragon and Aragon/Sicily. The importance of that ordering is shown by the fact that it was the very first stipulation of the *Acuerdo para la gobernación del reino* (better known as the *Concordia de Segovia*) that Isabel and Fernando signed in January of 1475, just weeks after her accession to the throne. The agreement required that Isabel’s arms precede Fernando’s on all chancery documents; the inverse order was stipulated for their signatures.[4]

Although they are not technically a part of the coat of arms, the yoke and arrows function as a visual foundation, just as the crowned eagle of St. John the Evangelist, also associated with Isabel, serves as a capstone, “protecting” it from above.[5] At the same time, the placement of the two devices inverts the priority given to Castile/Leon above, because the ox-yoke and severed yoke straps representing Fernando are on the left, followed by the five bundled

Figure 3.1. Heraldic shield of the Catholic Monarchs. From Faustino Menéndez Pidal de Navascues, *Heráldica medieval española,* vol. 1, La casa real de León y Castilla (Madrid: Instituto Salazar y Castro [Centro Superior de Investigaciones científicas], 1982), 198. Reproduced with permission.

arrows that symbolize the queen. As is standard in the courtly genre of the *invención,* which employed such devices, the visual symbols form the "body" of the *invención.* That body remains inert, however, until the viewer/reader couples it with its "soul," a verbal text.[6] In this case, the soul is the motto *Tanto monta* that is inscribed on the banderole that encircles the heraldic shield. The traditional and still often-repeated interpretation of the whole composition is that it represents and celebrates the marital and political union of Isabel and Fernando as coequal and harmonious.

The monarchs were eager to circulate this particular symbol of their shared sovereignty, expending considerable resources to do so. Art historian Joaquín Yarza Luaces has documented the proliferation of the yoke and arrows, either alone or in some combination with the motto or the royal initials F and Y, throughout the two kingdoms.[7] The symbols are quite literally strewn across the landscape of Castile, and to a lesser extent Aragon, ornamenting the interiors and exteriors of the many buildings the monarchs constructed to showcase their power.[8]

Perhaps the most impressive, and excessive, example of this royal ostentation of power is the church of San Juan de los Reyes in Toledo. It was commissioned in 1476 to commemorate an important victory in the war of succession that occupied Isabel and Fernando for the first five years of her reign, and it was originally designated by the monarchs as their final resting place.[9] The coat of arms, yoke and arrows, and royal initials cover the walls and ceiling of the church and cloister in exuberant profusion, a monogramming that proclaims both the power of the sovereign couple and the central role that religion played in their political agenda.[10] Even after their death, the symbolic equality of the royal couple continued to be celebrated, as in the medallion that graces the façade of the University of Salamanca, which enjoyed a close relationship with the monarchs.[11]

The royal devices, motto, and initials also appeared on royal seals and were incorporated into the municipal coat of arms of towns such as Ronda and Málaga, reconquered during the War against Granada (1482–92). Their broadest public dissemination was achieved through their imprinting on the coinage of the realm. However, the significance the symbols held for Isabel and Fernando is perhaps best illustrated by their ubiquity in their domestic space, where they were incorporated into tapestries; frontispieces, bindings, and slipcovers of books; and powder horns and oliphants.[12]

The message of unity and equality that the yoke and arrow devices and accompanying motto proclaim does not match the reality of the consequences of Isabel's marriage to Fernando. Their union did not significantly affect the separateness of their respective kingdoms, whose political structures and traditions were very different. Furthermore, the two realms could not be construed as equal in any sense. Because Castile was demographically and economically far stronger than Aragon, because Isabel inherited her kingdom five years before Fernando claimed his, because many of the rulers of the crown of Aragon had Castilian origins, and because Aragon was composed of distinct constituencies, each with its own parliament and traditional liberties, for all these reasons Isabel remained the stronger partner. Fernando clearly recognized this fact, and after an initial period of resistance, he threw a great deal of his energies and talents into Castilian affairs.[13]

I argue that the ostentation of political harmony and unity between Isabel and Fernando coexists in productive tension with the disunity, inequality, and violence attending the founding moment of what would become the nation-state of Spain.[14] The conjoined devices are best understood as a "nuptial fiction," a term coined by Abby Zanger in her analysis of the visual imagery disseminated on the occasion of another royal marriage with far-reaching dynastic consequences, the 1660 union of Louis XIV of France and the Spanish *infanta* María Teresa, daughter of Felipe IV.[15] Like the engravings on almanacs that Zanger studies, the royal emblem is a symbolic construct designed to mask the precarious nature of the union of the queen and her prince, to address the anxiety elicited by female sovereignty, and to both display and mystify the violence attending the founding of a new national identity.

What is being negotiated in the royal emblem is nothing more nor less than the sexual division of labor, albeit at the highest political level. Materialist feminist theory offers a useful theoretical frame for such a consideration. Judith Newton and Deborah Rosenfeldt introduced American scholars to materialism as a tool of feminist investigation.[16] Calling themselves materialist feminists, and explicitly diverging from the more strictly Marxist approach of early cultural materialists working in Britain, they grounded their work in Louis Althusser's extension of the meaning of the material beyond that of physical substance as realized in physical actions.[17] The Althusserian concept of the relative autonomy of ideology from economic conditions grants greater cultural significance to the power of images, myths, and discourses over our thinking and our lives. Political speeches, slogans, and symbols are examples of such material practices that Althusser classifies as ideological state apparatuses in contrast to, but not completely distinct from repressive state apparatuses such as the police or military.

In dealing with fifteenth-century Spain, it would clearly be anachronistic to speak of state apparatuses, or even of a state in the modern sense. It is evident, however, that Isabel and Fernando's keen appreciation for the ideological power of symbols and discourses anticipates the nature and function of modern political propaganda. Furthermore, as I discuss at the end of this essay, the symbols they created and assiduously propagated transcended their own age, so much so, that they were easily appropriated by the modern Spanish dictator Francisco Franco (1939–75) to impose fascist values on a painfully divided nation.

At this point, some historical background is called for.[18] Isabel's rapid and unexpected ascendancy began in 1468. From her birth in 1451 to the age of seventeen, she lived what Tarcisio de Azcona, Isabel's most objective modern biographer, calls "a hidden life."[19] She had been named third in the line of royal succession by her father King Juan II—after her half-brother Enrique, but also after her younger brother Alfonso. The order demonstrates the de facto sexism of the Castilian dynastic system, although there was no legal impediment against female rule in Castile as there was in Aragon, where Salic Law was in force. In 1462, the birth of a daughter to Juan II's son (and Isabel's half-brother), then reigning as Enrique IV (1454–74) and his queen Juana of Portugal complicated the line of succession, because the *infanta* Juana belonged to the direct line of succession, while Alfonso and Isabel were members of the collateral line.

Throughout the second half of Enrique's reign, a powerful if constantly shifting coalition of noblemen and prelates opposed the king's efforts to centralize and strengthen the power of the monarchy, curtailing the nobility's privileges and advancing men of lower rank. In their opposition to Enrique, which frequently bordered on outright rebellion, the grandees rallied around Prince Alfonso. The seignorial revolt finally erupted in outright civil war in 1464. Desperate to end it, Enrique made numerous concessions to the league of nobles, not the least of which was naming Alfonso heir to the throne instead of his own daughter Juana, thereby tacitly validating accusations that his daughter and heir was illegitimate.

Prince Alfonso's unexpected death in 1468 changed the course of Castilian history. It thrust his inexperienced seventeen-year-old sister into the forefront of the seignorial rebellion and made it inevitable that a woman—either Juana or Isabel—would wear the crown of Castile. From that moment on, Isabel and her supporters advanced her claim to the throne by discursively attacking the sexual body of the reigning king. They unleashed against the royal family the full force of a propaganda campaign whose goal was to discredit Enrique as a king and as a man. Official and unofficial accusations of sexual and gender-role transgressions against Enrique and his queen, Juana of Portugal, were circulated throughout the kingdom. Charges of impotence and sodomy against the king led inevitably to charges of adultery against the queen, and both king and queen were accused of illicit sexual relations with Enrique's favorite, Beltrán de la Cueva.

The ultimate goal of the accusations promoted by Isabel and her supporters against her half-brother and his wife was the reinforcement of the earlier imputation of illegitimacy to her niece and rival, Juana of Castile. From dubbing Enrique "the Impotent" and his wife Juana adulterous, it was a simple matter to taint the younger Juana as "la Beltraneja," that is, the shameful offspring of her mother and her mother's lover. This very accusation is made outright in the list of grievances presented to Enrique by the rebel faction in September of 1464 as a prelude to civil war.[20]

Because the accusations against Enrique and his wife and daughter still circulate in scholarly and popular publications, it bears stating that there is absolutely no documentary proof for any of the charges. As recently as 1992, Azcona made a moving plea for historians of Spain to stop applying the damaging sobriquet to Juana, the legitimate heir to Castile.[21] Azcona, however, does not affirm the inevitable corollary to the legitimacy of Juana's claim to the throne, namely, the *illegitimacy* of Isabel's claim. Like her great-grandfather Enrique II, the bastard founder of the Trastamaran dynastic line, Isabel was a usurper. The very stridency of the Isabelline accusations of illegitimacy against her rival Juana can be considered a measure of the tenuousness of her own claims. The zealousness with which she and Fernando disseminated the nuptial fiction of the royal devices should be viewed in a similar light.

Isabel's reinforcement of the medieval sex/gender system was instrumental to her rise to power and basic to her political agenda.[22] The subordination of women to men based on the need to control women's natural irrationality and concupiscence and the prohibition of nonprocreative sexual acts are central to the rhetorical battles waged in her name. She and her supporters mystified the major sociopolitical causes of the disorder of the final years of Enrique's rule—nobiliary rivalry, greed and power-grabbing, and the king's misguided politics of appeasement—constructing them as moral degeneracy and sexual corruption within the royal family. These abnormalities were then made the cause of a breakdown in dynastic continuity and succession. In this manner, Isabel and her supporters intentionally undermined the delicate balance of the medieval construction of the king's two bodies: a mortal, biological body and an immortal, political body.[23] The restoration of dynastic continuity, and therefore of the health of the kingdom, was the mission Isabel's supporters claimed God had set her. It was one she eagerly accepted.

To maintain the moral high ground in her opposition to Juana, Isabel had to marry and produce a legitimate, preferably male, heir. Unlike her English counterpart almost a century later, she could not choose to remain a virgin queen. Isabel's choice of Fernando, heir to the crown of Aragon, was a highly conscious one, due in part to his youthful vigor and reputation for bravery on the battlefield. These qualities suggested that the prince could not only father the desired heir, but that he would be capable of defending Isabel's succession on the battlefield. Beyond this, the marriage held the promise of uniting the two most powerful kingdoms of the peninsula.

At the same time, however, it is clear that Isabel had every intention of ruling Castile in her own right, as "queen and natural mistress" of the kingdom. Her determination not to yield her powers of governance is clear as early as 1469, in the *capitulaciones de matrimonio* drawn up for Fernando and signed at their betrothal, ten years before he inherited the kingdom of Aragon. She never wavered in that resolve. Thus, even as Isabel accused Enrique and his queen of subverting sanctioned gender roles and relations, she herself refused to accept the subordination that the roles of wife and queen entailed in the medieval and early modern periods.

A striking example of the kind of patriarchal pressure Isabel experienced is found in *Jardín de nobles doncellas,* addressed to the then princess by the Augustinian cleric Martín de Córdoba in the fateful year of 1468 when Isabel became a pretender to the throne and when she was deciding which of her several marriage suitors to choose. Fray Martín presents for the princess's edification a theory of monarchy derived principally from Aristotle's *Politics* and Seneca's *De clementia.* It is grounded in the divine right of kings and on the corporative concept of the state, including the common medieval metaphorization of the body politic as a macrocosm of the human body, and by extension, the association of the stability of social and political institutions with the stability of the family. In the preface, Fray Martín explicitly identifies his treatise as a defense of female sovereignty.[24] This assertion, however, is repeatedly undermined by the substance of his argument. For example, immediately after affirming the female right to rule, Fray Martín cites Aristotle to the effect that reason is what approximates man to God and qualifies him to rule over beasts and other intellectually inferior beings (137–38).

What then is the proper role of a queen? Just as a well-ordered earthly kingdom is a reflection of the divine, so it follows that "como en el reyno celestial el rey, Jhesu Cristo, es juez & la Virgen Reina es abogada, así ha de ser enel reyno terrenal, que el rey sea juez & la reyna abogada" (as in the celestial kingdom the King, Jesus Christ, is judge, and the Virgin Queen is the lawyer, so should it be in the earthly kingdom, that the king be the judge and the queen the lawyer) (201). In this intercessory role, the earthly queen, like the heavenly one, is limited to pleading on behalf of the people should the king oppress them. The royal division of labor that the cleric holds up as an example for the princess culminates with a striking military image: "la señora es escudo, ca no sólo ha de ser piadosa como madre, ni como abogada cerca del rey, mas ha de ser paués & adaraga & escudo, defendiendo los menudos de las fuerças de los mayores" (the lady is a shield, for not only must she be compassionate like a mother, or like a lawyer who is close to the king, but she must also be a pavis, buckler, and shield, defending the lowly against the force of the great) (88). In the patriarchal family of the *imperium*, the phallic sword of justice corresponds to the king in his two primary medieval functions, that of judge and warrior; the queen's uterine shield of compassion and clemency functions as the sword's supplement, separate and unequal.[25]

We have dramatic historiographic evidence of Isabel's first act of resistance to the patriarchal lessons proffered by tutors and advisers such as Fray Martín. It occurred at her precipitous accession to the throne in December of 1474, just days after Enrique IV's death. Diego de Valera, a much-admired arbiter of courtly etiquette, provides the most detailed account of a ritual that he surely witnessed. On the morning of her coronation, Isabel threw off her white mourning habit and donned a dazzling gown and brilliant jewelry to receive the oath of fealty and process through the streets of Segovia. Valera emphasizes the procession's ostentatious display of power, as the princess's trusted adviser Gutierre de Cárdenas preceded her in the procession holding aloft in his right hand "una espada desnuda de la vayna a demostrar a todos como a ella convenía punir e castigar los malhechores, como reyna e señora natural de estos reynos e señoríos" (an unsheathed sword so as to demonstrate to all how it was appropriate for her to punish and chastise wrongdoers, as queen and natural sovereign of these kingdoms and seignories).[26]

By flaunting the phallic sword of justice removed from its vaginal sheath, Isabel symbolically appropriated the power that Martín de Córdoba's theory of monarchy denied her. In doing so, furthermore, she boldly signaled a break with recent Castilian tradition, which designated as the symbol of monarchy a scepter topped by a gold orb and a cross, like the one that the tomb effigy of her father Juan II holds. As Peggy Liss observes, the queen's adoption of the sword, symbol of monarchic militant justice, signaled that the new queen was aligning herself with earlier, more "virile" times, disassociating herself from the perceived passivity and weakness, that is, "femininity," of her immediate predecessors, Enrique IV and even her own father, Juan II.[27] I shall return to this cross-gendering strategy.

Despite Valera's assertion, it was not accepted practice for a queen to act as judge, as the chronicler himself admits in recalling the grumbling about Isabel's manly act: "según algunas leyes que declaran acerca de las mugeres no aver lugar de juzgar" (according to some laws that declare that women have no right to judge).[28] The chronicler Alfonso de Palencia presents a more biting critique of the queen's self-ascribed role as judge: "Todos sabemos que se concedió a los Reyes; pero nunca supe de Reina que hubiese usurpado este varonil atributo" (we all know this was granted to kings, but I have never heard of a queen who usurped this manly attribute).[29]

The unequal balance of power between Isabel and Fernando was confirmed in the *Concordia de Segovia* signed by the monarchs on January 15, 1475. The document limited Fernando's governance rights and privileges in Castile, maintaining the power relations outlined six years earlier in the marriage *capitulaciones* and symbolically expressed in the coronation rituals and pronouncements. It affirmed Isabel's sole proprietorship of the crown of Castile, accorded her the right to grant all titles, offices, and privileges, and fixed the line of succession so that their daughter Isabel, and not Fernando, would inherit.[30]

The *Concordia* also provoked disagreement. Chronicler Fernando del Pulgar's version of the negotiations leading up to its signing cites one group of nobles (not surprisingly, the group with allegiances to Aragon) who maintained that Fernando, not Isabel, should rule Castile. Fernando, by virtue of being great-grandson of Juan I of Castile, was the rightful ruler of Castile on two counts: "ansí por pertenecer al Rey la sucesión destos Reynos, como por ser varón" (both because the succession of these kingdoms belongs to the king and because he is a man).[31] Alfonso de Palencia is typically more virulent in his attack on these departures from tradition. Assuming Isabel's feminine malleability, he attacks the *grandes* who influenced her to resist "el yugo que tal vez el ilustrísimo cónyuge, apoyado en la autoridad de marido, intentara imponer a las cervices castellanas" (the yoke that her most illustrious spouse, relying on the authority of a husband, attempted to impose on Castilian necks).[32]

Palencia's use of the etymologically related terms *yugo* and *cónyuge* (yoke and conjugal partner) brings us back to the royal heraldic shield. Most scholars attribute its composition to the renowned Castilian humanist Antonio de Nebrija and date it close to the signing of the *Concordia de Segovia* in the early spring of 1475. The royal shield is thus the product of a liminal event and as such is marked by ambiguity and flux.[33] Its liminality is overdetermined: not only was it created shortly after the death of a king, on the occasion of the contested coronation of his successor, and shortly before a war of succession, it also harks back to the royal wedding that had taken place five years earlier, when Isabel was still a princess and her spouse a prince.

The plurivalent field of signification contained in the royal shield makes it more complex and contradictory than tradition has acknowledged. It is an unstable construct of a tenuous union between a queen fully in possession of her kingdom and a prince who has yet to inherit his. A few scholars have recently begun to set the record straight regarding the multiple meanings of the royal shield.[34] Most helpful is Juan Gil's reminder that the yoke, yoke straps, and motto *Tanto monta* originally belonged solely to Fernando.[35] In its initial Aragonese context, the meaning of the device was not marital but martial. It represented the prince's much-admired gifts as a warrior and military strategist by associating them with no less grand a model than Alexander the Great and specifically, the Alexandrian legend of the Gordian knot. Whoever crafted the shield at the request of the monarchs, it is clear that it retains its kingly connotations: resoluteness primarily, but also royal power, territorial expansion, and the political principle of the ends justifying the means. These meanings were entirely apposite to the primary role of the medieval prince, that of warrior, a role that Fernando fulfilled splendidly, both before and after his marriage to Isabel. Furthermore, the motto's oracular associations befitted one who had been from birth the subject of messianic prophecies about a future conquest of Asia that would fulfill one of the most ancient longings of western Christendom: the reconquest of the Holy Land and the capture of Jerusalem.[36]

These associations could not so readily be applied to Isabel, whose gender barred her from the battlefield. The shield, however, brilliantly overcomes this obstacle. First, it truncates Alexander's classical motto *Nihil interest quomodo soluantur* (It matters not how the problem is solved) so that it becomes simply *Nihil interest.* It then translates the classical epigram, which in Latin would only have been understood by the cultured minority, into the more accessible but equally pithy and enigmatic motto, *Tanto monta.* The vernacular abbreviation brings into play the broader and more ambiguous semantic field suggested by the etymological association of *yugo* and *cónyuge.* Finally, the composition underscores the conjugal bond through visual and verbal chiasmus. As was already mentioned, by mutual agreement of the monarchs, the coat of arms Castile/Leon takes symbolic precedence through its placement in the upper left quadrant, over the coat of arms of Aragon and Aragon/Sicily in the upper right. The order of the emblems beneath the shield is reversed, however: the Aragonese yoke is placed on the left, before the Castilian arrows. The chiastic structure is reinforced phonetically through the inversion of the motto's a-o vowel sounds and the closed and open syllables in which they occur.[37]

In other manifestations of the royal devices, Fernando's *yugo* is often placed next to the initial Y of Isabel, and Isabel's *flechas* located next to the F for Fernando. These chiastic formulations are not merely romantic or celebratory, as is still often claimed.[38] They gesture toward yet another layer of meaning, a destabilizing cross-gendering of the kind we saw practiced by Isabel in her coronation march. The linguistic and visual chiasmus not only promotes the nuptial fiction, as commentators agree, it does so specifically through a kind of linguistic cross-gendering, an effect that transgresses gender and geopolitical boundaries, masculinizing the feminine Castile and feminizing the masculine Aragon, smoothing over real tensions and inequalities, and in the process enabling queenly power.

Nebrija and his royal patrons understood that the classical motto's strict sense of Alexandrian prowess would have been understood only by the educated minority. For that reason, they layered over the more popular, double-gendered symbolism of marital union over the abstruse and exclusively masculine sense.[39] The popular, even romantic connotations that the double-gendered yoke promoted are evident in the octosyllabic couplet that grew out of the motto "Tanto monta, monta tanto, Isabel como Fernando." The fact that the ditty is still memorized by Spanish schoolchildren attests to its lasting power.

For Juan-Antonio González Iglesias, the courtly connotations of *Tanto monta* respond to Fernando's desire to mask any overt proclamation of equality with Isabel and Castile, given the terms of the *Concordia de Segovia.* He does not completely exclude the latent presence of the original Alexandrian association of *Tanto monta,* however. Rather, he considers it a subtle reminder of Fernando's warrior role and masculine prerogatives.[40] This explains what Fernando stood to gain from the plurivalent symbolism of the emblems and motto, but it does not address the goals that Isabel sought in promoting an emblem that tied political equality to the affirmation that might makes right. I have argued for Isabel's awareness of her problematic status as female sovereign, especially in Aragon, and her agency in addressing it. We must conclude that she also approved of the shield's subtle way of simultaneously articulating and mystifying the imposition by force not only of Fernando's power but of her own as well.

Looked at from this perspective, the shield contains a much more explicit symbol of naked force than the yoke: the *haz de flechas* or bundled arrows associated with Isabel. As far as I know, no definitive explanation of its meaning exists. Part of the difficulty is that the number of arrows depicted there varies from the five seen on the heraldic shield to the eleven mentioned in a royal document of 1482.[41] González Iglesias suggests that the bundled arrows balance the yoke device not only visually but conceptually, the arrows tying together what has been severed in the yoke symbol.[42] Alberto Montaner associates the arrows with the union of the Iberian kingdoms and believes that the device carries with it a sense of religious evangelization as the means to that end.[43] Rafael Domínguez Casas suggests other possible meanings, including the possibility that the arrows represented heretical or diabolical threats that the sovereigns would overcome, or, because arrows were the weapon of foot archers, that they were meant to symbolize the small-town dwellers who helped Isabel rise to power.[44] It is significant in this regard that the arrows are always depicted with the arrowheads pointing downward, indicating readiness for use in warfare or in the execution of common criminals, as was traditional in Castile.[45]

I suggest that Isabel's symbolic *haz de flechas* contains its own classical subtext: the Roman *fasces,* the bundle of rods and axe with a projecting blade that Roman magistrates carried before them as a symbol of their power. The etymological link between *haz* and *fasces,* according to this reading, parallels the connection between *yugo* and *cónyuge.* It also points directly back to Isabel's recent dramatic performance of symbolic masculine power: the unsheathed sword held aloft in her coronation march.[46] The ease with which the Spanish Fascist Party adopted the yoke and arrows, as will be discussed, would seem to confirm that underlying meaning. Ultimately, what holds the two royal devices together are the proverbial ties that bind: the ties that bind the Aragonese subjects to Fernando and the Castilians to Isabel, as much or more than each of the rulers equally and irrevocably to the other. The notion of force contained in both royal devices—the queenly force of the bundled arrows or the kingly force of the severed yoke straps—encodes both an acknowledgment of the violence needed to forge the precarious political and kinship alliances that the devices express as well as a subtle threat to those who would undermine the sovereigns' political project.

Two notable texts dedicated to Isabel some time during the early years of her reign suggest that her subjects understood both the association of Isabel with force and the cross-gendering technique that the devices use. The first is the anonymous *La Poncella de Francia,* which narrates for Isabel's edification and "consolation" the story of Joan of Arc. The comparison of Joan's manly bravery and skill when facing the English and their French allies to Isabel's when confronting her enemies is overtly Alexandrian: "E no digan Alexandre aver fecho mucho en señorear el mundo, según el tiempo muy aparejado a sojuzgar las gentes que falló, que por mayor caso ternía una sola ciudad en vuestros reinos pacíficamente tomar, que en aquel tiempo señorear la redondez del mundo" (Let it not be said that Alexander accomplished a lot in conquering the world, because his era was more conducive to the subjection of the peoples he encountered, for he would find it harder to peacefully capture a single city in your kingdom than to master the whole globe in his own time).[47] Here Fernando's resoluteness and imperial ambitions are explicitly assigned to Isabel, recalling at once the yoke and the coronation sword that severed the patriarchal conjugal yoke straps.

The second work was written by Fray Íñigo de Mendoza, one of Isabel's court preachers. In Mendoza's extended verse gloss on Fernando's yoke and yoke straps, the king is depicted as a plowman, undoubtedly a reference to the humble origins of King Gordius in the Alexandrian legend. The yoke and yoke straps used to bind together the bulls that plow the fields are metaphors for the feudal ties that bind the lord's vassals to each other and to him. The binding of vassals depends on their condition, Mendoza explains. Those vassals submitting to Fernando out of love need not be bound at all—"sin coyundas, con dulçor / se deben de governar" (without yoke straps, with sweetness, they should be governed). Less compliant vassals require tighter binding—"los otros desenfrenados / . . . atarlos, pues que son locos" (the other uncontrolled ones . . . bind them, for they are wild).[48]

Mendoza's agricultural metaphor slides easily into a military one, as he exhorts the king to subjugate his kingdom (305). It also slips readily into conjugal imagery, however, as the poet imagines the king and queen after their victory in the war of succession: "los toros al yugo atados, / las vuestras manos reales / ararán los peñascales" (the oxen tied to the yoke, your royal hands will plow the rocky crags) (314). Plowing is productive here, and not only in relation to growing food for the nation. When Mendoza reminds Fernando of the need to have "buen aparejo, / buen arado" (good tools, a good plowshare) (314), we cannot discount the possibility that he is referring to yet another connotation of the motto *Tanto monta*. In animal husbandry, "montar" refers to "the horse or burro's covering of the mare, mounting."[49] In stressing the importance of Fernando's "tool," Mendoza associates the breeding and mating activity of bulls with the production of a fitting heir to the throne. The symbolism of the yoke strap extends to include the ploughshare, both symbols of kingly power to which the queen, no less than his subjects, must submit.

Zanger argues concerning Maria Teresa and Louis XIV that the sexual, mortal body of the queen threatens monarchical power not only because it undermines the divine image of the sovereign, but also because it is fundamental to the fictions of dynastic continuity.[50] Maria Teresa was a queen consort; queen regnants such as Isabel represented an even greater threat to sovereign fictions. Mendoza's bawdy use of *montar* speaks to the anxiety caused by the fact that Isabel had gone far beyond the traditional reproductive role of the queen (it is important to remember that at the time of the royal shield's creation, Isabel had not yet produced the desired male heir). Besides, if the queen was acting like a king, wielding swords and shooting arrows, what did that mean for Fernando's role in their marriage? Was it to be that of a mere stud animal?[51]

The symbolic power of the *yugo* and *flechas* has been extraordinarily long-lived in Spain. In the remainder of this essay, I examine their appropriation in the second half of the twentieth century, during the regime of Francisco Franco. The Spanish heraldic shield crafted for Franco shortly after he took power in 1939 is an intentional visual calque of the shield of Isabel and Fernando (fig. 3.2). The motto *Tanto monta,* however, has been transformed into the infamous *Una, grande, libre* (One, great, free), a reference to the *generalísimo*'s unification of a nation torn by a civil war far more devastating than the one that confronted Isabel upon her accession.

This is not the first official use of the royal devices in the twentieth century. They had previously been adopted by the Falange, the Spanish Fascist Party, at its founding (fig. 3.3). In 1932, Ernesto Giménez Caballero, an intellectual who went on to hold a variety of important ministerial positions in Franco's government, wrote the messianically titled *Genio de España: exaltaciones a una resurrección nacional y del mundo* (*The Spanish Genius: Exaltations of Its National and World Resurrection*) in which he claimed to have proposed the symbol, proudly stating "today it is the emblem of the nascent fascist movement in Spain."[52] The link between the Isabelline *fasces* and the Roman *fasces* posited earlier is here readily appropriated to symbolize the ideals of the new Spanish Fascist Party, which has its own ties to Rome, in this case, the Rome of Mussolini.[53] In the aftermath of the Nationalist victory in the Spanish Civil War in 1939, the yoke and arrow became a leitmotif of patriotic poetry, in ways often strikingly reminiscent of fifteenth-century Isabelline writers such as Íñigo de Mendoza.

The Castilian Isabel (not the Aragonese Fernando) soon became an icon of National Catholicism, which stridently insisted that the stability and strength

Figure 3.2. Heraldic shield of Spain under Francisco Franco <http://en.wikipedia.org/wiki/Image:Coat_of_arms_of_Spain_under_Franco.svg>. Reproduced with permission.

Figure 3.3. Banner of Falange political party (Falange Española de las Juntas de Ofensiva Nacional-Sindicalista), founded 1933.

of the state depended on the stability of the patriarchal family that, in turn, was dependent on the submissiveness of women.[54] The queen was one of two female role models—the other being Saint Teresa of Ávila—who were insistently held up to young Spanish women by Franco. Fundamental in the dissemination of these models was the Falange's women's auxiliary, the Sección Femenina, led by Pilar Primo de Rivera, sister of Falangist Party founder José Antonio Primo de Rivera. With over half a million members by 1939, the Sección was the largest women's organization in Spanish history. One of its publications for adolescents and young women was simply titled *Y,* a modern redeployment of the initial so widely disseminated four hundred years earlier. It is also significant that the Sección's most highly coveted service awards were gold and silver *Y*s.[55]

Pilar Primo de Rivera herself was to a great extent responsible for encouraging women to emulate Isabel, which meant to be cheerfully and silently self-sacrificing, to maintain their households in times of extreme deprivation, and to serve the nation by producing children to repopulate Spain after the devastation of the civil war. Primo de Rivera regularly addressed the nation's young women in advice columns published in *Y* and its companion publication *Medina,* where the yoke and arrows served as a seal of Falangist approval on her words of wisdom.

The confinement of women to the private sphere in the aftermath of the civil war went well beyond rhetoric. From 1942 on, labor laws stipulated the dismissal of married women, a variety of legislative policies were issued to boost the birth rate, and contraception and abortion were criminalized. As Helen Graham shows, however, the dire economic crisis of the postwar period created by Franco's autarkic economic policy meant that the reality of many women, especially poor urban working women, was quite different.[56]

The Sección harbored similar ideological contradictions. It took middle-class women out of their domestic routines to a greater extent than any single organization on the Republican side by enlisting (or requiring) their help in a wide range of desperately needed social services, from nursing to family and child welfare. Of course, by providing free labor in hospitals, food kitchens, schools, nursing homes, orphanages, and such, the Sección served the Francoist government by ameliorating the effects of a serious socioeconomic crisis, thereby promoting regime stabilization in the 1940s.[57] At the same time, however, despite its overt message of female subservience, it granted a measure of freedom and agency to the single, lower middle-class women who carried out its activities.[58]

A rhetorical flourish at the end of Primo de Rivera's December 1945 column in *Medina* illustrates the gender contradictions of the Sección. Recalling the cross-gendering images that we have seen in fifteenth-century texts, she states: "May we become so feminine in this that one day you will truly consider us men."[59] Intended to reinforce the essentialized feminine value of self-abnegation, this statement actually undermines it by revealing that gender identity and roles are in fact constructed.

In an even more striking instance of symbolic cross-gendering, Franco himself in the early years of his rule often explicitly identified with Isabel. In 1939, just after the end of the civil war, Franco promised that he would restore the Castillo de la Mota in Medina de Campo and donate it to the Sección Femenina for use as a training center. Not coincidentally, Mota was the site of Isabel's death in November 1504. On May 29, 1942, at the celebration marking the completion of the restoration, the dictator gave a speech. Using the royal we, he compared himself to the Catholic Queen, referring precisely to the moment of her accession that has been central to my discussion: "Lo mismo que nosotros recibimos a España, en forma similar la recibió Isabel de Castilla, dividida y enfrentada en luchas mezquinas, con grupos esquinados y nobles desenfrenados. . . . Entonces se corrigió con la sabiduría de un ideario, con el imperio del espíritu y con la fortaleza de la unidad" (Just as we received Spain, in a similar fashion did Isabel the Catholic receive it, divided and torn by petty conflicts, with difficult factions and uncontrolled nobles. . . . All of this she corrected with the wisdom of an ideology, the empire of the spirit, and the strength of unity).[60] On this same occasion, Franco bestowed on Pilar Primo de Rivera a medal in recognition of her work with the Sección: the golden *Y* bearing a crown, a move that symbolically makes her his political partner, his "queen."

Franco often constructed his modern-day struggle against the internal enemies of a pure Spain as a continuation of the Reconquest brought to a glorious conclusion by the Catholic Monarchs. In 1944, he triumphally connected the two crusades: "Un día tuvieron que ser los Reyes Católicos los que aquí vinieron, con el restablecimiento de la unidad y la autoridad, a suprimir las banderías y las divisiones. Y transcurridos varios siglos, es nuestro Movimiento quién renueva aquella tradición y en forma similar os devuelve, con la unidad, la autoridad, una dicha mayor y una espléndida certidumbre del porvenir de España" (One day it had to be the Catholic Monarchs who arrived here, with the reestablishment of unity and authority, to suppress factionalism and divisions. And several centuries later, it is our Movement which renews that tradition and in similar fashion returns it to you, with the unity, the authority, a greater joy, and a splendid certainty of Spain's future).[61]

These words demonstrate that the threat of force that I have argued subtended the visual propaganda of both Isabel and Fernando in the fifteenth century is very much present in Francoist propaganda as well. Both the Catholic Monarchs and Franco used repression and violence to build a unified nation founded on the exclusion or elimination of socially unacceptable elements. The twentieth-century dictator's appropriation of the centuries-old nuptial fiction of the Catholic Monarchs, and especially of Isabel, in this endeavor is proof of its lasting hold over the Spanish national imaginary, a hold that is only now being broken.

Notes

This chapter expands on ideas presented in my book *Isabel Rules: Constructing Queenship, Wielding Power* (Minneapolis: University of Minnesota Press, 2004). All translations from Spanish into English are my own, unless otherwise noted.

1. For a different approach to European monarchy in general and in particular to late medieval Iberia, see Theresa Earenfight, "Two Bodies, One Spirit: Isabel and Fernando's Construction of Monarchical Partnership," in *Queen Isabel I of Castile: Power, Patronage, Persona,* ed. Barbara F. Weissberger (Woodbridge, Suffolk: Boydell and Brewer, 2008), which argues vigorously against singling out queenship but rather considers the queen and king together as part of a dynamic, relational partnership.

2. Even recent biographical and critical studies that document Isabel's singular power have difficulty resisting the hagiographic and romantic strains that consciously or unconsciously reveal discomfort with female rule. See, for example, Peggy Liss, *Isabel the Queen: Life and Times* (1992; rev. ed. Philadelphia: University of Pennsylvania Press, 2004), 70: "Above all, nothing in Isabel's remarkable life is more remarkable than the love and respect she and Fernando demonstrated mutually, immediately, and ever after." The very title of another quincentenary biography, *Isabel, mujer y reina,* illustrates the author's need to contain the many gender-role inversions his own narrative records (Luis Suárez Fernández, *Isabel mujer y reina* [Madrid: Ediciones Rialp, 1992]). Tarcisio de Azcona, Isabel's best modern biographer, rejects such romanticized visions. *Isabel la Católica: Estudio crítico de su vida y su reinado* (1964; Madrid: Editorial Católica, 1992), 165.

3. The classic work on medieval Spanish heraldry is Faustino Menéndez Pidal de Navascues, *Heráldica medieval española.* Vol. I: *La Casa Real de León y Castilla.* Instituto Salazar y Castro (C.S.I.C.) (Madrid: Hidalguía, 1982); on Isabel I's shield, see 199–211. See also Martín de Riquer, *Heráldica castellana en tiempos de los Reyes Católicos* (Barcelona: Quaderns Crema, 1986). The particular rendering of the heraldic shield and accompanying devices depicted in figure 1 was apparently a favorite. Cf. the frontispiece of Alfonso X's *Fuero Real,* glossed by Alfonso Diaz de Montalvo in 1501 and the exquisitely carved ivory oliphant and powder horn attributed to the master of arms of Castile and Aragon sometime between 1492 and 1504 (*Isabel la Católica,* 270 and 355–56; for different versions of the shield, see 258, 265, and 267).

4. Azcona, *Isabel la Católica,* 248–50. I discuss the *Acuerdo*'s balancing of symbolic power below.

5. The eagle appeared on Isabel's personal seals while she was still Princess of Asturias (Menéndez Pidal, *Heráldica medieval española,* 199–200). The terminology associated with the paraheraldic (or protoemblematic) visual signs I discuss here is confusingly fluid; they are called variously devices, symbols, badges, and emblems. I will use the first two terms, more appropriate to the medieval period.

6. According to Riquer, monarchs and grandees first adopted such *divisas* in the first half of the fourteenth century as "their personal emblems or those created by them for chivalric orders . . . whose essential characteristic is that they are not placed within the outlines of the heraldic escutcheons but embroidered on clothing, engraved on expensive objects, or sculpted on stone facades or monuments, like the ancient preheraldic signs that continued to be used during heraldic times" (Riquer, *Heráldica castellana,* 27). On the *invenciones,* a form that originated in ceremonial tournaments and that was assiduously cultivated at Isabel's court, see Ian Macpherson, *The "Invenciones y letras" of the "Cancionero general."* Papers of the Medieval Hispanic Research Seminar 9 (London: Queen Mary and Wesfield College, 1998).

7. Joaquín Yarza Luaces, *Los Reyes Católicos: Paisaje artístico de una monarquía* (Madrid: Nerea, 1993).

8. Juan-Antonio González Iglesias, "El humanista y los príncipes: Antonio de Nebrija, inventor de las empresas heráldicas de los Reyes Católicos," in *Antonio de Nebrija: Edad Media y Renacimiento,* ed. Carmen Codoñer and Juan-Antonio González Iglesias (Salamanca: Universidad de Salamanca, 1994), 68.

9. From 1475 to 1479, Isabel defended her dynastic rights against the Castilians who considered her niece, Juana of Castile, daughter of Enrique IV, to be the rightful heir to the throne. The battle at Toro that San Juan de los Reyes commemorates marks the defeat of Juana's Portuguese allies.

10. *Isabel la Católica: la magnificencia de un reinado.* Ed. Sociedad Estatal de Conmemoraciones culturales (Salamanca: Ediciones El Viso, 2004), 161.

11. *Magnificencia de un reinado,* 170. The Greek inscription on the university façade—"The monarchs for the University; the University for the Monarchs"—may intentionally echo the sentiment of the *Tanto monta* motto.

12. *Magnificencia de un reinado,* 356, 501.

13. For an intelligent discussion of the precarious nature of the relationship between Castile and Aragon, see Emilia Salvador Esteban, "La precaria monarquía hispánica de

los Reyes Católicos: reflexiones sobre la participación de Isabel I en el gobierno aragonés." *Homenaje a J.A. Maravall,* ed. María Carmen Iglesias, Carlos Moya, and Luis Rodríguez Zúñiga (Madrid: Centro de Investigaciones Sociológica, 1985), 3: 315–27.

14. In his definitive study of Castilian heraldry, Riquer completely rejects the matrimonial meanings of the Catholic Monarchs' royal shield (Riquer, *Heráldica castellana,* 29). As will become clear, I do not entirely agree with Riquer's assessment.

15. Abby Zanger, *Scenes from the Marriage of Louis XIV: Nuptial Fictions and the Making of Absolutist Power* (Stanford, Calif.: Stanford University Press, 1997).

16. Judith Newton and Deborah Rosenfeldt, *Feminist Criticism and Social Change: Sex, Class, and Race in Literature and Culture* (New York: Methuen, 1985).

17. Ibid., xvii–xix; Louis Althusser, "Ideology and Ideological State Apparatuses," in *Lenin and Philosophy and Other Essays* (London: New Left Books, 1971).

18. For the summary that follows I have relied on Azcona, *Isabel la Católica,* and Liss, *Isabel the Queen.*

19. Azcona, *Isabel la Católica,* 52.

20. Referring to Beltrán de la Cueva, the nobles boldly asserted that both Enrique and others were aware that Juana was not his and his queen's biological daughter (Azcona, *Isabel la Católica,* 92).

21. Azcona, *Isabel la Católica,* 39.

22. See Elizabeth Lehfeldt, "Ruling Sexuality: The Political Legitimacy of Isabel of Castile," *Renaissance Quarterly* 53, no. 1 (2000): 31–56, for a different perspective on Isabel's manipulation of traditional sex and gender norms.

23. Ernst Kantorowicz, *The King's Two Bodies: A Study in Medieval Political Theology* (Princeton, N.J.: Princeton University Press, 1957). For Spain, see José Manuel Nieto Soria, *Fundamentos ideológicos del poder real en Castilla (s. XIII–XV),* (Madrid: EUDEMA, 1988).

24. "Some people, My Lady . . . take it badly when a kingdom or other state comes under the rule of a woman. But, as I will explain below, I disagree, since, from the very beginning of the World to the present, we see that God always gave woman responsibility for humanity's salvation, so that life would emerge from death" (Martín de Córdoba, *Jardín de nobles doncellas,* ed. Harriet Goldberg. North Carolina Studies in the Romance Languages 137 [Chapel Hill: University of North Carolina Press, 1974], 136). Subsequent citations are in text.

25. Catherine Soriano, "Conveniencia política y tópico literario en el *Jardín de nobles* doncellas (1468?) de Fray Martín Alonso de Córdoba," in *Actas del VI Congreso Internacional de la Asociación Hispánica de literatura Medieval* (Alcalá de Henares, 12–16 de septiembre de 1995). (Alcalá de Henares: Universidad de Alcalá, 1997), 1457–66, and Lehfeldt discuss *Jardín* in ways that complement my analysis.

26. Diego de Valera, *Memorial de diversas hazañas.* Vol. 3 of *Crónicas de los reyes de Castilla,* ed. Cayetano Rosell. Biblioteca de Autores Españoles 70. (Madrid: Atlas, 1953), 3–95.

27. Liss, *Isabel the Queen,* 98.

28. Valera, *Memorial de diversas hazañas,* 4.

29. Alfonso de Palencia, *Crónica de Enrique IV,* trans. Antonio Paz y Melia. Biblioteca de Autores Españoles 257, 258, 267. (Madrid: Atlas, 1973–75), 2: 162.

30. For a summary of the *Acuerdo*'s content, see Azcona, *Isabel la Católica*, 248–50.

31. Fernando del Pulgar, *Crónica de los Reyes Católicos*, in *Crónica de los reyes de Castilla*, ed. Cayetano Rosell. 3 vols. Biblioteca de Autores Españoles 70 (Madrid: Atlas, 1953), 1: 255.

32. Palencia, *Crónica de Enrique IV*, 2: 165.

33. As Zanger observes, following anthropologist Victor Turner, liminal events encourage the interrogation and reformulation of fixed ideas and established structures. The rituals and representations generated by liminal events are important because they are always related to or even constitute social ordering. Marriage rituals are at the heart of this liminal reordering, and royal marriage rituals, like royal funerals, engage many of the issues of dynastic continuity and succession constitutive of what we now call the fictions of sovereign power (3).

34. The first scholar to revisit the meaning of the emblems was Pedro Aguado Bleye, "Tanto Monta: La Concordia de Segovia y la empresa de Fernando el Católico." *Estudios segovianos* 1 (1949): 381–89.

35. Juan Gil, "Alejandro, el nudo gordiano y Fernando el Católico." *Habis* 16 (1985): 229–42.

36. Ibid., 232.

37. González Iglesias, "El humanista y los príncipes," 72.

38. Aguado Bleye, "Tanto Monta," 384.

39. González Iglesias, "El humanista y los príncipes," 66–67.

40. Ibid., 67.

41. The chancery document orders that a set of candlesticks donated by the queen to the cathedral of Santiago be engraved with "las armas del Rey mi señor y mías y con mi divisa que son once flechas atadas por medio" (the arms of the King my lord and mine with my emblem which are eleven arrows tied in the middle) (Menéndez Pidal de Navascues, *Heráldica medieval española*, 205).

42. González Iglesias, "El humanista y los príncipes," 72.

43. Alberto Montaner, "La emblemática de los Reyes Católicos: un error de interpretación histórica," *Universidad* (University of Zaragoza) 7 (1982): 24–26.

44. See Rafael Domínguez Casas, "The Artistic Patronage of Isabel the Catholic: Medieval or Modern?" in Weissberger, *Queen Isabel I of Castile*.

45. Liss, *Isabel the Queen*, 111.

46. On the representation of Isabel as judge and lawmaker in the historiographical and romance texts of Juan de Flores, one of her official chroniclers, see Weissberger, "Isabel's 'Nuevas leyes': Monarchic Law and Justice in *Triunfo de Amor*," in *Juan de Flores: Four Studies*, ed. Joseph J. Gwara. Papers of the Medieval Hispanic Research Seminar, 49 (London: Department of Hispanic Studies, Queen Mary, University of London, 2005), 91–113.

47. *"La Poncella de Francia": La historia castellana de Juana de Arco*, ed. Victoria Campo and Víctor Infantes (Madrid: Iberoamericana Vervuert, 1997), 91.

48. Íñigo de Mendoza, "Sermón trobado que fizo Fray Íñigo de Mendoza al muy alto y muy poderoso Príncipe, Rey y Señor, el Rey Don Fernando, Rey de Castilla y de Aragón, sobre el yugo y coyundas que Su Alteza trahe por divisa" in Íñigo de Mendoza, *Cancionero*,

ed. Julio Rodríguez-Puértolas (Madrid: Espasa-Calpe, 1968), 304. Further citations are in text.

49. *Diccionario de la lengua española*, 20th ed. (Madrid: Real Academia de la Lengua Española, 1984) 2: 924, no. 6.

50. Zanger, *Scenes from the Marriage of Louis XIV*, 5–6.

51. I owe this insight to Amanda Powell.

52. Giménez Caballero, *Genio de España*, 29. For more on Giménez Caballero and the "fascism of the intellectuals," see chapter 3 in Stanley Payne, *Fascism in Spain* (Madison: University of Wisconsin Press, 1999).

53. The dictator and founder of the Falange, José Antonio Primo de Rivera was an admirer of Mussolini (Payne, *Fascism in Spain*, 23–25).

54. Helen Graham, "Gender and the State: Women in the 1940's," in Helen Graham and Jo Labanyi, *Spanish Cultural Studies: An Introduction* (Oxford: Oxford University Press, 1995), 182–95. See also María Teresa Gallego Méndez, *Mujer, falange y franquismo* (Madrid: Taurus, 1983).

55. Manuel Ballesteros Gaibrois, *La letra "Y" (su historia y su presente)* (Madrid: Ediciones de la delegación nacional de la Sección Femenina de F.E.T. y de la J.O.N.S., 1939), establishes a Visigothic etymology for the grapheme *Y* and makes much of its grammatical function as a conjunction (34). On Francoist ideology of domesticity and motherhood, see Meriwynn Grothe, "Franco's Angels: Recycling the Ideology of Domesticity," *Revista de Estudios Hispánicos* 33 (1999): 513–37; and Aurora Morcillo Gómez, *True Catholic Womanhood: Gender Ideology in Franco's Spain* (Dekalb: Northern Illinois University Press, 2000).

56. Graham, "Gender and the State," 191.

57. Ibid., 193.

58. See also Victoria L. Enders, "Nationalism and Feminism: The Sección Femenina of the Falange," *History of European Ideas* 15, nos. 4–6 (1992): 673–80.

59. Reprinted in Luis Otero, *La Sección Femenina* (Madrid: EDAF, 1999), 38.

60. Francisco Franco, *Franco ha dicho . . .* (Madrid: Editorial Carlos Jaime, 1947), 212.

61. Ibid., 116–17.

4. Sword and Wimple

Isabel Clara Eugenia and Power

MAGDALENA S. SÁNCHEZ

Isabel Clara Eugenia (1566–1633)—Spanish *infanta* (princess), daughter of Philip II of Spain (r. 1556–98), joint-ruler (with her husband, Archduke Albert) of the Low Countries from 1599 to 1621, and governor from 1621, when Albert died, until her death in 1633—has so far received scant attention from scholars. This is unfortunate, because Isabel provides us with a fascinating example of early modern female sovereignty.

Isabel's actions as cosovereign with Albert suggest that she held a fairly traditional view of a married female sovereign: that is, that a married female ruler should not take a direct role in governing but should rather influence politics indirectly through her husband. She left conciliar meetings and negotiations to her husband and spent her days attending mass, visiting convents, and strolling through her gardens attended by her ladies-in-waiting. She also devoted herself to winning popular support for Habsburg rule in the Low Countries and to strengthening Catholicism in these lands. To those ends, she helped reform convents and purposely visited nearby villages to engage in public rituals that would bring her into greater contact with the populace. She cultivated an image of a benevolent, caring sovereign, who enjoyed life and welcomed occasions to mingle with her subjects.[1]

This is not to say, however, that she played no role in governing or that she was weak in exercising the power that she inherited. She conferred with her husband daily and affected policy indirectly through him. Once in sole authority, as she was after Albert's death in 1621, she showed confidence in her own ability to govern and did not hesitate to use her power to push for goals that were dear to her—in particular, the promotion of Tridentine Catholicism and the solidification of Habsburg dynastic rule throughout Europe. Both as cosovereign and later as sole governor, she worked within the framework available to her, at times clearly taking advantage of apparent limitations, in order to govern effectively and even forcefully.

Isabel and Albert were chosen as cosovereigns of the Netherlands by Isabel's father, Philip II of Spain. Philip had inherited the Low Countries from his father, Charles V, in 1555, but religious and political unrest there and Philip's inability to pacify and rule those territories effectively caused him to cede them to Isabel and Albert on their marriage in 1599. In choosing Isabel and Albert, Philip handed the Netherlands to two of his dearest and most trusted relatives. Isabel was Philip's eldest (and only surviving) daughter (by his third wife, Isabel de Valois) and his constant companion for the last decade of his life. Albert, youngest son of Philip's sister, Empress María, and Holy Roman Emperor Maximilian II, had been educated at Philip II's court, having arrived there at the age of eleven, and had served as viceroy of Portugal for a decade (1583–93) before returning to Madrid to help run the government and train the heir to the throne, the future Philip III. In 1595, Philip appointed Albert governor-general of the Netherlands, a position he held until becoming cosovereign of those territories. Isabel received the Netherlands as her marriage dowry and thus technically she was the principal ruler, although following her father's wishes and the terms of her marriage contract, she shared sovereignty with her husband (who as her husband administered her dowry). Jointly Isabel and Albert were (and are still) known as "the archdukes," derived from Albert's title of Archduke of Austria, and although Philip II considered giving them another title (such as dukes of Brabant), he ultimately decided against it. Isabel was often referred to as "la infanta" (princess in line to the Spanish throne) but the title of archduchess came through her marriage to Albert. Titles were actually of paramount importance, especially to Albert, who immediately after their marriage began a campaign in Madrid, Vienna, and Rome to gain the title of king and queen of Burgundy for himself and Isabel. He was ultimately unsuccessful in his efforts, but by 1610 turned his attention to an equally unsuccessful attempt to acquire an even more prestigious title: that of Holy Roman Emperor.[2] Albert's concern with gaining the title of sovereign demonstrates that he and Isabel worried about their credibility as sovereigns and their status vis-à-vis other rulers.

Scholars have noted all the limitations placed on Philip II's cession of sovereignty to Albert and Isabel—for example, a Spanish army, controlled by Madrid, would be based permanently in the Netherlands; the archdukes Isabel and Albert could not declare war or sue for peace without Madrid's consent; and they promised to do all in their power to bring the northern provinces under Spanish control and back into the Catholic fold[3]—and in noting these limitations, scholars have argued that Philip was merely giving the illusion of a cession while ensuring that Spain retained ultimate control over the Low Countries. Thus granting sovereignty to Isabel and Albert seemed merely a new means to achieve the same ends—the maintenance of those territories in Spanish hands.[4] All this may well be true; but even though Isabel and Albert always knew that their authority was limited, they took very seriously their promise to Philip II to make the Low Countries both Catholic and loyal to Spain. In adopting the rituals and symbols of sovereignty in the Netherlands, and in promoting themselves as independent rulers, Isabel and Albert tried to win the allegiance of their Dutch subjects, an allegiance Philip II had been unable to secure. If they were to succeed in making loyal subjects of the Dutch, the archdukes knew that they would in effect win Dutch fidelity to Catholic Habsburg rulers. They also no doubt welcomed the prestige, honor, and status associated with sovereignty, and their use of paintings to promote their sovereignty as God-given, along with their architectural projects and their gift-giving, indicate how willing they were to rival the magnificence of other sovereigns.[5] Their display of princely largesse and the creation of a large household financed only partially by Spain should caution us not to underestimate the archdukes' desire to emphasize their sovereignty and even their independence from Spain.[6] After all, both Isabel and Albert had reason to consider themselves at least as equals to other sovereigns. Philip II had thought to push Isabel's candidacy to the English and the French thrones and Albert for a time was considered a possible successor to Emperor Rudolf II. As the daughter of Philip II, the preeminent European monarch in the second half of the sixteenth century and a great proponent of using art to magnify royal power, Isabel knew how to display sovereignty, and no doubt felt justified in doing so.

The provisions of Philip's cession stipulated that sovereignty would devolve to the Spanish monarch at the death of either of the archdukes, should there be no direct heir. Isabel desperately wanted a child so that her line would continue in the Netherlands, which would then have a native-born prince to whom the Dutch could more easily give their allegiance. She undertook many pilgrimages to the church of Laeken (which had a miraculous ribbon that was supposed to help women conceive) to pray for an heir, an ultimately futile effort.[7] By 1616, when it became clear that there would be no heir, and desiring a peaceful transition of sovereignty from the archdukes to himself (and anxious to regain the Low Countries for himself and his heirs), Philip III (r. 1598–1621) demanded that deputies from all the provinces in Flanders publically swear allegiance to him. He had Archduke Albert serve as his proxy in receiving these oaths.[8]

At Albert's death in July 1621, Isabel accepted her consequent loss of sovereignty and was prepared to return to Spain to retire to the royal convent of the Descalzas, as her widowed aunts, Juana de Austria and Empress María, had done earlier. Retirement to a convent was also a time-honored and well-respected choice for widows and an appealing lifestyle for Isabel, who defined herself by her Catholic faith and who devoted much time to reforming and visiting convents. At Philip IV's request (Philip III had died in March 1621), however, and after careful consideration, she decided to remain in the Netherlands, even though her status had been reduced from that of sovereign to governor, subject to Spanish authority. In explaining her decision, Isabel stated that Albert, on his deathbed, had asked her to remain as governor because it was her duty to see to the future of the provinces and ensure that they remain Catholic and loyal to Spain. Isabel also claimed to be putting aside her personal wishes in order to follow those of her nephew, Philip IV. She refused to accept the office of governor in perpetuity as Philip wanted, however, leaving herself the option of stepping down if she so desired.

How did Isabel see her change of status in 1621? Was it particularly difficult for her to follow the orders of her nephew, Philip IV, who had not even been born when she left Spain, and who had no personal knowledge of the Low Countries? To understand Isabel's reaction to her demotion from sovereign to governor in 1621, we need to consider how Isabel approached sovereignty prior to 1621. In 1600, less than a year after her arrival in the Netherlands, she had participated in a ceremony in which she (and *not* her husband, Albert) was invested with a sword—a symbol of sovereignty. As she wrote to Philip III's royal favorite, the Duke of Lerma: "I forgot to tell my brother [Philip III] that at the oath-taking tomorrow, there is a ceremony that entails wearing a sword, and an abbot who has to carry it, and there is no other way but for him to gird me with it, and afterwards, if I command him, he will put it on my cousin [Albert]. Imagine how attractive I'll look."[9] Isabel was plainly amused that her sovereignty would be publically recognized with such military and implicitly male symbolism, and she also enjoyed the notion that *she* should decide whether Albert would have a role in a ritual confirmation and acceptance of sovereignty. Yet in the same letter (to the Duke of Lerma) in which she laughs at her superior and Albert's subordinate role in the investment ceremony, she also explicitly acknowledged her acceptance of the husband's authority in marriage. Commenting on disagreements between Philip III and his wife, Margaret of Austria, Isabel wrote that "if I were there I would tell his wife [Margaret] how important it is to do the will of one's husband, and that she, as a young girl, needs someone to counsel her."[10] Her remarks about the investment ceremony come at the end of her letter and appear almost an afterthought. Still, Isabel's surprise about her control over Albert's investiture, along with her earlier comments about Margaret's need for wifely obedience, suggest that as she was writing to Lerma, she had in mind the traditional relationship between husbands and wives and was aware of how her own sovereign position in the Low Countries was in some tension with the obedience and deference expected of her as Albert's wife.

Isabel was also clearly conscious of and even frustrated by the limitations placed on women. In a letter to the Duke of Lerma noting that Albert's High Steward (mayordomo mayor) Rodrigo Niño y Laso was taking a letter to Madrid, she commented that "I envy him [Niño y Laso] and indeed it is very bad that it is not socially acceptable for women to carry the correspondence and come and go as men do."[11] Isabel evidently discussed limitations placed on women with one of her ladies-in-waiting, the Countess of Uceda, because in another letter to the Duke of Lerma she noted that the countess had told her that she (the countess) had always wished she had been born a man, but that the protracted siege of Ostend had caused her to be glad to be a woman because otherwise she would have to go to the trenches and fight.[12] Isabel was pointing out the difficulties of the fighting and the harsh conditions suffered by the soldiers, but these comments indicate that she was conscious of how gender restricted a woman's actions, and while at times regretting these limitations, she still accepted them as necessary. When faced with certain rituals—such as the wearing or use of swords—that blurred or challenged gender distinctions, Isabel seemed uncomfortable.

As the investment ritual with the sword indicates, Isabel and Albert did not choose or control the rituals by which cities recognized the archdukes' sovereignty. As Isabel and Albert made their initial entry into the southern provinces of the Netherlands in 1599, these provinces swore their allegiance with oaths and ceremonies that emphasized that Isabel, and not Albert, was sovereign. Whereas Isabel was referred to as *domina* (mistress) and *princeps proprietaria* (proprietary prince), Albert was called only husband and guardian.[13] In the joyous entry into the city of Brussels, Isabel was given the keys to the city and the staff of justice.[14] In Brabant, Isabel, and not Albert, put her hand over the Bible to swear to uphold the laws of the territory. Female sovereignty was seen as gentle, peace loving, and even weak, and thus by stressing Isabel as the principal sovereign, these cities were pointing out the limitations on the archdukes' power. Moreover, the joyous entries also emphasized the conjugal love between Albert and Isabel, which in turn represented the ideal relationship between the sovereigns and the cities. Although a wife had to obey her husband, "in return for this obedience it was his duty to protect and support his wife. Moreover, his rights over her were conferred by contractual consent, and were not merely the result of possession."[15] In this way, the southern cities sought to emphasize that Albert and Isabel's rule was contractual and not absolute.

Even though these ceremonies and rituals were orchestrated by the separate territories and communities, indicating that they recognized Isabel as the primary sovereign and gave her precedence over Albert, the archdukes themselves sometimes chose to emphasize this distinction. For example, at Coudenberg palace, remodeled after Albert and Isabel's instructions, only Isabel's apartments (and not those of Albert) offered direct access to the royal chapel—a vital space for showcasing the archdukes' piety as well as promoting the divine nature of Habsburg rule. In fact, over the main altar of the chapel, the archdukes chose to place a painting of the *Adoration of the Kings* by Jan Gossaert, which carried the message not only that kings served God but also that they were God's representatives on earth and were to be venerated by their subjects.[16] Isabel's rooms led to a balcony overlooking the high altar of the chapel, and from this balcony, she usually heard mass, whereas Albert had no private balcony. Instead, he usually sat on the main level of the chapel, where courtiers and others sat. Isabel's balcony was reserved for the sovereign and put her on a higher, more prominent, and exalted level than anyone, including even her husband and coruler. Divine adoration was intertwined with devotion to sovereign, and the seating arrangement in the royal chapel seemed to emphasize Isabel, and not Albert, as the preeminent sovereign.[17]

Both Isabel and Albert made it a point to engage in popular celebrations as opportunities to mingle with their subjects and win their devotion. In 1615, Isabel took part in an annual contest hosted by the guild of archers in Brussels. A prize was given to the first person who could topple a popinjay tied to a pole, and Isabel won the prize. The guild decided not to hold another contest until after Isabel's death so as not to dethrone her as the champion. Isabel used the prize money to start a dowry for needy women.[18] Her participation in the contest was depicted in a series of paintings that Isabel commissioned, and as an avid huntress, she was exceedingly proud of her victory. In the portrait of Isabel and Albert painted by Otto van Veen some time after 1615, Isabel wears the insignia of the Brussels guild both on a brooch on her chest and on a hair decoration, and her hand rests on the brooch, drawing the viewer's attention to it.[19] Albert had been weak and ill in 1614 and therefore might not have been able to actively participate in such contests, but the archdukes seem also to have seen these public occasions as particularly suitable (whether because of her character or her gender) to Isabel. Isabel thus took on roles that helped connect her to the people of the Low Countries.

Although as cosovereign of the Low Countries, Isabel shared power with her husband, Archduke Albert, it was he who assumed all the day-to-day business of state, meeting with councillors, negotiating issues, and formulating policy. The state papers of their reign give the pronounced impression that Albert was the one in power, with Isabel taking a completely subordinate role (and scholars have not really challenged this view). Not until 1621, after Albert's death, does Isabel begin to figure prominently in the papers of state. We know from her surviving published correspondence, however, that from 1599 until at least 1612, she wrote constantly to the Spanish court (particularly to Philip III's favorite, the Duke of Lerma), asking for financial and military assistance, suggesting appropriate actions, warning about the dangers of any delay in financial support. The letters to Lerma were also filled with personal matters—news of court life, questions about Philip III and his family, and inquiries about Lerma's health and that of his family. Yet far from being simply cordial correspondence among family and friends, letters to the Spanish court were important political documents, designed to keep the Low Countries on the mind of the Spanish government and to influence Philip III to follow Isabel's advice. No doubt she knew that one of her principal responsibilities as coruler of the Low Countries was to use whatever leverage she had at the Spanish court to ensure Spanish assistance to her and Albert in the Netherlands. Although Albert also wrote extensively to Lerma, more often than Isabel did, his letters are much more formal than Isabel's. Whereas Isabel addressed Lerma as "Marquis" or "Duke," Albert addressed him as "Sir Marquis" (*señor marques*) or "Sir Duke" (*señor duque*). Albert also concerned himself primarily with detailing political events, requesting concrete assistance for Flanders, or other matters of concern to him. He seldom mentioned Isabel (and on the few occasions when he did, he referred to her simply as "*la infanta*"), nor gave details about their daily life. Isabel, on the other hand, filled her letters with chatty reports about her activities and with questions about her friends and relatives in Spain, interspersed with reports about political developments in the Low Countries and requests for assistance. When she referred to Albert, she always called him "my cousin," a term that implied familiarity, affection, and even equality, and never "husband," which would have suggested subservience. Thus Isabel's letters are a strong counterweight to Albert's and show that she took advantage of her greater familiarity with the Duke of Lerma to engage his attention and solicit his assistance.[20] Though not figuring largely in the official state papers before 1621, she was performing a crucial political role by writing to the Duke of Lerma, a role that no doubt she and Albert agreed on.

Furthermore, evidence suggests that Albert made few decisions on his own, but usually consulted Isabel. Francisco de Ibarra, captain of the Spanish lancers, commented in 1621 that servants noticed that whenever Albert went to see Isabel, his arms were full of papers.[21] The archdukes' historiographer, Erycius Puteanus, also observed that Albert "did everything alone, yet nothing without his wife," and Isabel was "a sharer in each affair though not a participant in it."[22] Albert would meet with her every afternoon around four o'clock and would inform her of matters of state, asking her advice and making decisions with her. Afterward, in the evening, Albert and Isabel would give separate audiences.[23] Ibarra's and Puteanus's observations suggest that in private, Albert asked for Isabel's opinion on matters of state, but that in public, Isabel preferred to assume the image of an obedient, submissive wife.[24] Whereas Albert and Isabel jointly granted titles of nobility, Albert knighted candidates—a ceremony that required dubbing the candidate with a sword—on his own. Thus Isabel and Albert seem to have followed a gendered approach to sovereignty and concluded that swords were unbecoming to female sovereigns. Such an attitude was more acceptable to the people of the Low Countries, to her servants, and to the court, and it was in keeping with the role that Isabel thought it best to project—that of an obedient wife who left political decisions to her husband. This was the role that she had suggested for her sister-in-law, Margaret of Austria, Philip III's wife. Although unofficially she must have readily expressed her opinions to Albert, helped him make decisions, and even shared in authority, officially Isabel believed it best to assume a subordinate role.

Until the signing of the Twelve Year Truce between the Low Countries and Spain in 1609, Albert was often away on military campaigns, and during those times, Isabel almost certainly took on a more direct role in governing. On some occasions, she also followed Albert to the front and organized relief measures for the wounded, even tending them herself.[25] During the siege of Ostend, which lasted from July 1601 to September 1604, Isabel visited the troops to encourage them and remained close to military headquarters at Ghent for at least six months.[26] The archduchess was so concerned about the siege that she supposedly vowed not to change her undergarments until Ostend was taken.[27] Close to the battlefront, she was also lending visible, public support to her husband at a time when he was being heavily criticized by the Spanish government. In this case, therefore, she demonstrated her devotion to her husband while also remaining close to the military action and to the making of crucial decisions.

Because of Albert's advanced age (he was 62 when he died) and weak health, the Spanish government had long considered what to do when the archduke died. The matter remained unresolved, however, until with Albert's death in 1621, Philip IV, who had succeeded his father as king of Spain only three months earlier, asked his aunt to remain as governor. Isabel accepted the position with little evident enthusiasm and quickly informed her subjects of the change in her status. One of her first acts was to write to all the provinces, councils, and governors of the Low Countries informing them that the territories had reverted to the Spanish king and that she governed them "by his command and in his royal name."[28]

The king and government in Madrid discussed what powers Isabel should actually hold, and the Marquis of Bedmar, who had been in Brussels at Albert's death and who knew the archduchess well, recommended that she be given greater power than previous governors because of her "age and the special goodness of Her Highness [Isabel] and so as not to give her any cause to leave governing, to which she is so little inclined."[29] Bedmar knew that Isabel had only reluctantly accepted her new role for the welfare of her subjects. Nevertheless, Bedmar's comments suggest that Isabel would consent to govern only if she held real power; she was not staying in Brussels and abandoning her long-held desire to retire to a convent in Spain merely to act as a figurehead for Philip IV. Bedmar's comments also echo those of the secretary to the papal nuncio in Flanders, who reasoned that Isabel was giving Philip time to reconfirm her independent sovereignty and that if he did not, she would retire to a convent, because the Dutch insisted on being ruled by their "natural princes" (and Isabel was seen as their natural princess), and not "tyrannized" by governors.[30] As a mere governor, the nuncio's secretary thought she would have no recognized authority and would face open revolt.[31]

Isabel evidently believed that she could govern the people of the Low Countries better than anyone else who might be sent by Philip IV, including her beloved and loyal general, Ambrosio Spínola. At the very least, she believed that her royalty, her connection to Albert, and her years of cultivating devotion and respect from the Dutch as their sovereign would now serve her well in attempting to maintain peace in those lands. Feeling a need to justify to her subjects her diminished status, she commissioned artwork and texts that depicted her as a spiritual mother to an orphaned people and emphasized that Albert lived on in her.[32]

The Spanish government, in considering what authority to give Isabel, researched carefully what earlier regents of Flanders had received, before deciding to give Isabel greater powers than those held by any previous

Spanish governor in the Netherlands, including her late husband, Archduke Albert, when he had governed the Low Countries for Philip II from 1595 until 1598. In the final instructions given her by Philip IV, Isabel retained the right to make appointments to most ecclesiastical and secular offices. The one area where she lost power was in her ability to reward nobles or to confer noble titles, because Madrid judged that this privilege belonged only to the sovereign, and she was no longer sovereign. In debating what type of Council of Flanders to create in Madrid, the Spanish government ultimately opted for a weak council so as not to detract from Isabel's authority and to give her greater freedom to make decisions. Philip IV and his councillors thought this was the best way to provide for continuity in the Low Countries and avoid more upheaval in those territories.[33] Isabel continued to maintain ambassadors at all European courts, and all European monarchs continued to send ambassadors to Brussels.

Isabel also immediately tried to work out her status vis-à-vis other rulers. She wrote to Philip IV about how she should address others now that she was no longer sovereign: "Those whom I treated as 'my cousin' I will continue to do so, and those whom I addressed as 'very dear and faithful' I will now address as 'very dear and well-loved' removing the word 'faithful' since it implies sovereignty, which does not belong to me."[34] Forms of address were important to Isabel, because she spent so much time writing and meeting with others, yet her letter to Philip suggests that she calmly accepted her change in status. Although she was no longer sovereign, she had to assume a more direct role in government and had to assume Albert's job of meeting with ambassadors and attending meetings of state. The papal nuncio reported that she followed her father's practice of commenting in the margins of all the state papers she received and also gave public audiences two days a week.[35] For all these public functions, she appeared dressed in the habit of a Franciscan tertiary (brown robes and a wimple), the dress she had assumed on Albert's death. This attire would have dramatically emphasized her piety and virtue, her widowhood, and her submission and obedience to her deceased husband. In a sense, by wearing a Franciscan robe, Isabel was sharing her husband's shroud, because Albert had been buried in Franciscan habit.[36] She was also following the powerful example of one of her patron saints and role models, Elizabeth of Hungary, who had also dressed as a Franciscan tertiary.[37] Her robe and wimple also had political significance, because it publicly proclaimed her devotion to the Catholic faith, her use of authority to promote that faith, and her power—or sovereignty—as derived from God.[38] Nevertheless, court splendor had been a principal means through which the archdukes emphasized their sovereignty, and by adopting a Franciscan habit and curtailing court entertainment and patronage, Isabel was sacrificing this visible means of proclaiming her authority at precisely the moment when she in fact had lost her sovereignty—perhaps the moment when she might have used courtly magnificence to counteract political changes. Isabel was criticized for her public display of humility and for making her court a virtual convent, but her ladies-in-waiting continued to dress (and be depicted) in magnificent attire and they became her vicarious way of exhibiting princely largesse.[39]

Other monarchs remained confused as to what Isabel's change in status actually signified. In 1622, James I of England sent an ambassador, Richard Weston, to ask for Isabel's assistance in bringing about a suspension of hostilities in the Palatinate (James's daughter Elizabeth was the wife of Frederick of the Palatinate). Frederick had accepted the Bohemian crown from the Bohemian Estates after they had deposed the Habsburg emperor, Ferdinand II, in 1618. By 1621, Catholic Habsburg forces had expelled Frederick from Bohemia and were attacking the Rhineland, his home territory. Even as negotiations for a peace were underway in Brussels, Habsburg forces were taking the Rhineland, and no doubt Isabel, knowing about the success of Habsburg troops, realized how futile peace efforts were. Weston asked Isabel to order the Spanish general, Don Gonzalo Fernández de Córdoba (who had been left there by Spínola, Isabel's general) to retreat from the Palatinate, to which Isabel replied that she lacked the power to do so because he was under the authority of Spain. Obviously frustrated by Isabel's response, Weston noted that had James known of her lack of power, he could have saved himself the trouble of sending an ambassador to her court and the embarrassment of having his ambassador treated so poorly. Isabel merely noted, again, that she would do all she could but that she lacked power. In truth, she had little interest in bringing about a cease-fire, because the Habsburg (Catholic) side was winning in the Palatinate, and a cease fire might have given the advantage to the Protestants. In this case, therefore, it was in Isabel's best interest to claim that she lacked authority, when she did indeed have influence over Spanish decisions.

In a subsequent interview with Petrus Peckius, Chancellor of Brabant, concerning Isabel's ability to mediate between the Emperor Ferdinand and the Prince Palatine, Weston argued that Isabel, as a member of the House of Austria, was partial to the emperor. Peckius replied, "for her own part, none can suspect that she has any design, because, though she is so great a princess by birth, and has her pretenses, yet she contents herself willingly with the condition of Governess of these countries; that she aims only at the public good and the satisfaction of his Majesty."[40] Another English ambassador involved in these negotiations, John Dickenson, observed that though he did not doubt Isabel's good intentions, the issue, rather, was "what power she might have to restore the places [in the Palatinate seized by Spanish forces], at this time being only governess," to which Peckius responded that he did not doubt that "the emperor and the King of Spain would confirm what she should undertake."[41] Thus Peckius believed that although she lacked sovereignty, Isabel had both influence and power and that Philip IV and the emperor would follow her wishes. Peckius emphasized that Isabel, because of her birth, was entitled to a much higher position than that of governor but did not demand more because she did not seek power for herself. As cosovereign Isabel had consistently and consciously minimized her share in decision making, and thus it is not surprising that as governor she would have continued to do so in order to make her governance more palatable to Spain. Peckius's comments suggest that Isabel was successful in appearing indifferent to political power while in fact exercising authority.

Statesmen and diplomats of the time were surprised that Isabel would calmly accept the change in status from independent sovereign to governor. Yet perhaps Isabel was less content with her status than she allowed. The war against the northern Dutch provinces, which resumed in 1621 after a twelve-year truce, consumed her attention and she struggled, much as she and Albert had done from 1599 until 1609, to secure Spanish military and financial assistance. Isabel was constantly frustrated at the Spanish government's inability to make speedy decisions and to give her sufficient and effective support. When the town of Breda fell in 1625 to Spínola after a nearly year-long siege, Isabel seems to have considered the victory her own. She commissioned a painting of the siege from Jacques Callot and had copies quickly sent to all the major European capitals, thereby publicizing not only the victory but also suggesting that she, and not Philip IV, was responsible.[42]

Toward the end of her life, she became increasingly convinced that the fighting in the Netherlands had to end, and when the notorious slowness of the Spanish government hampered her efforts, she took the initiative. Spínola, who by 1627 had left the Netherlands for Spain, wrote to her in 1633 (in cipher) that Philip IV and most of his councillors of state privately supported a truce but would make no firm commitment; he further advised her to act on her own, as she was not obligated to follow the opinions (*pareceres*) of the councillors of state, because if she waited the northern provinces would be lost forever.[43] In fact, Isabel had already sent her painter and ambassador, Peter Paul Rubens, on a secret mission in December 1631 to negotiate a truce with the Prince of Orange, and Rubens went to meet with the prince several other times in 1632.[44] These missions, which ultimately failed because

Orange recognized that he had the advantage, greatly angered the States General of Brussels (the parliamentary body of the southern provinces), who complained to Isabel that she needed to clear such attempts with them. In fact, Isabel knew that the Estates were also negotiating with the Prince of Orange and part of her purpose was to hinder the Estates, believing they were acting beyond their competence. Isabel's actions prompted Philip IV to remind her that "because of the love you have for these provinces and because you desire their greatest good, you will judge it convenient not to resolve anything related to a truce without first communicating it to all the councils and states."[45] Philip's scolding came too late, as Isabel had already done as she saw fit. Perhaps her advanced age (she was sixty-seven at the time) or experience in dealing with the Spanish government had given her greater confidence in her own ability to make decisions and take action, but her years as cosovereign and then as governor suggest that Isabel had all along trusted her own judgment and believed herself better equipped to deal with the situation in the Netherlands than anyone else.

Isabel's life from her marriage in 1599 until her death in 1633 indicates that far from shunning the traditional roles assigned to a royal woman, she embraced them, welcoming marriage, sharing authority with her husband, and longing for a child and heir. However, these roles did not prevent her from exercising influence and power; even her loss of sovereignty in 1621, which she accepted reluctantly, did not deprive her of authority. Her story ultimately illustrates that by displaying benevolence, humility, wifely obedience, and piety, royal women could in fact make their rule more acceptable to others.

Notes

I would like to thank Luc Duerloo and Dries Raeymaekers for their careful reading of and detailed comments on this paper, from which I have greatly benefited. I would also like to thank the Gettysburg College Grants Committee for the financial support that allowed me to conduct the archival research for this essay.

1. In part this might have resulted from Archduke Albert's problems with gout and his increasing difficulty in mobility. In public, Albert seemed serious and severe, whereas observers often noted that Isabel was lively and loved to laugh. It is difficult to know whether this was a studied, choreographed contrast or whether this accurately reflected Albert's and Isabel's personalities. See Johan Verberckmoes, "The Archdukes in their Humour," in Werner Thomas and Luc Duerloo, eds., *Albert and Isabella: Essays* (Leuven, Belgium: Brepols, 1998), 137–43; and Cordula Schumann, "Court, City and Countryside: Jan Brueghel's Peasant Weddings as Images of Social Unity under Archducal Sovereignty," in *Albert and Isabella: Essays,* 151–58.

2. I would like to thank Bernardo José García García and especially Dries Raeymaek-

ers for clarifying this issue for me. See Victor Brants, *La Belgique au XVIIe siècle, Albert et Isabelle. Études d'histoire politique et sociale* (Louvain, Belgium: n.p., 1910), 18–19, and Marie H. de Villermont, *L'Infante Isabelle: gouvernante des Pays-Bas* (Paris: Librarie S. François, 1912), 217–19.

3. Werner Thomas, "Andromeda Unbound: The Reign of Albert and Isabella in the Southern Netherlands, 1598–1621," in *Albert and Isabella: Essays,* 2–3; Rafael Valladares, "Decid adiós a Flandes. La Monarquía Hispánica y el problema de los Países Bajos," in *Albert and Isabella: Essays,* 52; Paul Allen, *Philip III and the Pax Hispanica, 1598–1621* (New Haven, Conn.: Yale University Press, 2000), 18; Geoffrey Parker, *The Dutch Revolt* (New York: Penguin, 1981), 233.

4. Valladares, "Decid adiós a Flandes," 52.

5. Thomas, "Andromeda Unbound," 12–13.

6. Dries Raeymaekers, "The Court and Household of the Archdukes Albert and Isabella, 1598–1621," pp. 9–13. Files under 2006-1, Birgit Houben and Dries Raeymaekers, "Changing Formats. Court and Household in the Habsburg Netherlands, 1598–1641" [paper for the Second Low Countries Conference, Antwerp, Belgium, 2006], Available at <www.lowcountries.nl/ workingpapers.html>, accessed September 28, 2008; Cordula van Wyhe, critical introduction to Jean Terrier, *Portraicts des S S Vertus de la Vierge contemplées par feue S.A.S.M. Isabelle Clere Eugenie Infante d'Espagne* (Glasgow: Glasgow Emblem Studies, 2002), xxxii.

7. Christopher Brown, "Rubens and the Archdukes," in *Albert and Isabella: Essays,* 125.

8. Alicia Esteban Estríngana, "Las Provincias de Flandes y la monarquía de España," in Antonio Álvarez-Ossorio Alvariño y Bernardo J. García García, eds., *La Monarquía de las naciones: Patria, nación y naturaleza en la Monarquía* (Madrid: Fundación Carlos Amberes, 2004), 216.

9. Letter from 29 January 1600 in Antonio Rodríguez Villa, ed., *Correspondencia de la Infanta Archiduquesa Doña Isabel Clara Eugenia de Austria con el Duque de Lerma y otros personajes* (Madrid: Fortanet, 1906), 10.

10. Letter from 29 January 1600, in Rodríguez Villa, *Correspondencia de la Infanta Archiduquesa Doña Isabel Clara Eugenia de Austria,* 8.

11. Letter from 18 January 1604, in Rodríguez Villa, *Correspondencia de la Infanta Archiduquesa Doña Isabel Clara Eugenia de Austria,* 102.

12. Letter from 11 August 1601, in Rodríguez Villa, *Correspondencia de la Infanta Archiduquesa Doña Isabel Clara Eugenia de Austria,* 41.

13. My discussion is based on Margit Thøfner, "Domina & Princeps proprietaria. The Ideal of Sovereignty in the Joyous Entries of the Archduke Albert and the Infanta Isabella," in *Albert and Isabella: Essays,* 55–66.

14. Isabel writes that it was a "vara muy larga que es de la justicia." *Relación de lo sucedido en el viaje de la Serenísima Infanta Dona Isabel Clara Eugenia de Austria,* reprinted in Rodríguez Villa, *Correspondencia de la Infanta Archiduquesa Doña Isabel Clara Eugenia de Austria,* 335. See also Ruth Betegón Díez, *Isabel Clara Eugenia: Infanta de España y soberana de Flandes* (Barcelona: Plaza Janés, 2004), 95.

15. Thøfner, "Domina & Princeps proprietaria," 62.

16. Thomas, "Andromeda Unbound," 12–13.

17. See Thomas, "Andromeda Unbound," 13. Much more research needs to be done on the use of space within the Coudenberg palace and the rituals accompanying worship within the royal chapel to gain a better understanding of the political messages that Isabel and Albert sought to convey.

18. Betegón Díez, *Isabel Clara Eugenia,* 157–58.

19. Luc Duerloo and Werner Thomas, eds., *Albert & Isabelle: Catalogue* (Leuven, Belgium: Brepols, 1998), 45, illustration on p. 46 and on catalogue cover.

20. When Isabel was born in 1566, the Duke of Lerma was a page (*menino*) in her mother's household. Isabel grew up with Lerma at the court and knew him and his family well. See Bernardo José García García, "Bruselas y Madrid: Isabel Clara Eugenia y el duque de Lerma," in *Albert and Isabella: Essays,* 67–68.

21. Cited in Cordula Schumann, "Humble Wife, Charitable Mother and Chaste Widow: Representing the Virtues of the Infanta Isabella Clara Eugenia (1599–1633)," (Ph.D. thesis, University of London, Courtauld Institute of Art, 2000), 48.

22. Quoted in Schumann, "Humble Wife, Charitable Mother and Chaste Widow," 49, notes 76 and 77. Luc Duerloo has also shown how Isabel and Albert worked together on a "devotional strategy" that reflected Habsburg commitment to a Counter-Reformation religiosity but that also emphasized the ties of the archdukes to their lands and subjects. See "Archducal Piety and Habsburg Power," in *Albert and Isabella: Essays,* 267–79.

23. Betegón Díez, *Isabel Clara Eugenia,* 149. Betegón Díez argues that Isabel would push Albert to action and when he was unable to make a decision, she would take one for him. See pp. 121–22. Betegón Díez does not cite her exact sources for these conclusions, but says she relies on the papers of Philippe Chifflet, chaplain to Isabel, for aspects of Isabel's daily life. I have not been able to consult Chifflet's papers, which are housed in the Municipal Library of Besançon, France.

24. Schumann, "Humble Wife, Charitable Mother and Chaste Widow," 49.

25. Villermont, *L'Infante Isabelle,* 270–74.

26. Rodríguez Villa, *Correspondencia de la Infanta Archiduquesa Doña Isabel Clara Eugenia de Austria,* 41, and Craig Harline and Eddy Put, *A Bishop's Tale: Mathias Hovius Among His Flock in Seventeenth-Century Flanders* (New Haven, Conn.: Yale University Press, 2000), 99.

27. Harline and Put, *A Bishop's Tale,* 99. This story, clearly apocryphal, was similar to that told of Queen Isabel of Spain, who supposedly vowed not to change her undergarments until the conclusion of the siege of Granada. I would like to thank Luc Duerloo for bringing this comparison to my attention.

28. Quoted in Alicia Esteban Estríngana, *Madrid y Bruselas: Relaciones de gobierno en la etapa posarchiducal (1621–1634)* (Leuven, Belgium: Leuven University Press, 2005), 22.

29. Bedmar to Philip IV, quoted in Esteban Estríngana, *Madrid y Bruselas,* 23.

30. Bernard de Meester summarizes the secretary to the nuncio's report in French and does not quote the original Italian. Crisogono Flacchio to Ludovisi, Brussels, 17 July 1621, in *Correspondance du nonce Giovanni-Francesco Guidi di Bagno, première partie (1621–1624),* ed. Bernard de Meester (Brussels: Palais des Académies, 1938), 29. Barbara Welzel quotes de Meester's summary and briefly discusses the secretary to the nuncio's report in "Princeps Vidua, Mater Castrorum: The Iconography of Archduchess Isabella as Governor of

the Netherlands," *Jaarboek Koninklijk Museum voor Schone Kunsten Antwerpen* (1999), 160.

31. Crisogono Flacchio to Ludovisi, in *Correspondance du nonce Giovanni-Francesco Guidi di Bagno,* 29.

32. See Schumann, "Humble Wife, Charitable Mother and Chaste Widow," 51–57, 165–66; Van Wyhe, critical introduction to Jean Terrier, *Portraicts des S S Vertus de la Vierge,* x–xiv.

33. On this issue see Esteban Estríngana, "Las Provincias de Flandes y la monarquía de España," 216–19.

34. Archives Générales du Royaume (hereafter AGR), Secrétairerie d'État et de Guerre, 186, fol. 13, Isabel to Philip IV, 6 July 1621.

35. Giovanni-Francesco Guidi di Bagno to Ludovisi, Brussels, 21 August 1621, in *Correspondance du Nonce Giovanni-Francesco Guidi di Bagno,* 53.

36. Schumann, "Humble Wife, Charitable Mother and Chaste Widow," 51.

37. Duerloo, "Archducal Piety and Habsburg Power," 278.

38. Cordula van Wyhe, "Court and Convent: The Infanta Isabella and Her Franciscan Confessor Andrés de Soto," *Sixteenth Century Journal* 35, no. 2 (2004): 413.

39. Van Wyhe, critical introduction to Jean Terrier, *Portraicts des S S Vertus de la Vierge,* xxxiii.

40. Public Records Office, London (hereafter PRO), State Papers (hereafter SP) 77/15 Part I, fol. 221v, 19 July 1622.

41. PRO, SP 77/15 Part I, fol. 222v, 19 July 1622.

42. Philip IV in turn had Diego Velázquez depict the victory in what has become the most famous rendering of the event. As Barbara Welzel has argued, "the many pictorial versions [of the siege of Breda] suggest a subtle struggle between Philip IV and Isabella for credit for the victory." Barbara Welzel, "Princeps Vidua, Mater Castrorum," 165.

43. AGR, Secrétairerie d'État et de Guerre, 126, 6 June 1633.

44. Ruth Saunders Magurn, ed., *The Letters of Peter Paul Rubens* (Cambridge, Mass.: Harvard University Press, 1971), 360.

45. AGR, Secrétairerie d'État et de Guerre, 206, fol. 264, Philip IV to Isabel, 12 June 1633.

5. "Princeps non Principissa"

Catherine of Brandenburg, Elected Prince of Transylvania (1629–30)

ÉVA DEÁK

Beginning with Giselle of Bavaria (ca. 985–ca. 1060), wife of Saint Steven, founder of the Hungarian Kingdom, powerful queen consorts at times played significant roles in its history. The long list of influential queens includes Queen Helena (ca. 1110–ca. 1146), wife of King Béla II, "the Blind"; Queen Gertrudis of Andechs-Meran (ca. 1185–1213), wife of Andreas II; and Elizabeth the Cuman (ca. 1239–ca. 1290), wife of Stephen V and later regent for their son Ladislaus IV. They were all married to kings of the first Hungarian ruling house, the Árpád dynasty, and contributed significantly to the governance of the country. Saintly princesses greatly enhanced the reputation of the dynasty—Saint Elizabeth and Saint Margaret are prominent examples.[1]

The age of the Angevins followed the demise of the Árpáds. Queen Elizabeth Piast (ca. 1305–80) was influential both as the wife of Charles Robert of Anjou and as dowager queen during the reign of their son, Louis I.[2] After the death of Louis Anjou, her daughters inherited the thrones of Poland and Hungary.[3] Although Mary (1371–95) was crowned queen regnant of the Hungarian Kingdom in 1382, first her mother, Elizabeth Kotromanić (ca. 1339–87) ruled as a regent instead of the young queen, and later Mary's husband, Sigismundus of Luxemburg governed the country.[4] After Mary's death, Sigismundus married Barbara of Cilly (1392–1451), daughter of an old Hungarian magnate family, to reinforce his power over the country. King Matthias Corvinus and his second wife Queen Beatrix of Naples (1457–1508) were iconic figures of Hungarian Renaissance culture. Louis II and Mary of Habsburg (1505–58) were the last king and queen who ruled uncontested the unified medieval Hungarian Kingdom.[5] Louis died in the battle of Mohács (1526) fighting against the Ottoman army.[6]

The battle of Mohács is traditionally accepted as the end of the medieval Hungarian Kingdom. The country was divided into three parts: the center of the country came under Ottoman rule; the northwestern part, Royal Hungary, was ruled by Habsburg kings; and the eastern part became an autonomous principality within the Ottoman Empire.[7] The Principality of Transylvania was independent in its home affairs, but was subordinated in foreign affairs to the Ottoman Empire and was compelled to pay an annual fee to Constantinople from the second half of the sixteenth century until the end of the seventeenth century.[8] In Transylvania, Isabelle of Jagiello (1520–59)—crowned queen of the Hungarian Kingdom—was a regent for her infant son John II (despite her title she ruled only Transylvania). Maria Christierna of Habsburg (1574–1617), wife of Prince Sigismund Báthory governed the country from time to time in the name of her husband and, after his resignation, in the name of her brother.[9]

This list of powerful women is far from complete. However, as in Western Europe, where women inherited the throne in most cases due to the lack of a male heir, there was no elected female ruler in the history of Hungary until the reign of Catherine of Brandenburg (1602–44), who was elected ruler of Transylvania. This makes her example particularly important.[10] Catherine's husband emphasized her special status in the political part of his testament in the following way: "perhaps no other illustrious princely woman has ever been elected."[11]

This chapter studies the life and reign of Catherine of Brandenburg with a focus on the years between 1626 and 1630. I examine her marriage to Gabriel Bethlen, the conditions of her election, her struggle for power, and the circumstances of her abdication. I do not challenge the rather negative evaluation of Catherine's short reign prevailing in the historiography. However, it should be emphasized that most of the arguments used against her rule—including arguments that she was a woman, extravagant, and immoral—were consistent with a wider discourse on the nature of women at the time. Sources used for my discussion include resolutions of the Transylvanian diet, historical works and chronicles of the period, the political part of Bethlen's last will and testament, memoirs, and correspondence.

The Marriage of Catherine of Brandenburg and Gabriel Bethlen

Gabriel Bethlen (1580–1629) was born into an influential Transylvanian noble family: his father, Farkas Bethlen, was princely councillor. Gabriel lost both his parents as a child.[12] Educated in the court of Prince Sigismund Báthori, he became an experienced commander and diplomat. He was one of the most influential politicians of Prince Stephen Bocskai (1602–6) and a pivotal figure during the reign of Gabriel Báthory (1608–13). Bethlen was elected prince of Transylvania with Ottoman support. The "golden age of the principality"—in terms of politics, culture, as well as foreign affairs—began with his reign (1613–29).[13] Bethlen led successful campaigns against Habsburg forces and concluded numerous peace treaties with favorable conditions during the Thirty Years' War.

Bethlen aspired to international recognition as a sovereign European ruler. To that end, in 1622, he asked for the hand of archduchess Cecilia Renata of Habsburg after the death of his first wife Zsuzsanna Károlyi, daughter of an important noble family. After lengthy deliberation, he was refused, and in 1625, the prince sent his deputation to the Hohenzollern family and proposed marriage to Catherine of Brandenburg, sister of the elector George William (1595–1640); the marriage contract was signed in the same year.[14] Through this marriage the prince of Transylvania became related to the Western European Protestant rulers—Christian IV of Denmark and Frederick V of the Palatinate—and became brother-in-law to the Swedish king, Gustavus Adolphus. The principality joined the alliance of the Protestant powers, in the year of the marriage.

Although the Principality of Transylvania was only formed during the second half of the sixteenth century and Bethlen became the first prince of his family, the Hohenzollerns had ruled the Electorate of Brandenburg since the fifteenth century. Catherine of Brandenburg was the daughter of elector John Sigismund (1572–1619) and Anna of Prussia (1575–1625).[15] She grew up in the electoral court of Brandenburg in Cölln an der Spree and was often a guest of the Königsberg court of her maternal grandparents.[16] After the marriage of her sister Marie Eleonore to Gustavus Adolphus, she lived at their court in Stockholm. Catherine was educated according to her dignity as a potential wife of a ruler.[17] Paul Strassburger, the Swedish ambassador, spoke highly of her: according to his report, she was "richly decorated with virtues suitable to a princely woman."[18] Bethlen was not the first prospective husband; previous negotiations over a possible marriage for Catherine to the Russian Grand Duke Nicolaus had failed in 1623.[19]

At the time of the wedding, the bride was twenty-four years old and a striking beauty (fig. 5.1). Although she was short, she had a shapely figure and an attractive face.[20] According to a later description by Don Diego de Estrada, master of ceremonies in the princely court of Alba Iulia (Gyulafehérvár, Weißenburg), "her skin was snow-white, her eyes and forehead really beautiful; her lips were somewhat thick and limp, showing similarities with that of the Habsburgs."[21] The groom was twice as old as his bride. According to contemporary descriptions and portraits, his appearance was rather unattractive: he had a large head and eyes, and a wide mouth (fig. 5.2); he wore a tuft of hair according to the Hungarian fashion; his long black beard became gray relatively early.[22] It was noticed at their wedding that some of the German ladies were frightened of him when he gave them his hand.[23] However, Bethlen loved luxurious clothes and in all likelihood this contributed to the fact that his appearance was referred to as "respectable."[24]

After a proxy marriage in Berlin, the main celebrations were held in Košice (Kassa, Kaschau) with great pageantry: banquets, fireworks, tournaments, a masked ball, a ballet, and other spectacles during the first week of March 1626. The new couple solemnly visited the most important cities and fortresses of the principality. The attendants of the bride also participated in the subsequent visitation before their return.[25] The representational role of the princely court of Alba Iulia increased significantly with the ambitious marriage plans of the prince, and this tendency continued during the marriage of Catherine and Gabriel as well. Masked balls, feastings, and ballets were organized more frequently in the princely court after the arrival of the princess.[26]

It is impossible to know whether their marriage was a happy one, though it seems unlikely that mutual love developed after the wedding.[27] As with

Figure 5.1. Portrait of Catherine of Brandenburg, 1620s (unknown artist and place).

Figure 5.2. Portrait of Gabriel Bethlen, oil on canvas, 1626 (unknown artist), Hungarian National Museum, Historical Picture Gallery, cat. no. 839. Reproduced with permission.

other dynastic marriages, communication between husband and wife was difficult in the beginning, for they could scarcely understand each other: Bethlen probably spoke some German, but Catherine did not speak Hungarian. Moreover, Bethlen began a military campaign only a few months after the wedding. There was a large age difference between them, and most probably, both of them had extramarital affairs. There were many rumors concerning Catherine's affairs during their marriage; after Bethlen's death, the rumors continued to circulate; it was said that Catherine had an affair first with a Moravian nobleman, then with her doctor. Her long relationship with Count István Csáky (1603–62), a married man, was common knowledge. Csáky was elegant, the same age as Catherine, and according to common opinion, the best-looking Hungarian at the time.[28] Moreover, he was educated and spoke excellent German.

Because marital infidelity was taken more seriously when committed by wives than by husbands, Catherine's "immorality" is stressed much more in the sources than that of her husband.[29] Yet it was not only Catherine who had lovers, for the love affairs of Bethlen also seem to have been well known. According to the official record of the Bavarian delegates at the wedding, the groom was forced to send away his twelve concubines, for had he not done so, the princess would not have appeared at the wedding. The source recorded the malicious remarks made by Hungarian lords that he would soon take them back.[30] During their marriage, the Swedish ambassador reported on Gabriel's numerous flirtations, love affairs, and concubines.[31] Gabriel also spoke openly about his active sex life. When his physician made a remark about the pains caused by edema in his sexual organs, the prince agreed that these parts had enjoyed more than enough pleasure during his life, therefore they deserved to suffer. This episode was recorded by one of his courtiers in a positive context, as an example of Bethlen's pious behavior during his last weeks.[32] Although in his last months Gabriel was seriously ill, according to the letters of Catherine written to her brother, she was much more interested in the last will of her husband than in his well-being.[33] Their marriage remained childless.

The Reign of Catherine of Brandenburg

The succession of the bride was an important condition of the marriage. It was used as an argument in the marriage proposal made to the Habsburg family and included in the marriage contract between Catherine and Gabriel.[34, 35] She was officially elected successor to Bethlen by the Transylvanian diet shortly after their marriage and swore a solemn oath (May 24–June 17, 1626).[36] Bethlen and the representatives of his allies—the English and the Dutch ambassadors—also used their influence to ensure Catherine's confirmation as his successor at the Porte.[37] The following summer, the envoy of the Ottoman Emporer arrived in Alba Iulia with the letter of appointment (*ahdnāme*) and Catherine received the princely insignia: a banner and a scepter, together with the presents customary for these occasions: a sword, *kaftan,* and a horse with a caparison.[38]

It was customary for the new prince to take a solemn oath. Moreover, the diet set conditions for the reign, although these were not confirmed by formal oath. The fundamental rights of the country were included in both the oath and the conditions. These were the right to practice freely the accepted religions, the preservation of the privileges of the orders and the country, and the right of the country to freely elect the prince.[39] Following tradition, Catherine formally swore to respect the freedom, customs, and religion of all orders; to administer justice to all; and to comply and enforce compliance with the privileges given by King Andreas II.[40]

The first known conditions were set for Sigismund Báthory in 1598. The conditions increased in number and varied considerably for the subsequent princes. Besides stressing the general rights of the country, they often related to actual problems or known weaknesses of the prince. Even the attitude of the prince toward an individual could be resolved under one of the conditions. Catherine's terms in addition included special restrictions for her as the only female ruler of the principality. Besides the usual conditions—respect for the privileges of the nobility and the different communities, for the four accepted religions, and the right of the country to freely elect her successor—she was obliged to share power with a governor and the princely council. Five of the thirteen articles dealt with the rights of the governor and the council. In public affairs, she was mandated to act with their knowledge and will; the income of the country would be handled separately by a treasurer in agreement with all the three parties; in case of the governor's death, the princess was obliged to choose his successor in accordance with the council's will. Usually, a governor was appointed power during a prince's minority or absence, and the council had a less important advisory function.[41]

Another of the special conditions under which Catherine ruled was that she could keep her power only so long as she remained a widow. Because she was not allowed to remarry, the possibility of founding a dynasty of her own was out of the question. The estates, most likely, could not imagine that she could rule independently if she had a husband. This concern had nothing to do with either their opinion of Catherine's personality (which was hardly known to them at that time) or her relatively young age (Bethlen had not been expected to die so soon). Similarly, the terms did not take into consideration the possible birth of a child by Bethlen, although the couple was recently married. Remarkably, the diet also considered the possibility of her abdication, believing that were the principality to be racked by turmoil, her relatives would advise her to leave the throne. The diet also enacted that the goods that Bethlen would leave to the country in his testament should remain intact.[42]

Under normal circumstances, the conditions did not in practice restrict the rulers. After the princes consolidated their power, the diet rarely interfered with state matters under the authority of the prince, such as military affairs or finances.[43] The above conditions, however, determined the reign of Catherine of Brandenburg following the death of Gabriel Bethlen on November 15, 1629. The council and the governor—István Bethlen (ca. 1580–1648), brother of the late prince—first counterbalanced princely power and later practically took over the leadership. Catherine's reign was characterized by a struggle for power between herself and her followers on the one side and the governor and the council on the other. Although her close followers tried to secure her absolute power by raising an army, the limits put down in the conditions of her election could not be lifted. On the contrary, the fact that her money was used to raise troops resulted in laws enacted by the diet that were even less favorable for Catherine.[44]

Moreover, the role of the diet and the orders temporarily increased at the expense of the ruler. The unusual frequency with which the diet met indicated the weakness of princely power from 1629 to 1630. Diets were usually summoned twice a year, though from 1623, it had been summoned only once. Extraordinary diets met only under special circumstances. In 1630, the diet met four times during Catherine's reign and two more times after her resignation.[45] The subsequent diets gave increasingly more authority to the council and the governor and set further limits on the ruler's fiscal and military power. According to the resolutions of the diet early in 1630, Catharine was allowed to confer offices or donate estates in agreement with the governor and the council only. Similarly, she was not permitted to make decisions concerning matters of property without their approval. Concerning finances, the diet ordered Catherine and the council to designate a treasurer together and instruct him.[46] Besides state revenues, the treasurer would handle the private incomes of the ruler; payments were allowed only with the knowledge of the governor and the council. As a result, the previous treasurer, Ferenc Mikó, was re-appointed. Later he was instructed to keep a record of all Catherine's expenses and present it monthly to the governor and the council for audit.

In July 1630, the diet authorized the governor and the council, that if anyone—including Catherine—raised an army without their knowledge, they were entitled to disband it. Moreover, if they detected significant hostility on her part, an army could be raised against her. In case of an emergency, the votes of the governor and the majority of the available councillors were sufficient to enforce this decision.[47]

A great number of Catherine's courtiers—including her most dedicated supporters—were Catholics. However, her inclination toward the Catholic faith reduced her popularity further in an overwhelmingly Protestant country. Toward the end of her husband's life, Catherine was compelled to make an official statement that she would not change her religion and to take the Lord's Supper publicly. The fact that the most influential supporters of her reign, as well as her lover Csáki, were Catholics worsened the situation. Although she tried to secure the sympathy of her Calvinist subjects by, for example, taking down the carved and gilded images of the Twelve Apostles from the pulpit of the "Great Church" and burning them, her faith remained a cause of concern during her reign.[48]

It seems that Bethlen, although fully aware of the uniqueness of the situation, did not consider his successor's sex a problem. When giving reasons for the promotion of Catherine's succession, he referred only marginally to the fact that she was a woman and explained to the diet, to the Ottoman court, and to his subjects how harmful an interregnum would be for the country, and that this was why he decided to provide a successor. In the part of his testament that addressed state government, Gabriel urged the country and its estates "to esteem and fear their prince and not to condemn that she is a woman because she was ordained by God and chosen by the country."[49]

Contemporaries had to deal with the problem of the title used to refer to female rulers. There are numerous examples of medieval queens using or being referred to with a male title by their chroniclers.[50] In medieval Hungary, the expression *rex feminus* is only used in connection with Mary, heiress of Louis I a' Anjou.[51] Elizabeth Tudor occasionally also referred to herself as prince or king.[52] Catherine of Brandenburg was referred to both as *fejedelem* (prince) and *fejedelemasszony* (princess) in contemporary Hungarian sources during her reign. The official sources preferred to use *fejedelem*, because *fejedelemasszony* meant primarily the wife of the prince.[53] When Catherine was elected, the diet formulated her status in the following way: "we elect her our prince unanimously"; a few lines below: "we, the country, chose Her Excellency, . . . our prince."[54]

The same use of male titles can be observed in the sources written in German and in Latin. The Saxon chronicler Georg Krauss explained the dispositions of Bethlen in his work as follows: the prince ordered in his last will and testament "to venerate her [Catherine] not as a princess but as a prince of the land."[55] Another seventeenth-century chronicle explained the uniqueness of her situation with the words "prince not princess" (*princeps non principissa*) in Latin.[56] Her official title during her reign began with the words "Catherine, by the Grace of God born Electress of Brandenburg, Prince of the Holy Roman Empire and Transylvania" (fig. 5.3).[57]

Her gender, however, was frequently used to attack her and question her capacity as a ruler. The agent of the Holy Roman Emperor exploited the issue to counteract the Ottoman confirmation of Catherine's succession in Constantinople.[58] Concern over her gender also emerged during her reign; it was stated that "the prince does not have a clear mind, she is a woman and she is German, it is impossible that she will be suitable for us."[59] The problem of her gender was particularly stressed at the time of her abdication (September 28, 1630). On one rare occasion, Catherine herself recorded why her sex was considered a problem in a letter written to her brother Georg William, describing the circumstances of her abdication. According to her account, the delegation of the orders threatened her: if she did not resign, she would be forced to do so. When Catherine asked why they were so hostile toward her, she received the answer that although she had done nothing against the country, she was "merely female" (*nur eine Weibperson*) while the country was burdened with war; in such a situation, it needed "a male prince" (*einen mänlichen Fürsten*).[60] This argument well expressed the contemporary opinion that held women to be unsuitable for military affairs.[61] Similarly, the diet that chose her successor established that she had to resign primarily because she was a woman: "After the grievous death of our . . . Lord her Majesty Catherine of Brandenburg im-

NOS CATHARINA DEI GRATIA, NATA MARCHIONISSA BRANDEBVRGICA, SACRI ROMANI IMPERII ET TRANSSILVANIÆ PRINCEPS, PARTIVM REGNI HVNGARIÆ DOMINA, SICVLORVM COMES, AC BORVSSIÆ, Iuliæ, Cliuiæ, Montium &c DVCISSA.

MEmoriæ commendamus tenore præſentium, ſignificantes quibus expedit univerſis. Quod Spectabiles, Magnifici, Generoſi, Egregij & Nobiles, cæteriq; univerſi Status & Ordines trium nationum Regni noſtri Tranſylvaniæ, & Partium Hungariæ eidem annexarum, in Generalibus eorum Comitiis, ad diem vigeſimum quintum menſis Ianuarij, Anni Domini Milleſimi Sexcenteſimi Trigeſimi, in Civitate noſtra Alba Iulia, ex edicto noſtro celebratis, congregati, exhibuerunt nobis & præſentaverunt quoſdam infraſcriptos Articulos, in eiſdem Comitijs, paribus ipſorum votis & unanimi conſenſu concluſos; Supplicantes Nobis humiliter, ut nos univerſos eos Articulos, omniaq; & ſingula in eiſdem cõtenta, ratos, gratos, acceptaq; habẽtes, benignè approbare, ratificareq; dignaremur. Quorum quidem Articulorum tenor talis eſt.

ARticuli Dominorum Regnicolarum trium nationum regni Tranſsylvaniæ et partium Hungariæ eidem annexarum, in Generalibus eorundem Comitiis, in Civitate Alba Julia, ad diem vigeſimum quintum menſis Januarii, Anno Domini Milleſimo Sexenteſimo Trigeſimo, indictis, celebratis concluſi.

Figure 5.3. Articuli dominorum regnicolarum . . ., Alba Iulia, 1630, National Széchényi Library, Collection of Old Books, cat. no. RMK I.592a. Reproduced with permission.

Figure 5.4. Strobel the Younger, The Banquet of Herod and the Decapitation of John the Baptist, Museo Nacional del Prado, cat. no. 1940. Reproduced with permission.

mediately succeeded him as prince; although for a short time she possessed and governed our poor homeland, her Majesty felt and experienced how hard and burdensome it is to reign as prince of Transylvania, and due to her Majesty's weak, feeble womanly status she could not perform her duties without endangering our homeland and her own well-being, therefore she resigned out of her own free will and we had to take care of the election of a new prince."[62]

The unusual conditions of Catherine's reign, as well as the persistent criticism of her gender, can be explained through the dominant patriarchal ideology of the period. In general, women were regarded as weaker and in need of male guidance. The assumption that they were subordinate to men and inferior in their capacities had a negative effect on their authority even when their right to the throne was indisputable.[63] In Catherine's case, these premises contributed to the swift end of her reign.

Other persistent charges during her reign included her "inclination to worldly pleasures"[64] and for luxury and conspicuous waste. Her lavish court life and her household expenses had been criticized even when Bethlen was still alive. According to the marriage contract, Catherine established a large court of her own. In the beginning, the size of her court was increased to

two hundred persons, allowing Germans to be included in their number. However, both the size of her court and the great number of her German courtiers gave rise to dissatisfaction in the principality. Despite the contract, the number of her household was cut down to seventy or eighty during her husband's reign, and most of her German followers were sent home. Bethlen's last will and testament also advised her to reduce the size of her household.[65] He considered it important that his wife learn the Hungarian language and customs, and a court with mainly Hungarian courtiers would serve that purpose.

The repeated negative comments about Catherine's extravagance can also be ascribed to contemporary opinion on the nature of women. According to the medieval church, women were especially inclined to the sin of *luxuria*. In the early modern period, they were the primary targets of moralizing literature and sermons against luxury.[66] Public opinion in Transylvania coincided with that abroad on Catherine's way of life, which may be gleaned from the allegorical painting by Strobel the Younger, *The Banquet of Herod and the Decapitation of John the Baptist* (fig. 5.4), which depicts a banquet attended by many of the important political personalities of contemporary Europe. The

Figure 5.5. Catherine of Brandenburg and Gabriel Bethlen, Genuinae effigies Principum Transilvaniae, Budapest, Library of the Hungarian Academy of Sciences, Department of Manuscripts and Rare Books—cat. no. Régészet 2–rét 3. Reproduced with permission.

different scenes of the painting are dominated by the idea of vanity. At the right side of the picture, a group of women surrounds Salome. These female figures have been identified as Elizabeth Stuart, widow of Frederick V of the Palatinate; Eleonore of Brandenburg, widow of the Swedish King Gustavus Adolphus; her daughter Christina; and her sister Catherine of Brandenburg.[67] The second woman from the right notably resembles Catherine as depicted in a portrait series of the princes of Transylvania (fig. 5.5, left) and to her other contemporary likenesses.

The other argument frequently used against Catherine was that she was a foreigner of German extraction and therefore not a real patriot. This was stressed even though the succession was offered to her because, as a member of a great ruling family, she was a good match for a successful prince seeking international recognition. Despite the political importance of international marriages, xenophobia existed in Europe also against foreign brides. Medieval examples show that these women were especially disliked because of their perceived divided loyalties, lack of patriotism, and strange customs.[68] Although Catherine learned Hungarian—according to a chronicle account she mastered the language to such a degree that her arguments and promises saved her position several times during her reign—she could not gain the favor of the majority of her subjects.[69]

In autumn 1630, immediately after Catherine's resignation, both her governor, István Bethlen, and George Rákóczi (1593–1648), a Hungarian aristocrat, were elected princes of Transylvania at about the same time. Catherine voted for Rákóczi in the diet and supported him. Later, however, their relationship deteriorated and there arose a protracted and acrimonious lawsuit between them concerning certain landed estates and movable goods. After her resignation, Catherine moved first to Royal Hungary, and then to Vienna. She officially converted to Catholicism and remarried in 1639. The husband freely chosen by her was Prince Francis Charles of Launenburg (1594–1660), a widower, soldier, and adventurer.[70] She died in the court of her widowed sister, Anna Sophie, in Schöningen in 1644.

As Gabriel Bethlen's widow and successor, Catherine of Brandenburg could not consolidate her power in Transylvania. Her reign is best characterized as a constant power struggle between the ruler on the one hand and the governor and council on the other. She was unable to overcome the unusually strict conditions set by the principality's diet. Her power was further curtailed, and then she was forced to resign. Without the proper support of the orders, she could not become a successful prince like Bethlen had been. Contemporary attitudes toward women played an important role in her failure, primarily because women were considered less suitable for the throne. Moreover, most of the arguments used against her—moral weakness, wastefulness, suggestibility, and incapacity—were also typical stereotypes of women in the era. Nevertheless, and despite the brevity of her reign, she is a remarkable example in early modern Europe of an elected female ruler.

Notes

1. Gábor Klaniczay, *Holy Rulers and Blessed Princesses: Dynastic Cults in Medieval Central Europe*, trans. Éva Pálmai (Cambridge: Cambridge University Press, 2002); Gábor Klaniczay, "Proving Sanctity in the Canonization Processes (Saint Elizabeth and Saint Margaret of Hungary)," in *Procès de canonisation au Moyen Âge: Aspects juridiques et religieux—Medieval Canonization Processes: Legal and Religious Aspects*, ed. Gábor Klaniczay (Rome: École française de Rome, 2004), 117–48; Ilona Sz. Jónás, *Árpád-házi Szent Erzsébet* [Saint Elizabeth of Hungary] (Budapest, Hungary: Akadémiai Kiadó, 1986).

2. Gyula Kristó, "Károly Róbert családja" [The Family of Charles I Robert], *Aetas* 20, no. 4 (2005): 14–28.

3. Oscar Halecki, *Jadwiga of Anjou and the Rise of East Central Europe* (Boulder, Colorado: Atlantic Research and Publications; Highland Lakes, New Jersey, 1991).

4. Sándor Márki, *Mária, Magyarország királynéja (1370–1395)* [Mary, Queen of Hungary (1370–1395)] (Budapest, Hungary: Magyar Történelmi Társulat, 1885); Erik Fügedi, "*Könyörülj, bánom, könyörülj*..." ["Have Mercy, My Bán..."] (Budapest, Hungary: Helikon, 1986).

5. On medieval Hungarian queens, see János Bak, "Roles and Functions of Queens in Árpádian and Angevin Hungary (1000–1386 A.D.)," in *Medieval Queenship*, ed. John Carmi Parsons (Stroud, UK: Sutton Publishing, 1998), 13–24; János Bak, "Queens as Scapegoats in Medieval Hungary," in Queens and Queenship in Medieval Europe, ed. Anne J. Duggan (Woodbridge, Suffolk, UK: Boydell Press, 1997), 224–33; Hajnalka Dobozy, *Királynéink az Árpád- és Anjoukorban* [Queens in the Árpád and Anjou Period] (Szeged, Hungary: n.p. 1934); Gyula Kristó, "Az első magyar királynék. 11. század" [The first Hungarian Queens. 11th century], *História* 22, no. 1 (2000): 10–12; Marianne Sághy, "Aspects of Female Rulership in Late Medieval Literature: The Queens' Reign in Angevin Hungary," *East Central Europe—L' Europe du Centre Est* 20–23 (1993–1996): 69–86; Attila Zsoldos, A királynéi intézmény az Árpádok korában [Queenship in the Árpád Era] (Budapest, Hungary: Magyar Tudományos Akadémia [Hungarian Academy of Sciences] Történettudományi Intézete, 2005); Armin Wolf, "Reigning Queens in Medieval Europe: When, Where, and Why," in *Medieval Queenship*, 169–88.

6. After Louis's death, Mary was regent of the country for the new king, Ferdinand I of Habsburg; from 1531, she was regent of the Low Countries. See Orsolya Réthelyi, Beatrix F. Romhányi, Enikő Spekner, András Végh, eds., *Mary of Hungary: The Queen and Her Court 1521–1531* (Budapest, Hungary: Budapesti Történeti Múzeum, 2005); Etienne Piret, *Marie de Hongrie* (Paris: Jourdan Editeur, 2005); Jane de Iongh, *Mary of Hungary: Second Regent of The Netherlands,* trans. M. D. Herter Norton (London: Faber & Faber, 1959); Bob van den Boogert and Jacqueline Kerkhoff, Maria van Hongarije: koningin tussen keizers en kunstenaars 1505–1558 (Zwolle, Netherlands: Waanders, 1995).

7. Transylvania constitutes a triangular plateau bordered by the Carpathians from northeast and south and the Bihor mountains on the west. The Principality of Transylvania also included eastern regions of Hungary on its west side, the so-called *Partium*.

8. For the history of the Principality of Transylvania during this period, see Ladislas Makkai, *Histoire de Transylvanie* (Paris: Les Presses Universitaires de France, 1946); Peter F. Sugar, "The Principality of Transylvania," in *A History of Hungary*, ed. Peter F. Sugar (Bloomington; Indianapolis: 1994), 121–37; Katalin Péter, "The Golden Age of the Principality," in History of Transylvania, ed. Béla Köpeczi (Boulder, Colorado; New York: Social Science Monographs, 2002), 2: 1–230.

9. Kálmán Benda, *Erdély végzetes asszonya* [The Fateful Lady of Transylvania] (Budapest, Hungary: Helikon, 1986), 39, 60.

10. On the reign of Catherine of Brandenburg see: Judit Bánki, "Brandenburgi Katalin az Erdélyi Fejedelemségben" [Catherine of Brandenburg in the Principality of Transylvania], *Történelmi Szemle* 36 (1994): 311–26; F. R. Krones, "Katharina von Brandenburg-Preussen als Fürstin Siebenbürgens 1626–1631," *Zeitschrift für Allgemeine Geschichte,*

Kultur-, Literatur- und Kunstgeschichte I (1884): 334–58; Róza Novák, *Brandenburgi Katalin* (Kolozsvár, Hungary [now in Romania]: Gombos Ferenc, 1903); Ágoston Ötvös, "Brandenburgi Katalin fejedelemsége" [The Principality of Catherine of Brandenburg], *Akadémiai Értesítő* II/2 (1861): 153–244; Georg Schuster, "Eine brandenburgische Prinzessin auf dem siebenbürgischen Fürstenthrone," *Hohenzollern-Jahrbuch* 5 (1901): 121–36; Helga Schultz: "Katharina von Brandenburg—zweite Gemahlin Gábor Bethlens," unpublished conference paper (1980). I wish to thank Professor Helga Schultz for allowing me to consult her paper.

11. József Koncz, comp., *Bethlen Gábor fejedelem végrendelete* [The Last Will and Testament of Gabriel Bethlen], offprint from Erdélyi Híradó (Marosvásárhely, Hungary: n.p., 1878), 19.

12. Katalin Péter, "Bethlen Gábor emlékezete. A fejedelem pályakezdése" [The Memory of Gabriel Bethlen. The Beginning of His Career], *Századok* 115 (1981): 744–49.

13. On the life and reign of Gabriel Bethlen, see László Makkai, ed., *Bethlen Gábor emlékezete* [The Memory of Gabriel Bethlen] (Budapest, Hungary: Európa Könyvkiadó, 1980); Graeme Murdock, "'Freely Elected in Fear': Princely Elections and Political Power in Early Modern Transylvania," *Journal of Early Modern History* 7, nos. 3–4 (2003): 213–44; Péter, "The Golden Age of the Principality," 1–230; Katalin Péter, "Two Aspects of War and Society in the Age of Prince Gabor Bethlen of Transylvania," in *From Hunyadi to Rákóczi: War and Society in Late Medieval and Early Modern Hungary*, ed. J. M. Bak and B. K. Király (New York: Brooklyn College of The City University of New York, 1982), 297–313.

14. Gyula Szabó, comp., "Bethlen Gábor házassága Brandenburgi Katalinnal" [The Marriage of Gabriel Bethlen with Catherine of Brandenburg], *Történelmi Tár* 4 (1888): 656–63.

15. On Anna of Prussia, see Toni Saring, "Kurfürstin Anna von Preußen," *Forschungen zur brandenburgischen und preußischen Geschichte* 53 (1941): 248–95.

16. Rita Scheller, *Die Frau am Preussischen Herzogshof (1550–1625)* (Cologne and Berlin: Grote Verlag, 1966), 171, 173.

17. Scheller, *Die Frau am Preussischen Herzogshof*, 173; Heidi Wunder, *He Is the Sun, She Is the Moon: Women in Early Modern Germany*, trans. Thomas Dunlap (Cambridge, Mass.: Harvard University Press, 1998), 155–59.

18. "Relatio Pauli Strasburgi de Catharina vidua principis Bethlen Gabor," in Alexander Szilágyi, *Georg Rákóczy I. im Dreissigjährigen Kriege 1630–1640* (Budapest, Hungary: Kilian, 1883), 47.

19. Schultz, "Katharina von Brandenburg," 2; Geheimes Staatsarchiv Preussischer Kulturbesitz (GStA PK), Brandenburg Preussisches Hausarchiv (BPH), Rep. 33, W., Nr. 68. Altere Remissionszettel über noch im Königl. Staats-Archiwe befindliche Acten betr. die projectirte Moscowitische Heirath (1623) der Markgräfin Katharina v. Brandenburg, die gleichfalls projectirte Vermählung derselben mit dem Prinzen Wladislaus von Polen (1630) und ihre mit dem Herzoge Franz Karl zu Sachsen-Lauenburg wollzogene Vermählung (1639).

20. *Vmbständtliche Relation deß Bethlen Gabors mit der Chur-Brandenburgischen Princessin Catharina zu Caschaw gehaltnen Beylagers* (Wien, Austria: Gregor Gelbhar; Prague: Paul Geste, 1626), A III.

21. Makkai, *Bethlen Gábor emlékezete*, 245.

22. Gizella Cennerné Wilhemb, "Bethlen Gábor metszet-arcképei" [The Engraving-portraits of Gabriel Bethlen], *Folia Historica* 8 (1980): 33–51.

23. August Ingler, comp., "Bethlen Gabor's Hochzeitsfeier: Nach dem handschriftlichen Berichte eines Augenzeugen," *Neue Folge* III (1874): 528.

24. Ingler, "Bethlen Gabor's Hochzeitsfeier," 528.

25. For accounts of the wedding, see Ingler, "Bethlen Gabor's Hochzeitsfeier," 517–43; "Des kurbaierischen Abgeordneten Maximilian Kurz Freyherrn von Senftenau Bericht über die im März 1626: vollzogene Hochzeit Bethlen Gabor's Fürsten von Siebenbürgen," *Zeitschrift für Baiern und die angränzenden Länder* II/2 (1817): 347–57; *Kemény János Önéletírása* [Autobiography of János Kemény], in *Kemény János és Bethlen Miklós művei* [The Works of János Kemény and Miklós Bethlen], ed. Éva V. Windisch (Budapest, Hungary: Szépirodalmi Könyvkiadó, 1980), 51–65; *Vmbständtliche Relation.*

26. On the court of Gabriel Bethlen, see Makkai, *Bethlen Gábor emlékezete*, 437–540; Horst Fassel, "Der Fürstenhof von Weißenburg (Alba Iulia) und seine Bedeutung für Wissenschaft und Kunst in Siebenbürgen zur Zeit Gabriel Bethlens," in *Europäische Hofkultur im 16. und 17. Jahrhundert*, eds. August Buck et al. (Hamburg: Dr. Ernst Hauswedell & Co., 1981), 3: 637–45.

27. Although a great number of letters written by Catherine of Brandenburg and Gabriel Bethlen remain, unfortunately the couple's correspondence is lost: only a single draft remains (of a letter written by Catherine to Gabriel: GStA PK, BPH, Rep. 33. W. Nr. 62. fol. 128–30.).

28. Farkas Deák, *Egy magyar főúr a XVII. században: Gr. Csáky István életrajza* [A Hungarian Aristocrat in the Seventeenth Century: The Biography of István Csáky] (Budapest, Hungary: Ráth Mór, 1883), 24.

29. Keith Thomas, "The Double Standard," *Journal of the History of Ideas* 20 (1959): 195–216; Margaret R. Sommerville, *Sex and Subjection: Attitudes to Women in Early-Modern Society* (London: Arnold, 1995), 141; Joan Kelly-Gadol, "Did Women Have a Renaissance?" *Becoming Visible: Women in European History*, eds. Renate Bridenthal and Claudia Koonz (Boston: Houghton Mifflin, 1977), 155, 160.

30. "Des kurbaierischen Abgeordneten," 355.

31. "Relatio Pauli Strasburgi de Catharina vidua principis Bethlen Gabor," 46–47.

32. *Kemény János Önéletírása*, 101–2.

33. GStA PK, BPH, Rep. 33. W. Nr. 80. fol. 33–36.

34. "Titkos utasítás Kamuthy Farkas számára Czecilia Renata főherczegnő kezének megkérése ügyében. Besztercze-Bánya 1624. január 11" [Secret Instructions for Farkas Kamuthy Concerning the Proposal of Cecilia Renata, Banská Bystrica, January 11, 1624], in Sándor Szilágyi, comp., "Adalékok Bethlen Gábor szövetkezéseinek történetéhez" [Contributions to the History of Gabriel Bethlen's Alliances], *Értekezés a Történeti Tudományok Köréből* II/8 (1872–73): 50–51.

35. GStA PK, BPH, Rep. 11. 255a, fol. 1–44.

36. "1626. máj. 24–jún. 17. A gyulafehérvári országgyűlés törvényei" [Laws Enacted by the Diet of Alba Iulia, May 24–June 17, 1626], in *Erdélyi Országgyűlési Emlékek: Monumenta comitialia regni Transsylvaniae 1540–1699*, 21 vols., comp. Sándor Szilágyi (Budapest, Hungary: Magyar Tudományos Akadémia, 1875–98), 8: 312–54.

37. *The Negotiations of Sir Thomas Roe in his Embassy to the Ottoman Porte from 1621 to 1628 Inclusive* (London: n.p., 1740), 549, 558–65, 586.

38. Sándor Szilágyi, comp., *Bethlen Gábor fejedelem kiadatlan politikai levelei* [The Unpublished Political Letters of Gabriel Bethlen] (Budapest, Hungary: Magyar Tudományos Akadémia, 1879), 435–45.

39. Sarolta Lakner, *Az erdélyi fejedelmek választási feltételei* [The Conditions of Election of the Transylvanian Princes] (Debrecen, Hungary: n.p., 1927); Krista Zach, "Fürst, Landtag und Stände: Die verfassungsrechtliche Frage in Siebenbürgen im 16. und 17. Jahrhundert," in Krista Zach, *Konfessionelle Pluralität, Stände und Nation: Ausgewählte Abhandlungen zur südosteuropäischen Religions- und Gesellschaftsgeschichte,* Herausgegeben von Joachim Bahlcke und Konrad Gündisch, eds. (Münster, Germany: Lit Verlag, 2004), 6: 59–62.

40. "Brandenburgi Katalin esküje az erdélyi rendek előtt" [The Oath of Catherine of Brandenburg Taken Before the Orders of Transylvania], in Ötvös, "Brandenburgi Katalin," 214–15.

41. Barna Mezey, *Government of the Transylvanian State in the 17th Century: Princely Power During the Reign of Gábor Bethlen* (Budapest, Hungary: ELTE, Department of Hungarian State and Legal History, 1991), 8–9; Zsolt Trócsányi, *Erdély központi kormányzata 1540–1690* [Central Government of Transylvania 1540–1690] (Budapest, Hungary: Akadémiai Kiadó, 1980), 19–22.

42. "1626. máj. 24–jún. 17. A gyulafehérvári orsággyűlés törvényei," 312–15.

43. Trócsányi, *Erdély központi kormányzata,* 400.

44. "1630. jan. 25.–febr. 17. A gyulafehérvári országgyűlés végzései s irományai" [Laws and Documents of the Diet of Alba Iulia, January 25–February 17, 1630], in Szilágyi, *Erdélyi Országgyűlési Emlékek*, 9: 76–108.

45. Zsolt Trócsányi, *Az erdélyi fejedelemség korának országgyűlései* [Diets of the Principality of Transylvania] (Budapest, Hungary: Akadémiai Kiadó, 1976), 16–18.

46. "1630. jan. 25.–febr. 17. A gyulafehérvári országgyűlés végzései s irományai," 85.

47. "A megyesi országgyűlés végzései s irományai" [Laws and Documents of the Diet of Mediaş], in Szilágyi, *Erdélyi Országgyűlési Emlékek*, 9: 114–15.

48. Georg Krauss, *Siebenbürgische Chronik des Schäßburger Stadtschreibers Georg Kraus 1608–1665*, vol. 1 (Wien, Austria: Österreichische Akademie der Wissenschaften, 1862), 84.

49. Koncz, *Bethlen Gábor fejedelem végrendelete*, 16.

50. John Carmi Parsons, "Introduction: Family, Sex and Power: The Rhythms of Medieval Queenship," in *Medieval Queenship*, 8.

51. Sághy, "Aspects of Female Rulership," 79.

52. Carole Levin, The Heart and Stomach of a King: *Elizabeth I and the Politics of Sex and Power* (Philadelphia: University of Pennsylvania Press, 1994), 1–2; Merry Wiesner-Hanks, "Women's Authority in the State and Household in Early Modern Europe," in *Women Who Ruled: Queens, Goddesses, Amazons in Renaissance and Baroque Art*, ed. Annette Dixon (London: Merrell; Ann Arbor: University of Michigan Museum of Art, 2002), 27–59.

53. Attila Szabó T., ed., *Erdélyi Magyar Szótörténeti Tár* [Historical Dictionary of the Hungarian Language in Transylvania], vol. 3 (Budapest, Hungary: Kriterion, 1982), 783–84.

54. "1626. máj. 24–jún. 17. A gyulafehérvári országyülés törvényei," 313.

55. "Derweill mit droben gehört, dass der Betthlen Gabor ex Testamentaria dispositione, sein Fürstl. Gemal Catharinam Brandeburgicam ihm Regiment gelassen, ihn welchem pfal seine Consiliarii sich ihm auch mit dem Jurament verpflichtet, sie nicht alss eine Fürstin sondern alss einen Fürsten des Landes zu veneriren . . .," Krauss, 83.

56. "Catharina Brandenburgica, quam iampridem in generalibus regni comitiis successorem principem, non principissam, creauerat," *Ioannis com. de Betlen Commentarii de Rebvs Transsilvanicis Proximis ab Obitv Gabrielis Betlenii Triginta Qvatvor Annis Gestis* (Viennae: Typis Iosephi Nobilis de Kurzböck, 1779), 8.

57. "Nos Catharina Dei gratia nata Marchionissa Brandeburgica, Sacri Romani Imperii et Transilvaniae Princeps, Partium regni Hungariae domina, Siculorum comes, ac Borussiae, Iuliae, Cliviae, Montium & c. Ducissa," in "1630. jan. 25.–febr. 17. A gyulafehérvári országgyűlés végzései s irományai," 76.

58. *The Negotiations of Sir Thomas Roe,* 563–64.

59. "1629. dec. 31. Csáky István Kornis Zsigmondnak" [From István Csáky to Zsigmond Kornis, December 31, 1629], in Deák, *Egy magyar főúr a XVII. században,* 228–32.

60. "Fogaras, den 29. Nov. 1630. Katharina von Brandenburg an ihren Bruder . . .," in Szilágyi, *Georg Rákóczy I.*, 7–8.

61. Cary J. Nederman and Elaine N. Lawson, "The Frivolities of Courtiers Follow the Footprints of Women: Public Women and the Crisis of Virility in John of Salisbury 83," in *Ambiguous Realities: Women in the Middle Ages and Renaissance*, eds. Caroline Levin and Jeanie Watson (Detroit, Michigan: Wayne State University Press, 1987), 82–95.

62. "1630. decz. 20–29. A fehérvári országgyűlés végzései" [Laws Enacted by the Diet of Alba Iulia, December 20–29, 1630], in Szilágyi, *Erdélyi Országgyűlési Emlékek* vol. 9, 149.

63. Charles T. Wood, "The First Two Queens Elizabeth, 1464–1503," in Louise Olga Fradenburg, ed., *Women and Sovereignty* (Edinburgh: Edinburgh University Press, 1992), 124; Natalie Tomas, "Alfonsina Orsini de' Medici and the 'Problem' of a Female Ruler in Early Sixteenth-Century Florence," *Renaissance Studies* 14/I (2000): 71–72; Karen Nicholas, "Women as Rulers: Countess Jeanne and Marguerite of Flanders (1212–1278)," in *Queens, Regents and Potentates,* ed. Theresa M. Vann (Dallas, Texas: Academia Press, 1993), 88.

64. János Szalárdi, *Siralmas magyar krónikája* [Miserable Hungarian Chronicle] (Budapest, Hungary: Magyar Helikon, 1980), 129.

65. Koncz, *Bethlen Gábor fejedelem végrendelete*, 28.

66. On the notion of luxury, see: Christopher J. Berry, *The Idea of Luxury: A Conceptual and Historical Investigation* (Cambridge: Cambridge University Press, 1994), esp. parts I-II; John Sekora, *Luxury: The Concept of Western Thought, Eden to Smollet* (Baltimore, Maryland: Johns Hopkins University Press, 1977); Maurice M. Goldsmith, "Liberty, Luxury and the Pursuit of Happiness," in *Languages of Political Theory in Early Modern Europe*, ed. Anthony R. Padgen et al. (Cambridge: Cambridge University Press, 1987), 225–51.

67. Jan Harasimowicz, "'Was kann nun besser seyn dann fuer die Freyheit streiten und die Religion.' Konfessionalisierung und ständische Freiheitsbestrebungen im Spiegel der schlesischen Kunst des 16. und 17. Jahrhunderts," in *1648 Krieg und Frieden in Europa*, eds. Klaus Bußmann and Heinz Schilling (Münster/Osnabrück, Germany: Westfälisches Landesmuseum für Kunst und Kulturseschichte, 1998), 2: 303.

68. Pauline Stafford, *Queens, Concubines and Dowagers: The King's Wife in the Early Middle Ages* (London and Washington, D.C.: Leicester University Press, 1983), 47, 58–59.

69. *Siebenbürgische Chronik des Schäßburger Stadtschreibers*, 1: 83–84.

70. A. E. E. L. von Duve, *Mittheilungen zur näheren Kunde des Wichtigsten der Staatsgeschichte und Zustände der Bewohner des Herzogthums Lauenburg von der Vorzeit bis zum Schlusse des Jahres 1851* (Ratzenburg, Germany: H. Linsen, 1857), 170; Christopher von Warnstedt, "Herzoglich Lauenburgische Regimenter in schwedischen Diensten im 17. Jahrhundert," *Lauenburgische Heimat N. F.* 37 (June 1962): 6; Peter von Kobbe, Geschichte und Landesbeschreibung des Herzogtums Lauenburg, vol. 2 (Altona, Denmark [now in Germany]: Johann Friedrich Hammerich, 1836), 412–13; Hermann Mayer, "Zur Familiengeschichte derer von Rautenkrantz als Nachkommen Herzog Franz-Karls," *Lauenburgische Heimat* 2 (April 1934), 37–43; U. von Rundstedt, "Die Söhne Franz' II. Franz Karl, Herzog von Sa.-Lbg.," *Lauenburgische Heimat* 4 (1928), 18–19.

PART II

Sovereignty and Representation

6. Juana of Austria

Patron of the Arts and Regent of Spain, 1554–59

ANNE J. CRUZ

From the late fifteenth to the mid-sixteenth century, Spain was led by a series of female sovereigns: Isabel of Castile (known as Isabel la Católica), queen regnant from 1474 to 1504; Isabel's daughter Juana of Castile (known as Juana la Loca), who, although considered mentally unstable, remained *de jure* queen until her death in 1555; and her granddaughter, Isabel of Portugal, whose marriage to Charles V in 1526 elevated her to the rank of empress. The rule of women in early modern Spain culminated with the regency of Juana of Austria, Isabel of Castile's great-granddaughter. None of these royal women has been viewed as governing independently from their husbands or sons; indeed, until very recently, Isabel of Castile's rule was inexorably linked to that of her husband, Fernando of Aragon.[1] Yet, as historians are now conceding, Spanish queens enjoyed a high level of autonomy at court.[2] Although Charles wielded immense political power as Holy Roman Emperor and had little communication with his mother, whose signature was nevertheless required on all official documents, he relied extensively on his wife, whom he appointed "lieutenant and governess of the realm" during his frequent absences from Spain.[3] Isabel's first-born, the future Philip II, was intensely attached to his mother and to his Portuguese governess and the empress's lady-in-waiting, Leonor de Mascarenhas. When he returned to Spain briefly in 1533, Charles, upset that his son was still living in his mother's household and could neither read nor write, set up a separate household for him and named the future cardinal of Toledo, Juan Martínez Silíceo, his tutor.[4]

The empress's death in 1539 deeply affected the prince and his two sisters, especially Juana, who was only four years old. All three of Isabel's children were reared without paternal support: Charles's final absence from Spain lasted from 1543 to 1556, when he returned to abdicate the throne. At only sixteen years of age, Philip was left as regent; as part of his royal responsibilities, the adolescent married his cousin, María of Portugal, fathered a son, don Carlos, and was left widowed in 1545. Three years later, he traveled officially through his Italian, German, and Dutch states, meeting with Charles in Brussels, where he stayed for several months.[5] In his absence, Philip's eldest sister María and her husband, the future Maximilian II, served as regents, but on the prince's return to Spain in 1551, the couple left the peninsula with their infant daughter Anna of Austria.

Following the complex endogamous arrangements typical of the Habsburg monarchy, in 1552, Juana married her cousin, Prince Juan Manuel of Portugal, the brother of Philip's late wife María of Portugal, both of whom were children of Charles V's sister Catalina. The ailing prince, two years younger than Juana, died less than two years after the marriage, and one week before the young princess gave birth to her only son, the future King Sebastian of Portugal. At that time, Charles's decision to marry the widowed Philip to Mary Tudor in order to achieve a political union with England again compelled Philip to leave Spain. With his father still in Austria, Philip recalled Juana from Portugal to serve as regent. She obediently left her son, at age four months, never to see him again.[6]

Juana's regency in Spain has been little studied, yet from the time of the empress's death in 1539 until 1554, the year the recently widowed Juana arrived from Portugal, no royal woman held a stable, lasting position at court.[7] While still only a child, the young princess had been responsible for the care of her motherless nephew, don Carlos, and of her sister María, who suffered from several maladies. Her ill-fated marriage to her Portuguese cousin and the forced abandonment of her son to return to Spain as regent no doubt cast a shadow on her personality. Dressed always in black (fig. 6.1), she created a myth as confusing and contradictory as that of her brother, and what has been published about her tends to be part soap opera and part black legend. As an example, in Antonio Mira de Amescua's entirely ahistorical play *La hija de Carlos Quinto* (ca. 1616), on her arrival from Portugal, Juana names Madrid the capital of Spain and rejects marriage to Archduke Matthias of Habsburg (her nephew, born in 1557) in order to found a convent where she will profess as a nun.[8] Rather than devoting herself entirely to spiritual matters, given Charles's penchant for utilizing dynastic marriages as a means to maintain and strengthen political alliances, she was prepared from an early age to assume sovereignty.

Indeed, in contrast to her legendary religiosity, early on Juana showed inter-

Figure 6.1. Juana of Austria by Alonso Sánchez Coello, ca. 1557, Archivo fotográfico del Museo de Bellas Artes de Bilbao. Reproduced with permission.

est in many secular pastimes. Educated with her brother at court, Juana shared with him a passion for hunting, painting, literature, and, especially, music. Geoffrey Parker has commented on Philip's "addiction" to music, mentioning in passing that "his sister Joana learned to play the viol and the vihuela (a sort of lute) with considerable skill."[9] He also recounts that Philip's tutor Juan Calvete de Estrella purchased a great number of books for him, including some works by classical authors, Aesop's fables, and books on theology and architecture, the collected works of Erasmus, Pico della Mirandola's *Immortality of the Soul*, and Copernicus's *De revolutionibus*. In 1547, Calvete purchased 135 books in bulk, including Pliny's *Natural History*, as well as works by Dante and Petrarch. The consignment also contained works on music, mathematics, astronomy, history, and geography, among other subjects. Philip's humanist readings provided him with an encyclopedic knowledge, which Juana evidently shared. The inventory made of her possessions in 1574, one year after her death, confirms that she had 249 books in her collection at the Convent of the Descalzas Reales, an unusually large library at her immediate disposal.[10] Among these are included not only a majority of devotional books (a book of hours, a breviary, a prayer book, a manual, the *Flos Sanctorum*, among others), but also chronicles, songbooks, Petrarch in the original Italian, Terence's *Pamphilus*, farces and autos, a French dictionary, grammar books, and several editions of the first Spanish pastoral novel, *Los siete libros de la Diana* (*The Seven Books of Diana)* by Jorge de Montemayor.[11] In addition to being reared by the retinue of her mother's Portuguese ladies-in-waiting, who took care of her household and spoke to her in her mother's first language, Juana studied with Philip's preceptors, including a Latin tutor who taught her several other languages.

Juana's return to Spain at nineteen years of age, after her husband's death, reinforced Portuguese influence at the Spanish court, as she brought with her a number of courtiers, musicians, and artists, including Montemayor, whose poems are dedicated to her.[12] She surrounded herself with Portuguese courtiers to protect her rights as possible regent of Portugal after the Portuguese king's death and until her son came of age.[13] Although it is rumored that she wished to join the Franciscan order, Juana's role as regent precluded any intention of religious enclosure. She set up her court in Valladolid and almost immediately began construction in Madrid of what was to serve as Philip's children's second home, the Convento de Nuestra Señora de la Consolación for discalced Claires, popularly known as the Convento de Descalzas Reales, a Franciscan convent built in the palace where she had been born in Madrid.

Juana faced several major crises during her regency caused by the political and religious factions at court and the increasing economic emergencies brought on by the wars against Flanders and Italy. In 1557, she was forced to suspend payment of state debts, due to the international monetary crisis.[14] Juana also attempted to quell the revolts in North Africa, which led to an armed intervention in the Maghreb. In Spain, the discovery of Lutheran cells in Seville and Valladolid precipitated two *autos de fe* and the issuance of the *Index of Forbidden Books* by the Inquisition.[15] Despite the tensions created by Charles's constant missives from Yuste, where he continued to rule from his retirement, and the divisions at court, Juana took strong, decisive military measures: she instructed the Marqués de Santa Cruz, Álvaro de Bazán, to lead a squadron against English corsairs, to head off an attack by the Turks at Orán, and to protect the fleet returning from the New World.[16] After the fall of Bougie (Bugía) in North Africa, Juana again took matters into her own hands and sent troops to recover the seaport and capture Algiers against her brother's express orders.[17] With little support, however, Juana's military strategy failed, compelling a stricter observance by Philip of his sister's political involvements. Juana had arranged Charles V's retirement at Yuste and the return of his two widowed sisters, María and Leonor, to Spain. After Charles's death, she refused to send Philip funds for him to stay any longer in the Netherlands, warning him that he needed to take care of Spain's growing economic problems.[18]

The princess's authority extended to both religion and politics: as with Jorge de Montemayor, whose religious poetry contrasts with the secular love scenes in his pastoral novel, Juana combined intense piety with a worldly understanding and enjoyment of courtly ritual and affairs of state. While in Portugal, she had allied herself with the Spanish Jesuits, especially Francisco de Borja, and with the Portuguese party known in Spain as the "ebolistas" after Ruy Gómez de Silva, the Portuguese politician given the title of prince of Éboli. On her return to Spain, the court was divided into two main parties, the "albista" party of the Duke of Alba; and Ruy Gómez's ebolista faction.[19] The two men were political enemies, but also expressed their conflict through their exclusive religious affiliations. The Alba party practiced a formalist and intransigent religiosity, unlike the Portuguese, who adhered to an interiorized spirituality known as illuminism or "recogimiento."[20] Juana's attachments to the Jesuits were well known: she was very close to Francisco de Borja and his wife, Leonor de Castro, who had come from Portugal in the empress's retinue. When widowed, Borja joined the Jesuit order and became Juana's spiritual advisor. The nuns who first occupied the Monasterio de Descalzas Reales were Borja's aristocratic relatives from Gandia, near Valencia.

Juana's extreme loyalty to the Jesuits led to several significant episodes in her relations with the order. The first was her secret request that she become a member of the Society of Jesus. The order's popularity had attracted many women, who either wished to join the order or to found a separate female branch. In 1545, Isabel Roser, a friend and patron of Ignatius of Loyola, successfully obtained a brief from Pope Paul III allowing her and two other women to take the vows of the society. Although the vows themselves made no mention of entrance into the society, Isabel's exorbitant demands for spiritual direction led Ignatius to ask the pope for dispensation from her vows. In 1547, Ignatius requested a papal brief forbidding the society to take communities of women under its obedience. Nevertheless, Juana was accepted into the society: not only was she the daughter of the Holy Roman Emperor, she had a close, personal affinity to Francisco de Borja—so close, that rumors were spread about their relationship.

Juana's entry into the Jesuit order was arranged secretly, under the pseudonym of Mateo Sánchez.[21] In practical terms, this meant that although she took the three vows of poverty, chastity, and obedience, she could separate from the society if she so desired. It is unlikely that she took two of her vows seriously: although she dressed austerely, she did not abandon her royal lifestyle, and her letters reveal her attempts to command both Ignatius and Borja.[22] Juana protected the Jesuit order and defended it against the Dominican Melchor Cano, who led the attack on fellow Dominican Bartolomé Carranza, the brilliant theologian and archbishop of Toledo. She was forced to take sides in the power struggle between the Inquisitor General Fernando de Valdés and Carranza.[23]

The five years of Juana's regency saw the rise and fall of the ebolista party. Until 1559, the lone member of the albistas at court, the Inquisitor General Fernando de Valdés, barely held on to power. Philip had asked Juana to expel him from court, but on the discovery of a Lutheran cell in Valladolid, Charles wrote from his retreat at Yuste asking that Valdés remain as inquisitor general. Valdés was also an enemy of Carranza, one of Philip's closest religious allies, who had accompanied him to England to catechize the Anglicans. Like the Jesuits, the ebolistas, and the royal family, Carranza practiced an interior form of religion that was considered close to heterodoxy by the dogmatic albistas. The conservative Valdés was quick to condemn Carranza, and the process against him found his catechism to be full of heterodox notions. The sweep was total: Carranza was arrested by the Inquisition; Francisco de Borja, also denounced and accused of sexual misconduct with Juana, fled to Portugal, where he wrote to Philip denying all the accusations. Charles ordered Juana to act with utmost rigor in punishing those indicted for religious dissidence.[24] Obeying her father's last directives, Juana lent support to the Inquisition trials against the royal preacher Agustín Cazalla and Carranza. She presided over the *auto de fe* against the Lutherans in Valladolid in May 1559, in which fourteen victims were "relaxed" by the Inquisition into the hands of the state, among them, members of Cazalla's family, friends, and acquaintances of the princess.[25] That same year, Valdés placed Carranza's catechism, along with Montemayor's religious poetry and Luis de Granada's spiritual treatises, on the *Index of Forbidden Books*.[26]

Until war broke out again with the Netherlands, however, Philip did not enforce religious controls; despite his strict adherence to Catholicism, the king responded pragmatically to political situations. During his stay in Germany, he had learned to live peacefully with the Protestants and, while in England, he did not take part in any persecution against Anglicans.[27] Similarly, Juana's brand of illuminist piety did not conflict with her appreciation for and enjoyment of the secular arts. Parker's categorical statement that Juana was "renowned for her coldness to other people" and that, like the king, she "preferred to be alone," contrasts with the energies she dedicated to the arts at court.[28] Juana patronized numerous court musicians, such as Antonio Cabezón, Tomás Luis de Vitoria, the composer and organist at the Descalzas Reales, and Miguel de Fuenllana,[29] and employed several court painters, having brought both the Flemish painter Antonio Moro and his student Alonso Sánchez Coello to Valladolid.[30] She also invited Rolam del Mois and Jooris van der Straaten (known as Jorge de la Rua in Spain) to court from Flanders.[31]

The Habsburgs were famous for their cultivation of portrait painters who specialized in what art historian Maria Kusche calls "portraits of representation," the Spanish school that portrayed members of the royal family in full or three-fourths length, in a more personal and less heroic dimension. According to Kusche, the portrait's function was "semi-private, familiar, and genealogical," with only a column, chair, or window alluding to their political power.[32] Representations of royals had a practical function as well; Lorne Campbell states: "The princes of Europe used portraits to keep themselves and their families in the public eye. . . . Princesses who were forced to live at great distances from their children were naturally anxious to have portraits of them . . . [and] when a marriage between princes was being negotiated, a portrait of the lady was often sent to the man so that he might have some advance knowledge of her appearance."[33]

The portraits' circulation was intended to overcome the distances between the European courts, and court painters fulfilled an essential political as well as decorative and familial role. Juana's collection of portraits at the Descalzas Reales was surpassed only by Philip's portrait gallery in the Pardo Palace.[34]

Two of the portraits in the king's gallery were of Philip's son don Carlos. Sánchez Coello had first painted the prince when he was ten years old; he painted him again at age eighteen as don Carlos neared marriageable age (fig. 6.2). Although the painter approached his models realistically, he tried to disguise the prince's shorter leg and his hunchback. The later portrait was sent to Vienna by the Austrian ambassador, who nevertheless noted that the youth had his mouth hanging open and one leg much longer than the other.[35]

Juana's compassionate attitude toward the increasingly unstable don Carlos demonstrates her deeply maternal feelings: on the occasion of the youth's near-mortal fall down a staircase, she led a procession barefoot to the Capilla del Obispo (Bishop's Chapel), next to the Church of San Andrés, a considerable distance from the palace. Despite his psychological and physical problems, the prince was the sole heir to Philip's vast empire and was therefore considered an ideal match for several European princesses: Catherine de' Medici's two daughters, Isabel and Margaret; the young widow Mary Stuart; Philip's niece Anna of Austria; and even Juana herself were seriously proposed as marriage partners. That Juana would consider marrying her brother's son, whom she had brought up as a child, underscores the immense importance placed on dynastic reproduction. The most significant

Figure 6.2. Don Carlos by Alonso Sánchez Coello, 1564, Kunsthistorisches Museum, Vienna. Reproduced with permission.

means of maintaining royal power was through direct succession and marriage alliances such as the endogamous unions practiced by the Habsburgs. Royal families were required to reproduce themselves, yet the extremely high number of women who died either in or immediately after childbirth surely sent a chilling message to young princesses that the fertility for which they were so greatly valued could in the end endanger their own lives. The requisite state imperative that they bear as many children as possible, due to the high infant mortality, further relegated them to the role of mere pawns in the much larger game of international politics.

It is probable that Juana joined the Jesuit order to keep her brother and father from bestowing her in marriage a second time, because she sustained the hope of returning to Portugal as queen regent until her son came of age. During Sebastian's childhood, Juana maintained constant communication with the Portuguese court; in 1565, she sent Cristóbal de Moura to obtain reliable news about her son's health.[36] She was well liked by the Portuguese, who perceived her as one of their own.[37] Juana never returned to Lisbon, however; instead, her acquiescence to a potential marriage with don Carlos speaks to her utter and complete devotion to the family's dynastic needs.[38] It also reveals the absolute separation that was understood to exist between sexual relations inspired by physical attraction and those obligated by reason of state, a separation that served Philip well in accepting his marriage to the older Mary Tudor.[39]

After Mary Tudor died childless in 1558, Philip planned his return to Spain. He had spent the previous year negotiating the marriage of don Carlos to Catherine de' Medici's daughter, Isabel de Valois. Because the young prince's health and mental condition had rapidly deteriorated, and because Mary's successor, Elizabeth I, had rejected him in his proposal, Philip agreed to marry Isabel himself. His union with the French princess, called Isabel de la Paz by the Spaniards to celebrate the signing of the Treaty of Cateau-Cambresis, temporarily resolved Franco-Spanish relations.

While Philip stayed in Madrid, Juana left for the Mendoza palace in Guadalajara, where the couple met after their wedding by proxy at Notre Dame in Paris, to prepare the wedding celebrations. Juana's dedication to her new sister-in-law was evident from the start. The fourteen-year-old Isabel (fig. 6.3) had not yet begun to menstruate when she arrived in Spain to meet Philip, who was then involved with one of Juana's ladies-in-waiting, Eufrasia de Guzmán.[40] Despite their eleven years' difference in age, Juana and Isabel immediately became fast friends, and the two spent the young queen's first year in Toledo dancing, playing cards, and gambling. Isabel's French court fought openly with the Spanish ladies-in-waiting for her attention.[41] An anonymous satirical sonnet dedicated to one of her ladies-in-waiting calls the young woman "a melancholy damsel," ridiculing her as a "whore-damsel" expecting, like her mistress, to be ravished by the king.[42] Isabel's boredom at Toledo (she called it "the dreariest place in the world were it not for my husband") may have helped persuade Philip to select Madrid as Spain's capital.[43] She was delighted to move from Toledo's austere climate to the new court, where she was not only ensured constant entertainment and picnics in the countryside, but where she was also closer to Philip.

Figure 6.3. Isabel de Valois by Alonso Sánchez Coello, 1560, Kunsthistorisches Museum, Vienna. Reproduced with permission.

Isabel's arrival in Spain marked one of the happier moments at the Philippine court. The young girl and her French ladies-in-waiting not only captivated the king and enlivened the vexed political atmosphere of Juana's regency, their presence brought forth a flourishing of musical, plastic, and literary arts that left an indelible imprint.[44] Juana devoted her artistic talent and her energies to keeping the young queen occupied in a flurry of activities. As Philip prepared to turn the small villa of Madrid into the Spanish capital, Juana, her Spanish retinue, and Isabel and her French ladies-in-waiting enjoyed riding and hunting; Isabel even attempted to teach Juana how to ride French-style, which ended in an embarrassing fall for the princess.[45] Summers were spent at the royal parks of Aranjuez, Valsaín, and El Pardo hunting deer, wild boar, and hares.[46] According to Isabel's biographer, Agustín González de Amezúa y Mayo, she also read often for entertainment (the queen owned at least seven novels of chivalry and purchased the

Amadís de Gaula in French) and occasionally for education (she owned the *Crónica General de España* and Gonzalo Illescas's *Historia Pontificial*).[47] Most court activities, however, centered on music and dance (*pavana*, *alemana*, *el pie de gibao*, *la hacha*), as Juana and Isabel shared an interest in music. Juana's beautiful singing voice and musical talent were well known; Isabel, who kept an organ, two harps, and a cithar in her room, had brought from France six musicians who played the vihuela, a Galician bagpipe player, and a flutist. They were all directed by Miguel de Fuenllana, musician of the Queen's Chamber and author of the *Libro de música para vihuela intitulado Orphenica Lyra*.[48] According to musicologist Higinio Anglés, no other court in the sixteenth century had so complete and distinguished a musical chapel as Charles V's daughters.[49]

Attentive to Isabel's education in the arts and a knowledgeable collector himself, Philip brought the young Italian painter Sofonisba Anguissola to Spain to serve as Isabel's teacher and portraitist. A child prodigy admired by Michelangelo, Anguissola is known for having developed the art of self-portraiture; after Albrecht Dürer, the first artist to represent himself, she painted the greatest number of self-portraits before Rembrandt.[50]

Anguissola's talent was quickly appreciated by Juana, who posed for a portrait shortly after her arrival in Spain (fig. 6.4). The artist's participation in court activities as a lady-in-waiting allowed her to better render Juana's complex personality: the resulting portrait evokes Juana's maternal role at court and commemorates her founding of the Descalzas Reales. The little novice's bouquet of three roses symbolizes the vows of chastity, poverty, and obedience she would later take as a nun, but they may have also referred to the secret vows taken by Juana as a Jesuit. Emphasizing both Juana's nurturing qualities and her piety, the portrait's simplicity and warmth contrasts with the colder, more detached image of Sánchez Coello's portrait.

Besides painting and music, the two young women dedicated much time to court spectacles. The renowned playwright Lope de Rueda was contracted as a theatrical producer at least six times in three years, from 1561 to 1563, receiving 100 reales for each play, and at times 100 extra.[51] Contemporary documents list several artists who were hired to play roles: Alonso de Capilla, Melchor de Herrera, Pedro de Medina, Alonso Rodríguez, Jerónimo Velázquez, Francisco de la Fuente, Gaspar Vásquez, Cristóbal Navarro.[52] In his biography of Isabel de Valois, Agustín González de Amezúa y Mayo includes a contemporary description of a mask organized in 1564. Two groups of seven ladies-in-waiting each were assigned to Juana and Isabel; one group staged an "invention" or charade that the other group then had to identify for prizes. The eleven inventions were elaborate constructions of vines, trees, running fountains, and even

Figure 6.4. Juana de Austria, Sofonisba Anguissola, 1559, Isabella Stewart Gardner Museum, Boston. Reproduced with permission.

a castle, with richly painted backdrops. Both courtiers and ladies took part in the charade, disguising themselves as savages, nymphs, Turks, and Moors. The two houses—Juana's and the queen's—often competed with each other over which of the two put on the best farce or masque.

In the last invention, considered the best, Juana and her ladies, including Anguissola, dressed as nymphs, appearing in a small hut constructed of flowering rosemary and surrounded by cages filled with canaries. One of the ladies, dressed as Diana, goddess of the hunt, and crowned with large pearls and a crystal crescent moon, played the lute near a fountain, while the princess and her other ladies played lutes, clavichords, and harps. Four satyrs guarded the fountain, decorated with lighted candles and ribbons that in turn were tied to the nymphs. These extravagant masques, which employed ornately costumed courtiers who took part in song, music, and dance in a highly artificial landscape, resemble the literary genres of the novels of chivalry and, especially, the pastoral. It is not coincidental that Montemayor's *Diana* included scenes very similar to the masques. Quite likely, these artistic diversions were intended to domesticate through artistic ritual the court's potentially warring factions.

Juana's attention to games and sport helped Isabel adapt to her regal role. Conscious of her dynastic responsibilities, Isabel, who had earlier given birth to her first child, the infanta Isabel Clara Eugenia, a year later gave birth to her second daughter Catalina Micaela. That same year (1566), the Flemish nobility rebelled against the Spanish regent Margaret of Parma; in 1567, Philip sent the Duke of Alba to the Netherlands, whose Tribunal of Blood sentenced over 1,200 rebels to death. In 1568, the Count of Egmont was beheaded. Taxed and persecuted, the Dutch rebels would continue the war until the next century. The year 1568, labeled by the historian Joseph Pérez an "annus horribilis," effectively saw the end of the joyful, luminous court graced by Juana, Isabel, and their ladies-in-waiting. It also witnessed the mental unraveling of the young prince don Carlos, who schemed to lead a militia against the Dutch. Philip could ill afford to have his unstable son take up arms; claiming that he was doing so in the interest of the state, the king, accompanied by the Council of State, burst into his son's room and placed him under house arrest. After alternatively starving and bingeing, don Carlos died in the Alcázar on July 24, 1568.

The prince's death gravely affected the entire court. Isabel lived only two months longer than her stepson did after giving birth to a stillborn daughter. Philip's "black legend" began almost immediately; in pamphlets that circulated throughout Europe, William of Orange accused Philip of having his son murdered and of poisoning Isabel. The queen's household was soon dismantled and her possessions sold at auction, and most of her ladies-in-waiting were sent back to France. Juana was desolate: not only had she lost a surrogate son, she had also lost a beloved sister. In a letter expressing her true emotions on Isabel's death, she wrote to Catherine de' Medici, Isabel's mother: "You are right, your Majesty, as you state with such Christian feeling, that of the immense loss everyone has suffered at the death of our most Serene Queen, my lady and sister who is now in glory, our greatest and truest comfort is to have witnessed her most Christian death; . . . although despite this, I must confess to you that I loved her so dearly, that I cannot begin to find consolation for the enormous loneliness her absence causes me."[53] She tried to find some solace in her role of surrogate mother to Isabel and Philip's two daughters. Profoundly touched by Isabel's death, Philip retreated to a monastery for over two weeks. However, he was without any male heirs, and Catherine de' Medici was already pressing for a union with Isabel's young sister Margot.[54] Considering the difficulty that a Valois had had in producing a son, Philip opted instead to marry his niece, Anna of Austria (fig. 6.5).

Philip's fourth marriage was intended to bring peace to Europe, since it was planned as one of a series of marriages: his daughter, Isabel Clara Eugenia, would be wed to the French King, Charles IX, and his sister Margot to Juana's son, King Sebastian of Portugal. Although the other two marriages failed to take place, Philip and Anna's marriage consolidated Spanish hegemony in Central Europe and Italy at a time when Spain was embattled on two fronts: the continuing Dutch rebellion and the expansion of the Ottoman Empire in the Mediterranean.[55] According to Kamen, Anna was Philip's most significant spouse.[56] She consolidated relations between the Spanish and the Austrian Habsburgs, and what was most important for the Spanish realm, she produced an heir who would ascend to the throne as Philip III.

In 1570, Juana moved permanently to the Descalzas Reales, where she was informed of the death of another close friend, Francisco de Borja. Although in ill health, Juana attended Philip and Anna's wedding. The marriage took place during the last year of the rebellion of the Alpujarras; in the preceding year, Philip had established the Inquisition in Mexico and Peru. Increasingly serious and taciturn, he personally prescribed the etiquette for Anna de Austria's household, stressing an orderly and solemn life. Yet Juana

Figure 6.5. Anna of Austria, Sofonisba Anguissola, 1570, Museo Nacional del Prado, Madrid. Reproduced with permission.

continued in her role of surrogate mother, not only for the young bride, but also for her children. Anna's first son Fernando was born in 1571, the same year as the battle of Lepanto; a second son, Diego, was born in 1573. As she had done regularly in the past with Isabel, she accompanied the queen in her ninth month to El Escorial. Wishing to have the child in Madrid, the queen, accompanied by Juana, made it as far as Galapagar, where she gave birth to don Diego. Both these sons would die in childhood; Juana did not live to see Anna's fourth and final son, who would reign as Philip III.[57]

After giving birth, the queen continued on to Madrid. Juana, feeling ill, returned instead to El Escorial, fittingly perhaps, because that had been her brother's favorite palace and where he entombed his Habsburg ancestors. She died there, still regal at 38 years old, a widow who had been mother to all the royal children but her only son, Sebastian. Even though Juana did not rule as queen regent in Portugal, she accomplished much in Spain through her political influence and in the arts. On her death, her inventory included "masks for different faces, dresses of many colors, with baggy pants, long skirts, capes, capelets, and painted leggings, and their corresponding beards, bags, and gourds, attire typical of rustics and shepherd."[58] The costumes indicate Juana's continued interest in theater, perhaps as a desire to keep intact her memories of a vanished past. Yet Juana of Austria's legacy remains important to Spanish history; although she would not live to see the crisis of the Portuguese succession, her unfailing support of the Portuguese alliance, maintained through her courtiers, Ruy Gómez and Cristóbal de Moura among them, prepared the way for Philip's accession to the Aviz throne.

Notes

1. See Barbara Weissberger, *Isabel Rules: Constructing Queenship, Wielding Power* (Minneapolis: University of Minnesota Press, 2004), and her chapter in this volume.

2. See Magdalena Sánchez, *The Empress, the Queen, and the Nun: Women and Power at the Court of Philip III of Spain* (Baltimore: Johns Hopkins University Press, 1998).

3. Isabel was given the titles of *lugarteniente general y gobernadora del reino*, ensuring her command in the event of the emperor's imprisonment or death. See María del Carmen Mazarío Coleto, *Isabel de Portugal: emperatriz y reina de España* (Madrid: Consejo Superior de Investigaciones Científicas, 1951), 159–60. Charles and Isabel communicated in code and he fully backed her decisions of state. For the history of royal women who assumed the official title of lieutenant in Spain, see Theresa Earenfight, "Absent Kings: Queens as Political Partners in the Medieval Crown of Aragón," in *Queenship and Political Power in Medieval and Early Modern Spain*, ed. Theresa Earenfight (Aldershot, UK: Ashgate, 2005), 33–51.

4. Manuel Lacarta, *Felipe II. Biografía histórica* (Madrid: Silex, 1994), 27.

5. Carlos Gómez-Centurión Jiménez, "El felicísimo viaje del príncipe don Felipe,

1548–1551," in *Felipe II. La Monarquía y su época. La Monarquía Hispánica* (Madrid: Real Monasterio de San Lorenzo de El Escorial: Sociedad Estatal para la Conmemoración de los Centenarios de Felipe II y Carlos V, 1998), 81–95.

6. A sickly youth, Sebastian was raised by his grandmother, Catalina of Portugal. There are numerous references to his early contraction of a sexually transmitted disease and to his possible abuse by his male teachers. See Harold B. Johnson, *Dois Estudos Polemicos* (Tucson, Ariz.: Fenestra Books, 2004); and Harold B. Johnson, "A Pedophile in the Palace: or The Sexual Abuse of King Sebastian of Portugal (1554–1578) and its Consequences," <http://www.people.virginia.edu/~hbj8n/pedophile.pdf>, 18 May 2007. Sebastian's death at the battle of Alcázarquivir in North Africa allowed Philip II to claim the throne of Portugal. See Geoffrey Parker, *The Grand Strategy of Philip II* (New Haven, Conn.: Yale University Press, 1998), 102.

7. I am grateful to Kelli Ringhofer, who is completing a dissertation on Juana de Portugal under the directorship of Carla Rahn Phillips at the University of Minnesota, for the bibliography she has made available to me on Juana de Portugal.

8. Although Juana founded the Convento de Descalzas Reales, she never professed as a nun. The play stresses Juana's zealotry by having her send Bishop Juan de Cazalla, who was accused of Lutheranism, to the Inquisition:

> Bind the beast at my feet
> so he may be taken to the Holy Office
> and may he pay with fire
> his cruel intentions. (III.2339–50; my translation)

9. Geoffrey Parker, *Philip II* (Chicago: Open Court, 1995), 9.

10. María Luisa López Vidriero, "Introducción: Notas sobre Libros y lecturas en el Monasterio de las Descalzas Reales," in *Catálogos de los Reales Patronatos: Manuscritos de impresos del Monasterio de las Descalzas Reales de Madrid* (Madrid: Patrimonio Nacional, 1999), 1: 3.

11. López Vidriero, "Introducción," 4–7.

12. Juana appears as the "great Princess Augusta Cesarina" in Jorge de Montemayor's *Los siete libros de la Diana*, ed. Enrique Moreno Báez (Madrid: Editora Nacional, 1981), 100. Juana has also been taken to be the protagonist Felismena; see Pilar Gómez Bedate, "Felismena y doña Juana, princesa de Portugal: Una hipótesis para los enigmas de la *Diana* de Jorge de Montemayor. *Revista Salina* 16 (Nov. 2002): 79–90.

13. José Martínez Millán, "Familia real y grupos políticos: la princesa doña Juana de Austria," in *La corte de Felipe II*, ed. José Martínez Millán (Madrid: Alianza Editorial, 1998), 78.

14. Martínez Millán, "Familia real y grupos políticos," 92–97.

15. Carmen Sanz Ayán, "La regencia de doña Juana de Austria. Su dimensión humana, intelectual y política," in *Felipe II. La Monarquía y su época: La Monarquía Hispánica* (Madrid: Real Monasterio de San Lorenzo de El Escorial: Sociedad Estatal para la Conmemoración de los Centenarios de Felipe II y Carlos V, 1998), 139.

16. Luis Fernández de Retana, *Doña Juana de Austria* (Madrid: El Perpetuo Socorro, 1955), 128.

17. Sanz Ayán, "La regencia de doña Juana de Austria," 139.

18. Parker, *Grand Strategy*, 151.

19. Following several historians, Boyden notes that care must be taken not to divide the factions into an "open vs. closed" dichotomy between family blocs or large philosophical issues, as there were strong personal reasons fueling the division. See James M. Boyden, *The Courtier and the King: Ruy Gómez de Silva, Felipe II, and The Court of Spain* (Berkeley: University of California Press, 1995), 94–95.

20. The conflicts at court were not due solely to religious differences, since members of the same orders fought for political power at court and within the church. The power struggle between two members of the Dominican Order, Inquisitor General Fernando de Valdés and the Archbishop of Toledo Bartolomé Carranza, who accompanied Philip II to England and authored the controversial *Comentarios sobre el Catechismo Cristiano* (Commentaries on the Christian Catechism), resulted in Carranza's long inquisitorial process and imprisonment. For the process and Juana de Portugal's role in it, see J. I. Tellechea Idígoras, "El proceso del arzobispo Carranza," in *Historia de la Inquisición en España y América*, ed. Joaquín Pérez Villanueva and Bartolomé Escandell Bonet (Madrid: Biblioteca de Autores Cristianos, Centro de Estudios Inquisitoriales, 1984), 556–99.

21. For Juana's participation in the order, see Ricardo García-Villoslada, S.J., *San Ignacio de Loyola: Nueva biografía* (Madrid: Biblioteca de Autores Cristianos, 1986).

22. John Padberg. "A Woman Jesuit: Secret, Perilous Project." <www.companysj.com/v171secret.html>, 18 May 2007.

23. See Joseph Pérez, *La España de Felipe II*, trans. Juan Vivanco (Barcelona: Crítica, 2000), 60 ff.

24. Pérez, *La España de Felipe II*, 66.

25. In May 1559, Charles wrote to Juana: "Believe me, daughter, this business has caused and still causes me more anxiety and pain than I can express, for while the king and I were abroad these realms remained in perfect peace, free from this calamity. But now that I have returned here to rest and recuperate and serve Our Lord, this great outrage and treachery, implicating such notable persons, occurs in my presence and in yours. You know that because of this I suffered and went through great trials and expenses in Germany e, and lost so much of my good health. Were it not for the conviction I have that you and members of your councils will find a radical cure to this unfortunate situation, punishing the guily thoroughly to prevent them from spreading, I do not know whether I could restrain myself leaving here to settle the matter" (quoted in and translated by Henry Kamen, *The Spanish Inquisition: A Historical Revision* [New Haven, Conn.: Yale University Press, 1998], 94).

26. José Martínez Millán, "Familia real y grupos políticos: la princesa doña Juana de Austria," in *La corte de Felipe II*, ed. José Martínez Millán (Madrid: Alianza Editorial, 1998), 94–95.

27. Henry Kamen, "La política religiosa de Felipe II," *Anuario de la Historia de la Iglesia* 7 (1998): 22.

28. Parker, *Philip II*, 81–82.

29. Fernández de Retana, *Doña Juana*, 191–92.

30. Sánchez Coello brought Juana a portrait he painted of Sebastián at one year of age. See Stephanie Breuer-Hermann, "Alonso Sánchez Coello, vida y obra," in *Alonso Sánchez Coello y el retrato en la corte de Felipe II*, ed. Alfonso E. Pérez Sánchez (Madrid: Museo del Prado, 1990), 19.

31. Maria Kusche, "El retrato cortesano en el reinado de Felipe II y el arte de su tiempo," in *Felipe II y el arte de su tiempo* (Madrid: Fundación Argentaria, 1998), 356.

32. Kusche, "El retrato cortesano," 348.

33. Lorne Campbell, *Renaissance Portraits: European Portrait-Painting in the 14th, 15th, and 16th Centuries* (New Haven, Conn.: Yale University Press, 1990), 197.

34. Kusche, "El retrato cortesano," 360.

35. Campbell, *Renaissance Portraits*, 197.

36. Sebastián suffered from urinary tract infections that may have left him impotent. See Paulo Drumond Braga, "D. Joana de Áustria (1535–1573): Uma releitura da sua intervencao na vida portuguesa," *Arquivos do Centro Cultural Calouste Gulbenkian* 34 (1996): 237.

37. The Castilian ambassador to Portugal, Luis Sarmiento, wrote to Philip in 1553 that "all adore [Juana] and with good reason" [todos la adoran y con mucha razón] (Drumond Braga, "D. Joana de Áustria," 238).

38. In the end, it was don Carlos who rejected the marriage, stating that he thought of Juana as his mother (Martínez Millán, "Familia real y grupos políticos," 100).

39. Philip's marriage to Mary Tudor, eleven years his senior, was considered a marriage of state only, with the express purpose of producing an heir. His marriage to Isabel de Valois proved to be a happy union, although it lasted less than a decade. His last marriage to Anna of Austria was forced by the need for male succession, because don Carlos had died and Isabel bore only daughters. See Bianca María Lindorfer, "Ana de Austria, La novia de un hijo y la esposa de un padre," in *La Reina Isabel y las reinas de España: realidad, modelos e imagen historiográfica*, ed. María Victoria López-Cordón and Gloria Franco (Madrid: Fundación Española de Historia Moderna, 2005), 411–25.

40. Philip would maintain relations with Guzmán until at least 1564, when he bestowed the pregnant lady-in-waiting in marriage to the courtier Antonio de Leyva, Prince of Áscoli. See Henry Kamen, "El secreto de Felipe II: Las mujeres que influyeron en su vida," *Torre de los Lujanes: Boletín de la Real Sociedad Económica Matritense de Amigos del País* 32 (1996): 60. See also Henry Kamen, *Felipe de España* (Madrid: Siglo XXI, 1997), 214. Philip's bastard son, Antonio de Leyva, perished off Ireland serving in the "Invincible Armada."

41. Agustín González de Amezúa y Mayo, *Isabel de Valois Reina de España* (Madrid: Dirección General de Relaciones Culturales, Ministerio de Asuntos Exteriores, 1949), 1: 167.

42. To a maid of Isabel of Peace, Damsel and slightly melancholic
You're melancholic, whore-damsel
cover of peace, good taste, and behavior
. . . and since your Lady extends her blankets,
extend yours as well, Mary-armpit
that your skirts also serve the same purpose.

[A una criada de Isabel de la Paz, Doncella y un poco melancólica
Melancólica estais, puti-donzella
cobertor de la paz, buen gusto y trato . . . Y pues tu ama tiende sus fracadas,
tiéndelas tú también, mari-sobaco,
Que no son para menos tus faldillas].

González de Amezúa y Mayo, *Isabel de Valois*, 166 n. 54.

43. "El más fastidioso lugar del mundo si no fuera por mi esposo" (Fernández de Retana, *Doña Juana*, 181).

44. Despite her apparent frivolity, Isabel developed into an astute political mediator between her mother, Catherine de' Medici, and Philip, who challenged his mother-in-law's concessions to the Protestants. See Margarita García Barranco, "Isabel de Valois (1546–1568): Reinterpretación del papel de una reina consorte en la monarquía española," in *La Reina Isabel y las reinas de España*, 397–410.

45. González de Amezúa y Mayo, *Isabel de Valois*, 184ff.

46. Ibid., 281.

47. Ibid., 247–48.

48. Ibid., 244.

49. Higinio Anglés, *La música en la corte de Carlos V* (Madrid: Consejo Superior de Investigaciones Científicas, 1944), 75.

50. For biographies of Anguissola, see Fiammetta Basile, *Le rughe di Sofonisba* (Palermo: Edizioni della Battaglia, 2004); Sylvia Pagden and Maria Kusche, *Sofonisba Anguissola: A Renaissance Woman* (Washington, D.C.: National Museum of Women in the Arts, 1995); Ilya Sandra Perlingieri, *Sofonisba Anguissola: The First Great Woman Artist of the Renaissance* (New York: Rizzoli, 1992); Orietta Pinessi, *Sofonisba Anguissola: Un 'pittore' alla corte di Filipo II* (Milan: Selene, 1998); and Daniela Pizzagalli, *La signora della pittura: vita di Sofonisba Anguissola, gentildonna e artista nel Rinascimento* (Milan: Rizzoli, 2003).

51. AGS Simancas: Casa Real. Obras y Bosques, leg. 52; cited in González de Amezúa y Mayo, 231.

52. Cristóbal Navarro, who was known for his role as a cowardly scoundrel, was likely the actor whom Cervantes eulogizes in his prologue to his *Ocho comedias y ocho entremeses nuevos* (1615). According to Cervantes, he improved the theater by changing the sacks of clothing to trunks, ridding the actors of false beards, and inventing stage machinery, clouds, thunder and lightning, and staging battles (Miguel de Cervantes, *El rufián dichoso: Pedro de Urdemalas*, ed. Jenaro Talens and Nicholas Spadaccini [Madrid: Cátedra, 1986], 102).

53. "Señora: . . . Y es assí cierto, como V. Md. muy christianamente lo dize, que de tan gran pérdida como fue para todos la muerte de la Serenísima Reyna, mi señora y hermana que está en gloria, el mayor y más verdadero consuelo que nos ha quedado es hauer visto que hizo un fin tan christiano . . . Aunque con todo esto, no puedo dexar de confesar a V. Md. que yo la amaua tan tiernamente, que no me puedo acauar de conortar de la gran soledad que me haze su ausencia" (cited in Martínez Millán, "Familia real y grupos políticos," 104).

54. Parker, *Philip II*, 106.

55. Henry Kamen, "Anna de Austria," in *Felipe II. La Monarquía y su época: La Monarquía Hispánica* (Madrid: Real Monasterio de San Lorenzo de El Escorial: Sociedad Estatal para la Conmemoración de los Centenarios de Felipe II y Carlos V, 1998), 267.

56. Kamen, "Anna," 271.

57. Of Anna's five children—two sons and three daughters—only the heir, Philip III, lived to adulthood. Lindorfer, "Ana de Austria," 424.

58. González de Amezúa y Mayo, *Isabel de Valois,* 233 n. 27.

7. Elizabeth I as Sister and "Loving Kinswoman"

CAROLE LEVIN

Elizabeth Tudor had one older half-sister and one younger half-brother by the first and third of her father Henry VIII's wives. During her father's reign, the young Elizabeth spent a fair amount of time with one or the other of her siblings either at court or one of the other residences where she lived. Though her relationship with her brother Edward was easier, Mary, seventeen years older than her younger sister, could be kind to the child who had lost her mother in such a horrific manner—even though she loathed Elizabeth's mother Anne Boleyn. This essay interrogates the relationships Elizabeth had with both Mary and Edward. These were not, however, the only siblings Elizabeth had. She not only referred to fellow sovereigns as her sisters and brothers, but Henry VIII fathered, or at least was rumored to have fathered, other children. In this essay, I examine Elizabeth's sibling relationships in these other contexts as well. I also discuss the legends and rumors about Henry VIII's illegitimate children, and why certain individuals were thought to have been Elizabeth's siblings even if that assertion is questionable. Though as Queen Elizabeth often used the rhetoric of family, she found her relationships with her siblings to be problematic and dangerous. Given the competing claims for power as well as different religious practices, it was often difficult for royal children to have close bonds.

Henry had each of his daughters declared illegitimate when he ended the marriages with their mothers, but in 1543 in his will, ratified by Parliament, he placed them back in the succession after his son Edward if he died without children of his own. Mary, as the elder, was the more immediate heir. Elizabeth's life in her father's reign was difficult but improved considerably with the coming of her final stepmother, Katherine Parr, who was kind to all three of the children. In the final year of his reign, 1546, no doubt at Katherine's instigation, Henry invited Elizabeth to court. Mary and Elizabeth were listed as the queen's ladies-in-waiting.[1]

Edward and Elizabeth were brought together in January 1547 to be told the news that their father had died; Edward's advisors thought the boy would deal with the news better if he were with his sister. This seems to have been the case; Elizabeth met the news with fortitude, and Edward congratulated her on her stalwartness: "There is very little need of my consoling you, most dear sister, because from your learning you know what you ought to do, and from your prudence and piety you perform what your learning causes you to know . . . I perceive you think of our father's death with a calm mind."[2]

Yet once Edward was boy-king at the age of nine, he spent little time in the company of his sister Elizabeth, and she in turn lived in different households from her older sister Mary. Elizabeth did attempt to stay in touch with Edward through letters, and several times she visited him at court. Though Elizabeth was writing to a younger brother, she was also well aware that she was addressing her sovereign. In a letter written to Edward only a month into his reign, she told him that her "feelings, indeed, proceeding not so much from the mouth as from the heart, will declare a certain due respect and faith towards your majesty." A year later, after a visit with Edward she wrote, "Of your love towards me no more numerous or illustrious proofs can be given, king most serene and illustrious, than when I recently enjoyed to the full the fruit of a most delightful familiarity with you. . . . I perceive your brotherly love most greatly inclined towards me, by which I conceive no small joy and gladness."[3]

Though she may well have felt fondness for her brother, and possibly her sister, for that matter, at this point in her life, from her early teens, Elizabeth must have been all too well aware that for her to ever ascend the throne, her siblings had to die. Those around Edward and later Mary were equally aware of what a threat to these reigns the young princess was. In early 1549, at only fifteen, Elizabeth was at great risk because Thomas Seymour, among other plots to gain power as Edward's younger maternal uncle, attempted to marry her. Though she had no one to advise her, Elizabeth learned very early to keep her own counsel and to hold back her trust. She also early used her position as the king's sister to advantage. After Seymour and both her servants were lodged in the Tower, the council sent Sir Robert Tyrwhitt to examine Elizabeth.

Perhaps as a way to humiliate Elizabeth and to force a confession, Tyrwhitt told Elizabeth that there were rumors circulating that she was with child. But this did not break Elizabeth's will. She responded with a forceful letter to the lord protector, asking to come to the court so that she could demonstrate that she was not pregnant. Furthermore, aware of the importance of being well thought of by the English people, Elizabeth requested that Somerset publicly deny this slander and do so because she was the king's sister: "But if it might so seem good unto our lordship and the rest of the Council to send forth a proclamation into the countries [counties] that they refrain their tongues, declaring how the tales be but lies, it should make/both the people think that you and the Council have great regard that no such rumors should be spread of any of the king's majesty's sisters (as I am, though unworthy)."[4] Elizabeth managed to survive this crisis and protect both Ashley and Parry. As for Seymour, she certainly did not publicly mourn his death. She did, however, carefully remember his fate, that he had been executed at the command of his own elder brother.

In May 1549, a few months after the crisis was over and life was more tranquil for Elizabeth, she sent her brother the present of her portrait that he had requested from her. She also hinted to him in the accompanying letter that she wished she could come to court and see him more often: "I shall most humbly beseech your majesty that when you shall look on my picture you will witsafe to think that as you have but the outward shadow of the body afore you, so my inward mind wisheth that the body itself were oftener in your presence."[5]

For the rest of Edward's reign, Elizabeth presented herself as a demure young Protestant woman who kept the council and her brother fully abreast of her doings. This self-presentation was successful. At the end of that year of crisis, Elizabeth was invited to spend Christmas at court with her brother. The Spanish ambassador noted that Elizabeth "was received with great pomp and triumph, and is continually with the King."[6] Elizabeth visited court a second time in early 1551. As Edward's health became more fragile, Elizabeth sent her brother letters demonstrating her great concern. In April 1552, she wrote: "What cause I had of sorry when I heard first of your majesty's sickness all men might guess but none but myself could feel." In the spring of 1553, she wrote to Edward that the news of his ill-health "grieved me greatly. . . . I shall pray God forever to preserve you."[7]

However, Edward's health only worsened in the spring and summer of 1553. Edward, at the behest of the Duke of Northumberland, or at least with his assistance, made a new will that excluded his sisters in favor of his cousin Lady Jane Grey, fortuitously married to the duke's youngest son Guilford. Edward was deeply concerned about the continuation of Protestantism, and Northumberland about the continuation of his power.

Edward's "Devise for the Succession" was illegal. Edward was not of age, and though his father's will had been ratified by Parliament during Henry's lifetime, Edward's was not.

Despite his supposed closeness particularly to Elizabeth, the argument that she, like Mary, might wed a foreigner, seemed to be a justification for Edward to exclude her in favor of the safely married Jane. In the devise both Mary and Elizabeth are declared "illegitimate and not lawfully begotten." Edward added the hope that after his death his sisters would "live in quiet order, according to our appointment," a vain hope indeed.[8] Edward failed rapidly. For this plan to work, Northumberland knew that he had to have both princesses under his control before he announced Edward's death and Jane's accession. Events were moving too fast for the duke, and with the king's death kept secret, Northumberland sent both Edward's sisters the message that his last wish was to see them.

Whatever the news that Edward was dying might have meant personally to either sister, it also meant that according to the succession as dictated by Henry VIII, Mary was the next queen. She immediately took to the road with a small entourage to London but was stopped on the way with the message that she was riding into a trap—some members of the King's Council, though they might publicly support Northumberland thinking they had little choice, in fact did not want to upset the succession or see him continue in power. While Mary had immediately flown to action, Elizabeth, concerned with what might be going on and sensing a trap, sent word that she herself was too ill to travel—a ploy she would use again in her dealings with a sibling.[9]

Mary became queen without a battle; on July 19, the Duke of Northumberland was arrested, and Mary proclaimed ruler of the realm. Jane's brief rule was over. Ten days later, Elizabeth came to London to await Mary's triumphant entry, and on July 31 rode out of London to meet Mary and escort her into the city. Elizabeth may well have been concerned over how her sister would respond to her—their sisterhood depended on their father and their mothers had been bitter rivals. In the first euphoria of becoming queen, Mary greeted her younger sister with great affection and on August 3 when Mary rode in state, Elizabeth was immediately behind her sister, the queen. This warm state of affairs cooled rapidly, however, and Mary went so far as to deny her relationship to Elizabeth altogether, claiming to those close to her that Elizabeth instead resembled the musician Mark Smeaton, "a very handsome man," but also the one of lowest status of the five executed as Anne Boleyn's lovers.[10] Few people accepted Mary's claim. Redheaded Elizabeth was proud that people saw her very much as a Tudor.

Though Edward VI and Elizabeth had shared similar religious beliefs, which one would have thought would make her an acceptable heir, at the end of his reign, the dying Edward had apparently acquiesced or even initiated a change in the succession that would have denied Elizabeth her rights and placed her in extreme danger. With her sister Mary, Elizabeth had to also contend with personal bitterness over their mothers' rivalry and their very different religious beliefs. For Mary, her religious faith was the guiding force of her life.

As Mary returned England to obedience to Rome, she must have been all too aware of how her younger sister was the Protestant alternative. At first, Elizabeth boycotted the Catholic services at court, but by September 1553, it was clear her position was too dangerous to continue that. Elizabeth begged Mary for instruction in the "true faith," but though Elizabeth claimed conversion, Mary must have been suspicious, especially because on September 8, the first day Elizabeth was to attend Mass, the princess asked to be excused because of a stomachache. When the queen insisted on her presence, Elizabeth, according to the Spanish ambassador, "complained loudly on the way, keeping up a pretence of illness."[11]

Elizabeth must have become even more concerned the following month when Parliament passed an act that upheld the legality of Henry's marriage to Catherine of Aragon. Many might well argue that because Elizabeth was legally a bastard, she had no right to succeed the throne. Elizabeth, upset with the political and religious mood at court, became even more sporadic in her attendance at mass. Though at the beginning of the reign Elizabeth had had precedence over all ladies at court save the queen, by November, French Ambassador Antoine de Noailles was noting that Mary was ceding that position to their cousin Margaret, Countess of Lennox, and sometimes even to "Madame Frances, who is the Duchess of Suffolk," and also mother of the condemned Lady Jane Grey.[12] This clearly put even more strain on the sisters' relationship. Mary was furious when she heard that Elizabeth was meeting secretly with the French ambassador; Elizabeth managed to convince Mary's representatives that these meetings had never happened, but it was becoming more and more evident that Mary was eager to believe the worst of her younger sister. The Venetian ambassador wrote home of Mary's "scorn and ill will" toward Elizabeth.[13]

Elizabeth requested permission to leave court for her residence at Ashridge but begged to see Mary before she left. Elizabeth assured her sister of her devotion to the Catholic doctrine, but Mary was not convinced. Though Mary gave Elizabeth a gift of a coif of rich sables, it was not out of sisterly affection; Renard, the Spanish ambassador, had suggested it would be unwise for Elizabeth to leave court feeling disaffected. What Elizabeth wanted much more from her sister than an expensive gift was the promise that she would allow Elizabeth to defend herself to her personally if Mary heard anything to her discredit, begging Mary, de Noailles heard, "not to put faith in stories to the disadvantage of the Princess without giving her a hearing."[14] Mary, however, by this time felt great hostility toward her sister; she was convinced that Elizabeth would "bring about some great evil unless she is dealt with."[15]

The evil Mary feared turned out to be the rebellion led by Thomas Wyatt against her marriage to Philip of Spain in early 1554. Though the rebellion was defeated on January 29, Mary demanded that Elizabeth return to court and respond to charges that she had known and approved of the plot. Elizabeth responded that she was too ill to travel. Mary did not believe her sister; she sent three members of her council, Lord William Howard, Sir Edward Hastings, and Sir Thomas Cornwallis, who were accompanied by two doctors, Thomas Wendy and George Owen. The doctors admitted that though Elizabeth was unwell, travel would not be life threatening. Elizabeth was not so sure. This decision was made on February 12, the same day her cousin Jane Grey was executed. Elizabeth may well have believed that traveling to the capital could be fatal. While Elizabeth did seem to truly be in ill health, she also appears to have exploited her physical condition so that she could prolong the travel time. The entourage moved slowly, taking five days to travel the thirty-three miles to London.

Mary's confidante, Simon Renard, wanted Elizabeth sent directly to the Tower, as did Mary's chancellor, Stephen Gardiner, Bishop of Winchester. Several members of Mary's council, however, were uncomfortable with the idea of imprisoning the *sister* of the queen. Elizabeth was held for nearly a month in her rooms in Whitehall while Mary and her council argued about her fate. Because no one was willing to guard Elizabeth under house arrest, Mary decided she would indeed send her to the Tower. Henry Radcliffe, Earl of Sussex, and another member of the council were sent to take Elizabeth to the Tower by barge, as Mary and her council feared there might be attempts to rescue her if she were taken through the streets of London. When Elizabeth was told she was being sent to the Tower, she begged for an audience with Mary before the order was carried out. The order to the Tower without a chance to see Mary was what Elizabeth had most feared and was exactly what she had begged from her sister at their last meeting. Sussex knew the queen would not see Elizabeth, but when this request was denied Elizabeth pleaded that she might at least write to Mary before she was moved. Sussex yielded; Elizabeth was, after all, like Mary, the daughter of Henry VIII.

In her letter Elizabeth beseeched Mary to see her before imprisoning her in the Tower. At this moment of crisis, Elizabeth not only recognized the need to be able to see and talk with her sister, she understood the importance of carefully crafting her request. Elizabeth urged Mary to grant her an interview so that she can respond to the charges against her:

> And to this present hour I protest afore God . . . that I never practiced, counseled, nor consented to anything that might be prejudicial to your person any way or dangerous to the state by any mean. And therefore I humbly beseech your majesty to let me answer afore yourself and not suffer me to trust your councillors—yea, and that afore I go to the Tower (if it be possible); if not, afore I be further condemned.[16]

It is perhaps not surprising that at this time of crisis, Elizabeth would recall a previous threat to her personal and political safety, the Seymour incident. As she begs Mary to see her, Elizabeth refers to Seymour's death at the order of his brother, Somerset:

> I have heard in my time of many cast away for want of coming to the presence of their prince, and in late days I heard my lord of Somerset say that if his brother had been suffered to speak with him, he had never suffered. . . . Therefore once again, with humbleness of my heart because I am not suffered to bow the knees of my body, I humbly crave to speak with your Highness.[17]

Elizabeth hoped that if she could actually see and talk with her sister, she could convince Mary of her innocence, despite their differences. But Mary was furious that Sussex allowed Elizabeth to write to her, and she refused her fervent plea for a meeting; perhaps Mary did not trust herself to remain firm if she and her sister Elizabeth actually talked. Simon Renard was convinced that Elizabeth wrote the letter for the express purpose of delaying her imprisonment, but it seems likely that Elizabeth truly believed that were she able to see and speak with her sister, she might avert this catastrophe. The letter only gained Elizabeth a one-day reprieve; the next day she was taken to the Tower. In the next months, Elizabeth became so convinced that her sister would have her executed she considered begging Mary for a French swordsman, so she could die in the same manner as her mother.

Although Elizabeth feared Mary greatly, the queen in the end did not have her younger half-sister killed. When Mary was dying in November 1558, she sent word to Elizabeth begging her sister to continue the Roman Catholic faith. But Elizabeth's father had broken with the pope to marry her mother, and when Elizabeth became queen she reestablished the Church of England.

The new Protestant queen had lost both her brother and sister. While she was queen, however, she used the rhetoric of family often in her letters to other monarchs, on occasion calling herself sister to both her cousin Mary

Stuart and Mary's son James. For example, Elizabeth a number of times called herself the "dear" or "good" "sister" to Mary Stuart, and later addressed Mary's son James as her "good brother and cousin the king of Scots." Elizabeth's erstwhile suitor Henry III of France was also referred to and addressed as "our good brother." To add to the confusing family relations, Elizabeth also addressed Henry's mother, Catherine de' Medici, as her "very affectionate sister and cousin." As Lena Orlin points out, Elizabeth "turned to political purpose her membership in the figurative family of European sovereigns"[18] Indeed, the special relationship of monarchs was such she even called herself "sister" when she signed a letter to the king of Morocco.[19]

The official siblings of Elizabeth I were her two predecessors, Edward and Mary, who had both ruled before her, but Henry VIII had other children about whose illegitimacy there was no question. Elizabeth's relations with these siblings were much less clear, but they also played some role in her development as queen as well as sister. Henry VIII's acknowledged illegitimate son, Henry Fitzroy, was close to his father and had been discussed as a possible heir in the last years of Henry's marriage to Catherine of Aragon, particularly once Henry had given him the title of Duke of Richmond and Somerset; in the end, his clear illegitimacy presented too large a problem. The boy did come to pay his respects to his new half-sister, and then heir to the throne, soon after her birth. It must have been, however, a great disappointment to the young man that yet another sister was heir rather than himself. In the spring of 1536, Richmond was probably not grief-stricken at the charges against his father's second wife. At the very least, Anne took Henry's time and attention away from his son. To further the split between Henry and Anne, rumors circulated that May that Anne had intended to have Richmond murdered. There is no evidence to support this charge, which was apparently manufactured by the Seymours to protect their interests.[20] Henry, however, seems to have believed it. The Imperial Ambassador Eustaches Chapuys claimed that when Richmond came to say good night to his father on the evening of Anne's arrest, Henry was moved to tears at the sight of his son, and told him that "he and his sister, meaning the Princess, were greatly bound to God for having escaped the hands of that accursed whore" who had been determined to poison them both.[21] Anne Boleyn's fall potentially could have made an enormous difference to Richmond's possibilities. On May 17, 1536, Thomas Cranmer, Archbishop of Canterbury, who had declared Henry's marriage to Catherine null and void and married Henry to Anne three years earlier, now declared this marriage also unlawful, making Elizabeth illegitimate. With all three of his recognized children now legally bastards, Henry Fitzroy, as the male, would have precedence if the next marriage of Henry's, to Jane Seymour, had no offspring. Jane Seymour, however, was to give birth to the indubitably legitimate son Edward in 1537, and anyway Fitzroy had died the year before, two months after witnessing the execution of Elizabeth's mother, Anne Boleyn. Richmond's biographer Beverley Murphy remarks that Richmond had "elegant handwriting, not unlike that used by his half-sister Elizabeth." In the seventeenth century, Thomas Fuller argued that it was very much in Elizabeth's, as well as in Mary's, interest that Fitzroy had died when he did: "Well it was for them that Henry Fitzroy, his natural son (but one of supernatural and extraordinary endowments,) was dead; otherwise (some suspect) had he survived King Edward the Sixth, we might presently have heard of a King Henry the Ninth, so great was his father's affection."[22]

We will never know what made Fuller consider Fitzroy to be "unnaturally or extraordinarily great,"[23] a meaning of supernatural in the early modern period. Because Fitzroy had died before Edward was even born, however, there seems to have been little connection between Elizabeth and Fitzroy, except for the wild theory that Elizabeth died in 1542 and Katherine Ashley and Thomas Parry, in fear of Henry VIII's reaction, substituted the illegitimate son of Henry Fitzroy for Elizabeth. According to this belief, the dead Elizabeth's nephew thus was able to carry this deception off without a hitch for the next sixty years.[24]

Henry Fitzroy died young and had no children of his own. Henry VIII, however, may have had other children, including another son. Some people have argued that Mary Boleyn, wife of William Carey and briefly Henry's mistress before he fell in love with her sister Anne, had a son and/or possibly a daughter by the king. It is impossible to know with complete certainty who was the father of Mary's children, Henry and Catherine, her husband or the king. It depends in part on how old Mary was at the time of her marriage; whether it was arranged so that Henry could have Mary without concern about another illegitimate son or whether she became Henry's mistress some years after she wed Carey; and how long she was actually the king's lover. A further difficulty is the debate over the date of the birth of her daughter Catherine.

We do not know exactly how old Mary Boleyn was at the time of her marriage to William Carey in 1520. Jonathan Hughes follows Eric Ives in dating Mary Boleyn's birth as occurring in 1499. Kathy Lynn Emerson, however, puts Mary's birth date in 1504. Although most scholars believe that Mary was the older daughter, Retha Warnicke believes that she was a year younger than Anne, and that both were considerably younger than other scholars such as Ives argue. Warnicke suggests alternatively that Mary was born in 1508, was only twelve when her marriage was arranged with William Carey, and that the marriage was not consummated for several years.[25] Just as we do not know Mary's age, nor do we know exactly when or how long the relationship with Henry lasted. Because Henry was the principal guest at the Boleyn-Carey wedding, some would argue that the marriage was a cover for the Boleyn affair with the king. Most scholars, however, assert that the affair did not begin until 1522 or 1523, the year Henry named a ship *Mary Boleyn*. Warnicke argues that the brief affair did not begin until after the birth of Catherine, which she believes happened in 1524, an often accepted date, though it has been given as early as 1522 and alternatively as after the birth of Henry, which we know occurred March 4, 1526. Catherine became maid of honor to Anne of Cleves in November 1539, and maids of honor to adult queens were usually, though not always, at least sixteen.

Eric Ives argues that after having a very public illegitimate son with Elizabeth Blount, "perhaps Henry realized that it was much safer to risk begetting children whose paternity could be denied than bastards who only emphasized his lack of legitimate heirs." Another reason that Ives argues that Henry VIII was not the father of either of the Carey children was that the king was "a man of such known low fertility" and adds that "once she had begun to cohabit with William Carey her two children came in quick succession." He believes that the older of the two was Henry and that Mary became pregnant with him early in June 1525.[26]

Anthony Hoskins argues that not only Henry but also his sister Catherine Carey were the children of Mary Boleyn Carey by Henry VIII. The evidence Hoskins presents is quite problematic, however, and is for the most part based on the fact that there was a rumor that Henry Carey was the son of Henry VIII floating around in the 1530s. The rumor was spread, however, by supporters of Catherine of Aragon, and much of what they said about Anne Boleyn and those close to her was completely inaccurate. In 1535, John Hale, Vicar of Isleworth, in his confession to the council asked for forgiveness for his slander of Henry VIII and Queen Anne, and added that two years before "Mr. Skydmore dyd show to me young Master Carey, saying that he was our [sovereign] Lord the King's son by our sovereign Lady the Queen's sister, whom the Queen's grace might not suffer to be in the Court." The Catholics would certainly have encouraged any negative comments about Henry and the Boleyns, and this statement, though interesting, does not prove that Henry Carey was Henry's son. Hale was certainly wrong that Anne refused to allow her sister Mary Boleyn to come to court. Also, Henry Carey became Anne's ward after the death of his father, and she made sure that he received a fine education. As Paul Friedmann, a nineteenth-century biographer of Anne Boleyn, pointed out when he presented Hale's evidence, "I hasten to say that I know of no other evidence in support of this . . . assertion."[27] William Carey acknowledged the boy as his, and the king never suggested otherwise, nor did Henry Carey.

Katherine was appointed a maid of honor to Anne of Cleves in November 1539, but only six months later, she married Sir Francis Knollys, and the next year gave birth to Lettice, the first of sixteen children. Katherine apparently became close to Elizabeth during the reign of Edward. She and her husband were at court with Sir Francis in the position of master of the horse for the young king, and apparently Katherine spent time with Elizabeth during the times she visited her brother's court. Katherine and her husband were committed Protestants, and in 1556, during the reign of Mary, the Careys fled abroad with five of their children. Katherine's departure deeply grieved Elizabeth, who signed her farewell letter to Katherine, *cor rotto* (broken heart).[28] When Elizabeth became queen the Careys returned; Katherine was named one of the four waged ladies of the bedchamber for her friend and cousin, a position she had until her death, despite her many children.

Queen Elizabeth hated to have those she cared about not at her beck and call, and Sir Francis Knollys was distressed that he was separated from his wife, especially after May 1568, when he was placed in charge of Mary Stuart, first at Carlisle Castle, then at Bolton Castle. He repeatedly asked both the queen and Sir William Cecil to allow him to return to court. He was especially upset that the queen refused to allow him to come Christmas 1568, as Katherine had been ill with a fever. Cecil wrote to Knollys to assure him that Katherine was better; Sir Francis, however, was so distressed that at the end of December he wrote to Katherine suggesting that they retire to live simply in the country. Tragically Katherine's recovery was only temporary; she became seriously ill again. The queen visited her often, but Katherine died January 15, 1569. Elizabeth was devastated, so grief-stricken that there was concern for her own health; she devised an elaborate and expensive (640 £, 2 s. 11 d.) funeral ceremony for Katherine, who was interred in Westminster Abbey. Warnicke comments that "until her death in early 1569, Catherine was one of her *cousin* Elizabeth's closest friends" (emphasis mine).[29]

Henry Carey was a gentleman in Elizabeth's household when she was princess. Once she became queen, she quickly knighted him and gave him the title of Baron Hunsdon. She also provided him with a substantial grant of lands. When Henry died almost forty years later in 1596, he too received an extremely lavish funeral. Elizabeth clearly loved Katherine Carey, and cared very much for Henry as well, but she never recognized either of the Careys as her half-siblings. Jonathan Hughes states that some scholars believe that "the deep affection" that the queen showed to both the Careys was "more appropriate for half-siblings than for cousins. But the fact that Katherine . . . and Henry were the only blood relatives Elizabeth had after her accession is probably sufficient explanation. . . . There is no need to postulate that they were the children of Henry VIII."[30] In a letter to Henry Carey, Elizabeth signed herself "Your loving kinswoman."[31]

Elizabeth's fondness for Henry and especially Katherine Carey might actually argue more for her belief that the Careys were her maternal cousins rather than her half-siblings. Elizabeth treated some people with mercy or generosity; her treatment of her royal cousins, Katherine and Mary Grey, however, suggests that she felt deeply threatened by close relatives on her father's side.

Katherine's secret marriage without the queen's permission to Edward Seymour, Earl of Hertford, in December 1560, did present a real risk to Elizabeth, as many at court perceived Katherine as a close heir to the throne. The marriage was discovered when Katherine became pregnant, and both Katherine and Hertford were placed in the Tower, where Katherine gave birth to a son in September 1561. Elizabeth did not want the marriage recognized because that would discredit Katherine and her child as potential heirs; the queen was pleased that Katherine and Edward Seymour could not prove they had legally wed. Neither Katherine nor Edward knew the name of the minister, and Katherine had mislaid their certificate. The one witness, Edward's sister, who had arranged the secret wedding, was dead. Though the couple was kept separately in the Tower, sympathetic jailors allowed them to meet, and Katherine was soon pregnant again. After the birth of their second son, Katherine and the younger boy were placed in the charge of her uncle, Lord John Grey, and Hertford and the older boy were lodged with the Duchess of Somerset. Katherine and Hertford were never allowed to see each other again, and Katherine died in 1568; romantics considered that she died of a broken heart, and in the seventeenth century, Thomas Fuller referred to her as the "Lady of Lamentation."[32]

While Elizabeth's harshness to Katherine Grey is politically understandable, her like treatment of the youngest Grey, Mary, is far harder to justify. Mary at full height was only a little over four feet tall, and her physical condition was such she was called "Crouchback Mary" when she lived at court. The Spanish ambassador described her as "little, crook-backed, and very ugly."[33] In 1565, she secretly married a gentleman porter, Thomas Keyes, a widower with several children of whom Mary was apparently very fond. According to Thomas Fuller writing a century after her death, Mary thought it would add to her safety to marry "one whom she could love and none need fear."[34] Keyes was six-and-a-half feet tall, leading to some merriment at court when the marriage was discovered, with claims that the giant had married the dwarf. Elizabeth was not amused, and Mary's situation became much less safe rather than more. Keyes was sent to the Fleet, and Mary was forced to live with various relatives. Keyes died in 1571, and two years later, Mary was given her freedom, buying a home in Aldersgate Street, London, where she may have raised her stepchildren until her own death five years later. Though technically also an heir to the throne, no one including Mary had considered her a real possibility. Mary had genuinely cared for Keyes and his children and, after the examples of what had happened to her two older sisters, had wanted to live as quiet and normal a life as possible. When Mary died, one of her belongings was John Foxe's *Actes and Monuments,* which detailed her oldest sister Jane's tragic life in great detail. There was no reason for Elizabeth's cruelty other than the antipathy she felt for her paternal relations.[35]

While neither Carey ever claimed to be a sibling of Elizabeth, a number of Elizabethans believed that Sir John Perrot, born in 1528, was a son of Henry VIII, and in the investigations in his supposed treason it was claimed that "he had boasted that he was King Henry's son."[36] Sir Robert Naunton's *Fragmenta Regalia* (1641) helped to popularize this belief, and by the mid-seventeenth century, it was frequently mentioned that Sir John Perrot referred to himself as the illegitimate son of Henry VIII, that he looked greatly like the old king, and that Elizabeth believed he was her brother. For example, in 1643, Sir Richard Baker wrote of Perrot that "he was a man of goodly personage, stout and cholerick, and one whom (many thought) the Queen had the more reason to respect, for her Father King Henry the Eights sake."[37] Roger Turvey's research has demonstrated that Mary Berkeley Perrot was never the mistress of Henry VIII, thus making it impossible that Sir John Perrot was the king's illegitimate son.[38] What is significant, however, for this essay is that Perrot may well have believed he was Henry's bastard son or at least suggested to others that he was, and many people at Elizabeth's court, possibly even including the queen herself, may well have believed it to be possible, particularly given Perrot's temperament and physical appearance.

Although not actually the son of the king, Perrot did play a significant role in the politics of Elizabethan England. He was knighted as part of Edward VI's coronation. His Protestantism did not endear him to Mary, however, and he was briefly imprisoned during her reign for sheltering heretics; after his release, he fled abroad. Perrot returned upon Elizabeth's accession and in fact was one of the four bearers who carried her canopy of state during her coronation. Perrot had a talent for making enemies at court, however. He angered Christopher Hatton by suggesting that he had danced his way into the queen's favor.

In the 1570s, Perrot was put in charge of Munster, and the queen was pleased enough with what he accomplished there that in 1584, two years after Lord Grey was recalled, she offered him the appointment of lord deputy of Ireland. Ireland was a hard place for many of Elizabeth's men, but Perrot was quite successful. As Hiram Morgan points out, however, Perrot acted more as a viceroy than a lord deputy and communicated directly with James VI of Scotland; he also did not please Elizabeth by making independent overtures to the English Parliament for funds. While Elizabeth stated in a letter to Perrot that "I know you do nothing but with a good intent for my service," she added that he "better heed ere you use Us so again."[39] The queen reduced both Perrot's budget and the number of troops allotted. She ordered him to listen to the advice of his senior privy councilors.

Perrot had what some have called an expansive and dynamic personality, and he was quick to anger and intemperate in expressing it, even if it were against the queen. When she sent orders he did not care for he exclaimed, "Ah, now silly woman, now she shall not curb me, she shall not rule me now." He also stated that "she may command what she will, but we will do what we list." Another time he was even more furious: "God's wounds, this it is to serve a base bastard piss kitchen woman."[40] He had also apparently stated publicly that Elizabeth was "ready to pisse herself for fear" of Philip of Spain.[41]

Sir John was recalled from Ireland to help against the threatened invasion by the Spanish in the summer of 1588, but Ireland, in a rare state of peace, was not a problem for England then because before he left Perrot had had rounded up any potential troublemakers and imprisoned them. Within days of his return, he was appointed lieutenant-general of the three south-west shires of Wales to ensure they were ready for possible Spanish invasion. By early 1589, Elizabeth had made him a member of the Privy Council. However successful Perrot might be, his personality was a problem, and although Henry VIII could get away with saying anything he might choose, a man who may have called himself Henry's son was not so fortunate. In March of the same year, Thomas Windebank, Clerk of the Signet and confidential and private secretary to Elizabeth, had his audience with the queen immediately after she had met with Perrot. Windebank wrote to Sir Francis Walsingham that he did not know what had been said but it left the queen "out of tune."[42]

Perrot's real problems began, however, when he began to lobby to return to Ireland as lord deputy, a move that made his successor, Sir William Fitzwilliam, a cousin of Mildred Cecil, and under the protection of her powerful husband, very nervous. He had been Perrot's second-in-command, and apparently involved in wide-scale corruption. According to Hiram Morgan, Fitzwilliam and Lord Burghley "concocted a huge conspiracy against" Perrot that led to him being tried for treason.[43] In April 1590, Sir Francis Walsingham died. He had protected Perrot, and his death was a disaster for the cantankerous knight.

In December 1590, Perrot was examined and then charged with treason and imprisoned in the Tower, though the trial at Westminster did not take place until April 1592. The charges were on four main counts: his outbursts had demonstrated an evil disposition toward the queen, he had aided traitors, he had conspired with England's enemies, specifically Philip II, and he had supported Irish rebels.[44] Evidence of a treasonable correspondence between Perrot and Philip II was shown to be a forgery by Denis O'Roughan, who had previously been imprisoned for counterfeiting Perrot's signature. Despite this, Perrot was found guilty of treason and sentenced to be executed.

But Elizabeth was reluctant to have the sentence carried out. According to Naunton, Perrot's response to his death sentence was to question, "will the Queen suffer her brother to be offered up a sacrifice to the envy of his frisking adversaries?"[45] Whether she believed he was her brother or not, Elizabeth may well have remembered decades earlier how she felt in the Tower waiting for word whether or not Mary would order her death. In his final testament, written in the Tower in May, Perrot maintained that he had "been most falsely accused through the malice and envy of some wicked and evil disposed persons." Perrot, however, also stated he could deny that "far otherwise than did become me" were "some fond and eager words"—in sixteenth-century terms he meant his words were "idiotic," "mad," and "biting," which unfortunately was the case. He stated how this caused him "sorrow in heart and soul" and "upon the knees of my heart," he begged Elizabeth's forgiveness.[46] While rumors were circulating that Elizabeth intended to pardon him, Sir John died on November 3, 1592, most likely of natural causes, though rumors swirled through court that he had been poisoned. Elizabeth restored the estates to his son Thomas.

Despite what people may have believed in the latter part of the sixteenth century and since, Henry VIII never could have admitted to the paternity of Sir John Perrot, because he was not his father. The king did, however, acknowledge that he was the father of Ethelreda Malte, though he had her raised as if she were the natural child of his tailor, John Malte, who was paid well for the privilege. Ethelreda's mother was Joanna Dyngley, but she had no hand in her upbringing. Ironically and indirectly, Ethelreda may have done more than any other sibling to establish a sense of family for Elizabeth because of her marriage to John Harington and the Haringtons' close relationship to Elizabeth. John Harington of Stepney was treasurer of the king's camps and buildings at Stepney and intensely loyal to Henry. In payment for

Harington's fidelity, the king arranged a marriage for him in 1546 with his illegitimate daughter, and at the time of the marriage gave Ethelreda a large grant of forfeited monastic land, which Harington inherited on Ethelreda's death, some time between 1557 and 1559.[47] The lands Harington inherited on her death made his fortune, and he showed his gratitude to the king by the steadfast devotion to his younger daughter, Elizabeth. Harington, as a servant to Thomas Seymour, had been in Elizabeth's household when she lived with Katherine Parr early in Edward's reign. Though still married to Ethelreda, by early in Mary's reign, Harington was very much in love with Isabella Markham, one of Elizabeth's six gentlewomen of her household.

In 1554, John and his wife Ethelreda accompanied Elizabeth to wait upon her when she was imprisoned in the Tower. While in the Tower, Harington wrote to Mary's Chancellor Stephen Gardiner. After describing his own duty to Elizabeth he added, "My wife is her servant, and does but rejoice in this our misery, when we look with whom we are held in bondage. Our gracious King Henry did every advance our families' good estate . . . wherefore our service is in remembrance of such good kindness." Suggesting a close relationship with Elizabeth, Harington described how she "does honor us in tender sort, and scorns not to shed her tears with ours."[48] Harington's marriage to Ethelreda may have had its difficulties, especially given his love for Isabella, whom he married early in Elizabeth's reign. When John and Isabella's son John was born in 1561, Elizabeth agreed to be his godmother, creating a different kind of family relationship for Elizabeth.

Elizabeth's relationships with her siblings caused her danger and anxiety. In many ways, Elizabeth had little freedom over how she would relate to her siblings; these relationships were predetermined by the political and religious constraints of the time that made uncomplicated familial affection impossible. Elizabeth, however, was able to structure some positive family feelings. Being a godmother apparently gave the queen some joy. As her godson Sir John Harington said of her, "We did all love her, for she said she loved us. . . . When she smiled it was pure sunshine."[49]

Notes

This essay is a much expanded and in many ways different version of an earlier piece on the same subject, "Sister Subject/Sister Queen: Elizabeth I and Her Siblings," in Naomi Miller and Naomi Yevnah, eds., *Sibling Relations and Gender in the Early Modern World: Sisters, Brothers, and Others* (Aldershot, UK: Ashgate, 2006), 77–88. I appreciate Hiram Morgan's help with John Perrot. I would like to thank Sara Mendelson, Jo Carney, and Retha Warnicke for their help with this work and so much else. Elizabeth Darocha, Lisa Schuelke, Natasha Luepke, and Erica Wright all helped with the research. I am very grateful.

1. Anne Somerset, *Elizabeth I* (New York: St. Martin's Press, 1992), 14.

2. Frank A. Mumby, *The Girlhood of Queen Elizabeth: A Narrative in Contemporary Letters* (London: Constable and Co., 1909), 81.

3. Leah S. Marcus, Janel Mueller, and Mary Beth Rose, eds., *Elizabeth I: Collected Works* (Chicago: University of Chicago Press, 2000), 13, 15–16.

4. Ibid., 32–33.

5. Ibid., 35.

6. Somerset, *Elizabeth I,* 28.

7. Marcus, Mueller, and Rose, *Elizabeth I,* 37, 38, 39.

8. Somerset, *Elizabeth I,* 30.

9. Mumby states, "Elizabeth, according to most accounts, had one of her real or feigned attacks of illness at the hour of the Northumberland's temporary success." *The Girlhood of Queen Elizabeth,* 81.

10. Henry Clifford, *The Life of Jane Dormer, Duchess of Feria,* ed. Joseph Stevenson (London: Burnes and Oates, 1887), 80.

11. Mumby, *The Girlhood of Queen Elizabeth,* 82.

12. Ibid., 92.

13. *Calendar of State Papers and Manuscripts, Relating to English Affairs, Existing in the Archives and Collections of Venice,* VI, Part II, ed. Rawdon Brown (Orig. pub. 1881; Nendeln, Liechtenstein: Kraus Reprint, 1970), 1058.

14. Mumby, *The Girlhood of Queen Elizabeth,* 97.

15. *Calendar of State Papers, Spain,* XI, 418.

16. Marcus, Mueller, and Rose, *Elizabeth I,* 141.

17. Ibid., 141–42.

18. Lena Orlin, "The Fictional Families of Elizabeth I," *Political Rhetoric, Power, and Renaissance Women,* ed. Carole Levin and Patricia A. Sullivan (Albany: State University of New York Press, 1995), 94.

19. The point about the king of Morocco was made by Professor Nabil Mater in his talk at the symposium, The English and the Others, December 5, 2003, the Newberry Library.

20. Beverley A. Murphy, *Bastard Prince: Henry VIII's Lost Son* (Thrupp, Stroud, UK: Sutton, 2001), 164.

21. *Letters and Papers, Foreign and Domestic, of the Reign of Henry VIII,* ed. James Gairdner (London: Her Majesty's Stationery Office, 1887), X, 908 (p. 377). See also *Calendar of Letters, Despatches, and State Papers, Relating to the Negotiations Between England and Spain Preserved in the Archives at Simancas and Elsewhere, Vol. V, Part II: Henry VIII, 1536–1538,* ed. Pascual de Gayangos (London: Her Majesty's Stationery Office, 1888), item 55 (p. 125).

22. Thomas Fuller, *The Church History of Britain* (1655), ed. J. S. Brewer (Oxford: Oxford University Press, 1845), III, 232.

23. "Supernatural," Oxford English Dictionary online; *Oxford English Dictionary* <http://dictionary.oed.com/>, accessed February 13, 2008.

24. This is one version of the "Bisley boy" legend that has Elizabeth replaced by a boy. See for example Bram Stoker, *Famous Impostors* (New York: Sturgis and Walton Company, 1910). It has about as much historical accuracy as the idea of Elizabeth as the mother of

the Earl of Oxford, who wrote all the great literature of the Elizabethan age. Perhaps she was both a male and a mother.

25. Kathy Lynn Emerson, *Wives and Daughters: the Women of Sixteenth Century England* (Troy, N.Y.: The Whitston Publishing Co., 1984), 41.

26. Eric W. Ives, *Anne Boleyn* (London: Blackwell, 1986), 20.

27. Anthony Hoskins, "Mary Boleyn's Carey Children—offspring of King Henry VIII?" *Genealogists' Magazine* 25.9 (March 1997), 345–52; Paul Friedmann, *Anne Boleyn*, II (London: Macmillan and Co., 1884), 324; *Letters and Papers of Henry VIII*, VIII, item 567.

28. Sally Varlow, "Knollys, Katherine, Lady Knollys (*c.* 1523–1569)," *Oxford Dictionary of National Biography,* online edition, Oxford University Press, October 2006 <http://0–www.oxforddnb.com.library.unl.edu:80/view/article/69747>, accessed December 23, 2006.

29. Historical Manuscripts Commission, *Mss. of the Marquis of Salisbury, etc. Part I* (London: Eyre and Spottiswoode, 1883), 400, 415; Retha Warnicke, *The Rise and Fall of Anne Boleyn* (Cambridge: Cambridge University Press, 1989), 238.

30. Jonathan Hughes, "Stafford, Mary (*c.* 1499–1543)," *Oxford Dictionary of National Biography,* Oxford University Press, September 2004; online edition, October 2006 <http://0–www.oxforddnb.com.library.unl.edu:80/view/article/70719>, accessed December 23, 2006.

31. Marcus, Mueller, and Rose, *Elizabeth I,* 126.

32. Thomas Fuller, *The Worthies of England* (1662), ed. John Freeman (London: George Allen & Unwin, Ltd., 1952), 317.

33. *Calendar of the Letters and State Papers Relating to English Affairs, Preserved Principally in the Archives of Simancas. Vol. I: Elizabeth, 1558–1567,* ed. Martin A. S. Hume (London: Her Majesty's Stationery Office, 1892), 468.

34. Fuller, *The Worthies of England,* 317–18.

35. For more on Katherine and Mary Grey, see Richard Davey, *The Sisters of Lady Jane Grey and Their Wicked Grandfather* (New York: E. P. Dutton and Co., 1912); Hester W. Chapman, *Two Tudor Portraits: Henry Howard, Earl of Surrey, and Lady Katherine Grey* (Bath: Chivers, 1960); Mary Luke, *The Nine Days Queen* (New York: William Morrow, 1986); and especially Susan Doran, "Seymour [Grey], Katherine, countess of Hertford (1540?–1568)," *Oxford Dictionary of National Biography,* Oxford University Press, 2004 <http://www.oxforddnb.com/view/article/25157>, accessed January 17, 2007, and Susan Doran, "Keys [Grey], Lady Mary (1545?–1578)," *Oxford Dictionary of National Biography,* Oxford University Press, September 2004; online edition, May 2006 <http://www.oxforddnb.com/view/article/15503>, accessed January 17, 2007. At the end of Elizabeth's reign, her young cousin Arbella Stuart felt greatly aggrieved by the queen's treatment of her. Arbella's situation was far more dire in the reign of her cousin James I, when she reenacted Katherine Grey's secret marriage with Katherine's grandson William Seymour. Once the marriage was discovered, Arbella was separated from her husband and eventually spent the last years of her life a prisoner in the Tower.

36. *Calendar of State Papers, Domestic Series, of the Reign of Elizabeth, 1591–1594,* ed. Mary Anne Everett Green (London: Longmans, Green, Reader, and Dyer, 1867), 167. Hiram Morgan states that "a number of contemporary statements do show that he was held to be the son of Henry VIII" in "The Fall of Sir John Perrot," in *The Reign of*

Elizabeth I: Court and Culture in the Last Decade (Cambridge: Cambridge University Press, 1995), 123.

37. Sir Robert Naunton, *Fragmenta Regalia, or Observations on the Late Queen Elizabeth, Her Times and Favorits* (London, 1641), 25–27. Although Roger Turvey is correct that the book by Naunton, Perrot's grandson-in-law, widely circulated the belief, he is incorrect in stating that Naunton began it. Roger Turvey, "Perrot, Sir John (1528–1592)," *Oxford Dictionary of National Biography,* Oxford University Press, 2004 <http://0-www.oxforddnb.com.library.unl.edu:80/view/article/21986>, accessed December 23, 2006. Turvey's work on Perrot, however, is otherwise very useful as is the excellent work on Perrot in Ireland by Hiram Morgan. Hiram Morgan, "'Never Any Realm Worse Governed': Queen Elizabeth and Ireland," *Transactions of the RHS* 14 (2004), 295–308, and "The Fall of Sir John Perrot," in *The Reign of Elizabeth I: Court and Culture in the Last Decade,* ed. John Guy (Cambridge: Cambridge University Press, 1995), 109–25. I am grateful to Professor Morgan for discussing with me the Elizabethan beliefs that Perrot was the son of Henry VIII. Sir Richard Baker, *A Chronicle of the Kings of England From the Time of the Romans Government Unto the Death of King James, Containing All Passages of State and Church, With All Other Observations Proper for a Chronicle* (London, 1643), 380.

38. R. K. Turvey, "Sir John Perrot: King Henry VIII's Bastard? The Destruction of a Myth," *The Transactions of the Honourable Society of Cymmrodorion* 1992 (actually published 1994), 79–94.

39. Morgan, "Never Any Realm Worse Governed," 301; *Calendar of State Papers Relating to Ireland, of the Reign of Elizabeth, 1586–88,* ed. Hans Claude Hamilton (London: Her Majesty's Stationery Office, 1877), 43.

40. Morgan, "The Fall of Sir John Perrot," 121.

41. Naunton, *Fragmenta Regalia,* 26.

42. *Calendar of State Papers, Domestic, 1581–90,* ed. Robert Lemon (London: Longman, Green, Longman, Roberts, and Green, 1865), 584.

43. Morgan, "Never Any Realm Worse Governed," 302.

44. Hiram Morgan, *Tyrone's Rebellion: The Outbreak of the Nine Years War in Tudor Ireland* (Woodbridge, Suffolk, UK: The Boydell Press, 1993), 58.

45. Naunton, *Fragmenta Regalia,* 26.

46. Historical Manuscripts Commission, *Calendar of the Manuscripts of the Most Hon. the Marquis of Salisbury Preserved at Hatfield House, Hertfordshire* (London: Her Majesty's Stationery Office, 1892), IV, 195.

47. Jason Scott-Warren, "Harington, John (c. 1517–1582)," *Oxford Dictionary of National Biography,* Oxford University Press, 2004 <http://www.oxforddnb.com/view/article/12325>, accessed January 19, 2007.

48. Ruth Hughey, *John Harington of Stepney: Tudor Gentleman* (Columbus: Ohio State University Press, 1971), 45.

49. John Harington, *The Letters and Epigrams of John Harington,* ed. Norman Egbert McClure (Philadelphia: University of Philadelphia Press, 1930), 140–41.

8. Fashioning Monarchy

Women, Dress, and Power at the Court of Elizabeth I, 1558–1603

CATHERINE L. HOWEY

The reign of Elizabeth I (1558–1603) began and ended with gifts of cloth and clothing. Coronation cloth was distributed to members of the royal household, from the nobility and gentry to the lowly servants. The men and women who received yards of crimson or scarlet fabric to wear during the queen's coronation ceremony would be visibly demarcated as members of the queen's royal court. Just as an ocean of scarlet and crimson cloth formally signaled the beginning of Elizabeth I's reign, a somber sea of black and purple signified its end.[1] Once more, a range of fabric and garments was distributed among the funeral participants. The portioning out of cloth for both the coronation and the funeral spanned the social hierarchy within the royal household. For example, the funeral account book reveals that, in addition to the nobility receiving black cloth, humble court servants, such as the footmen, also collected their allotted four yards apiece of black fabric.[2]

It was not only the beginning and end points of a reign that were demarcated by the gift of cloth. Throughout her reign, Elizabeth gave and received sartorial gifts, exchanging fabric, clothes, and dress accessories with her male and female courtiers. One institutionalized form of English royal gift giving was the exchange of gifts between the monarch and select subjects on New Year's Day. On the first day of January, the peers of the realm, high government officials, bishops, and members of the queen's household presented gifts to the queen who in return gave her loyal subjects presents of gilt plate. Over the course of her reign, Elizabeth received a large range of presents, from purses filled with money to hundreds of gifts of clothing, cloth, dress accessories, and furniture. Periodically throughout the rest of the calendar year, Elizabeth also showed her favor by giving a courtier new clothes or clothes from her own wardrobe. It was also standard operating monarchical procedure to send foreign ambassadors away with gifts of jewelry and gilt plate. In personal and diplomatic correspondence, courtiers, subjects, and foreigner ambassadors recorded their efforts to choose gifts for the queen, and the queen's reception and wearing of these gifts.

The ways in which Elizabeth I and her subjects used gifts fits into the framework established by anthropologists and used by historians for analyzing gift giving in preindustrial societies.[3] As Marcel Mauss argued, gift giving in archaic societies was not a purely altruistic act, but rather the purpose of the gift was to bind the giver and the receiver in a mutually reciprocal relationship. The gift could be used as a means to show gratitude for past favors or to build up credit for future requests.[4] Mauss's theory of gift giving has been critiqued for divorcing gift exchange from the realm of politics. As scholars have argued, during Elizabethan New Year's gift giving, politics were very much embedded in the strategies behind the subjects' gifts to their monarch. Families and individuals gave gifts of money, jewels, or clothes as an implicit appeal to keep the lands and government offices that maintained their elite social status.[5] An important facet of this argument focuses on the types of gifts many Elizabethan female courtiers gave to Elizabeth, namely gifts of clothes and other articles of hand-wrought needlework, which had an intimacy that endowed them with more "authority and efficacy" than gifts of cash.[6] Other scholars have also demonstrated how women used needlework to fashion their political identities and aspirations as well as to forge political networks.[7]

Politics were deeply embedded in the multitiered system of courtly gift exchange. Elizabeth's subjects used gifts to the queen in an attempt to exercise power over her by making the queen feel obligated to return a favor to the gift giver.[8] As this essay will argue, gifts of cloth, clothes, and clothing accessories were important tools of domestic and international statecraft creating ties between the giver and the receiver of the gift. Systematized exchanges of dress and its accessories at Elizabeth's court constituted a space in which subject and monarch could fashion each other's political identity. This system of sartorial exchange had many levels: consulting others on what to give, helping people obtain gifts, presenting the gift, recording or relaying Queen Elizabeth's reactions to gifts, and maintaining the gifts once received. Although both men and women actively participated on every level of this courtly system of gift exchange that mutually bound the queen to her subjects, this chapter highlights the ways in which court women, especially the women who served in the privy chamber—the two to three rooms used by the monarch for private repose—engaged in the politics of the Elizabethan gift exchange. Historians can more accurately and centrally analyze the role of women in Elizabethan politics by examining the courtly system of sartorial gift exchange, because it was through sartorial gifts that women were able to participate in multiple political acts, including the construction of Elizabeth's public image and the creation of ties to the monarch that could be used for political favors. Through the analysis of the circulation of gifts of dress and dress accessories, our understanding of the use of clothing and the creation of majesty becomes more nuanced. Monarchs did not simply use gorgeous dress to create a majestic setting to awe a passive audience, but rather, courtiers often participated in the performance of monarchical majesty and supplied the media that manufactured it.

Taking female courtiers' power seriously in the economy of gift giving at Elizabeth's court dramatically revises historians' understanding of the role of the queen's privy chamber women. Until recently, most scholars assumed that the privy chamber women's responsibilities for Elizabeth's clothes and person was a "domestic" matter, and thus divorced from politics.[9] For the past twenty years, the scholarship on Elizabethan court women was trapped in a very narrowly defined debate about politics and the privy chamber first articulated in David Starkey's work on the court of Henry VIII. According to Starkey, under Henry VIII, the privy chamber became the center for politics, patronage, and power. The politics of intimacy was revived in the early sixteenth century; those physically closest to the monarch, acting as both private attendants and government officials, held the most influence over the monarch and were subsequently the first to receive rewards for their service.[10] Within this physically narrow space, historians have tried to discern the role of women at court and the possibility of their political agency, and have debated whether or not the removal of the privy purse and the dry stamp from the charge of the chief gentlewoman was an indicator that Elizabeth stripped the privy chamber and its female attendants of any political function.[11] Although this body of scholarship has laid an important foundation for our understanding of Elizabethan court women, it unnecessarily limits our awareness both of the spaces in which women could wield power and influence and of the activities by which they were able to do so. Therefore, examining this system of sartorial gift giving reveals new areas for political participation at Elizabeth I's court and introduces new political players that have been hitherto overlooked.

Cloth Connections

The importance of gifts of dress and accessories at court and the crucial roles women played in this courtly sartorial system are richly illustrated by Elizabeth's January 1559 coronation. The account book for Elizabeth I's coronation lists men and women from the Duke and Duchess of Norfolk, the highest ranking peers in the kingdom, to the lowly footmen, and the book states who received what type of cloth or clothes for the coronation and its preceding festivities. For example, Mistress Catherine Asteley, chief gentlewoman of the queen's privy chamber, was allotted seven yards of scarlet for the actual coronation ceremony and fifteen yards of crimson velvet and two yards of purple tinsel to enable her to "attende vppon the Quenes maiestie on The Even of hir Highnesses Cornation."[12] A portrait exists that records another example of a royal gift of fabric for the coronation (fig. 8.1). Although the portrait is entitled, *Portrait of a Woman, Aged 16, Previously Identified as Mary Fitzalan, Duchess of Norfolk,* the second wife of the Duke of Norfolk, and was painted in 1565 by Hans Eworth, the sitter's clothes suggest that it is actually a 1565 copy of an earlier portrait of Margaret Audley, Norfolk's first wife.[13] The first duchess had been one of the forty-two female participants in the coronation ceremony, and the records indicate that she was designated two yards of cloth of gold for turning up the sleeves along with her sixteen yards of crimson velvet.[14] Not only do the materials depicted in the portrait appear to represent the types of materials dispatched to Audley for the coronation, but the style of dress also follows the general line of fashion for 1558 and is out of date for the 1560s.[15]

The lavish outfit worn by the duchess in her portrait speaks to the public function of clothing in constructing monarchical splendor. The duchess was one of hundreds of individuals dressed in such distinctive, eye-catching gar-

Figure 8.1. Portrait of a woman, aged 16, previously identified as Mary Fitzalan, Duchess of Norfolk, 1565. Hans Eworth, oil on panel, 35 × 28 in., Yale Center for British Art, Paul Mellon Fund. Reproduced with permission.

ments.[16] A pamphlet commemorating Elizabeth's procession through London to Westminster the day before her coronation, recorded the spectacle of the queen's retinue: "the most noble and Christian princesse, oure mooste dradde soueraigne Lady Elizabeth . . . marched . . . through the citie of London towarde Westminster, richly furnished, and most honorably accompanied, as well with gentilmen, Barons, & other nobilitie of this realme, as also with a notable trayne of goodly and beawtiful ladies, richly appoynted."[17]

Both the above passage and the coronation account book speak to how majesty was created and maintained by the monarch surrounding himself or herself with men and women appropriately dressed. As R. Malcolm Smuts has argued, although royal entries and other public displays of monarchical power used allegory, most of the public only witnessed fragments of the overall production. Although the majority of the crowds may not have heard the speeches or saw the tableaux vivants, they would have been impressed with courtiers dressed in elaborate silks and rich jewelry.[18] In the case of a coronation, appropriate dress was lavish velvets, silks, and satins. For a royal funeral, the proper attire was traditional mourning costume, which mostly consisted of cloaks and hoods. Both Elizabeth I's coronation and funeral were state-sponsored events that required their participants to be dressed in a very particular way. The clothes were so important that they were issued by the royal wardrobe of the robes and were considered government expenses because they were all used for displaying royal power.

Whereas the account books of Elizabeth I's coronation and funeral and the printed pamphlet of the last Tudor coronation entry provide evidence that clothing was an important part of constructing the fitting backdrop for displaying monarchical power, the portrait of the Duchess of Norfolk speaks of an additional role played by clothing at the early modern court. Dress and its accessories acted as more than just a passive mirror reflecting the glory of the ruler; gifts of cloth, clothes, and dress accessories bound subject and monarch, and enhanced a subject's prestige. If the portrait does commemorate the first duchess's role as a participant in the coronation, it records in paint the gift of cloth from the queen and testifies not only to the prominent role played by the woman at her monarch's coronation, but also to the importance of her family. Clothes acted as a link, connecting the monarch not only to individuals but also to groups such as families and towns. This portrait is more than just an individual statement; it is a visual declaration of the ties between the queen and the families connected to the Duke and Duchess of Norfolk.[19] Portraits and (as will be discussed) letters all bear witness to the active agency of sartorial gifts in forging and perpetuating connections between the queen and her subjects.

Dressing a Queen, Fashioning a Monarch

Creating connections through gifts of cloth to bind subjects to monarchs was not a strategy monopolized by the ruler. Elizabethan subjects, including women, also could initiate sartorial ties by offering gifts to their queen. Over her forty-five year reign, Elizabeth I received hundreds of gifts of cloth, articles of dress, and jewelry from her courtiers. There is a manuscript trail consisting of inventories, New Year's gift rolls, and lists of what jewels were in whose custody that provides detailed information on exactly what type of clothing and accessories Queen Elizabeth I received from her subjects. Although scholars cannot with absolute certainty match jewels and garments to specific portraits, Elizabeth did receive jewels similar to those depicted in some of her state portraits. Many of the jewels and the embroidery that decorated the clothing depicted in her portraits functioned as symbols used by Elizabeth to craft her public persona. For example, in one of the more famous portraits of Elizabeth I, the so-called *Pelican Portrait,* painted by Nicholas Hilliard around 1575, now located at the Walker Gallery in Liverpool, an enameled jewel of a pelican hangs at the queen's breast, symbolizing her Christ-like willingness to sacrifice herself for her subjects.[20] Although this jewel does not match any jewel given to the queen by one of her courtiers, the queen often received gifts of jewels in the form of symbols that Elizabeth appropriated to construct her monarchical image. A few years before this portrait was painted, Elizabeth received from Lady Woodhouse as a New Year's gift "a juell being a dyall, and a pellycane with three byrds, sett in golde with an emeralde, smale rubyes and dymondes being broken."[21] The description of Lady Woodhouse's gift reveals that through gifts courtiers could actively contribute to the maintenance and perpetuation of Elizabeth's chosen monarchical image by supplying her with symbolically resonant objects.

Historians have debated how much control Elizabeth exerted over her public image. The arguments have ranged from claims that Elizabeth was the architect of her cult to contentions that she passively allowed her male councilors to construct her image for her. Other scholars have convincingly argued that there was constant negotiation between Elizabeth and her male councilors over her image and other policies.[22] Nonetheless, in this debate the possible participants in the construction of Elizabeth I's public personae have always been limited to the queen and the men who surrounded her. The New Year's gift rolls, however, demonstrate that women too contributed to Elizabeth I's symbolic arsenal of clothes and jewels. For example, Lady Woodhouse presented Elizabeth with a pelican jewel. Another important symbol Elizabeth appropriated was that of the phoenix whose connotation of resurrection and regeneration allowed the unmarried, childless Elizabeth to calm people's fears about the succession by proclaiming through symbols that the monarchy would not die with her.[23] In 1576, a gentlewoman by the name of Mrs. Townsend gave the queen a "a Girdell of grene S^rceonet powderid w^t spangells w^t a border . . . enbraudered w^t a smale Ringe of golde w^t a phenix in it garnisshed about w^t a Rrose of eight Rubies."[24] It was probably no mere coincidence that Mrs. Townsend gave the queen a garment with the embroidered symbol of the phoenix in 1576, as it was around this time that the portrait commonly known as the *Phoenix Portrait* of Elizabeth I was painted by Nicholas Hilliard. Both male and female courtiers/subjects were aware of Elizabeth's strategies of self-presentation and assisted her in implementing them.

Not only did Elizabeth receive gifts that reinforced her public image, but she also gave gifts of jewels that symbolized the traits she proclaimed as hers, thus creating a circulation of symbolic jewels at court.[25] For example, Elizabeth gave the 1571 New Year's gift of an enameled red and white rose jewel that she received from Blanche Parry, who became chief gentlewoman of the privy chamber in 1565, to Elizabeth Howard, a woman who served the queen as a privy chamberer in the 1570s.[26] This jewel was surely meant to represent the Tudor rose, a symbol of Elizabeth's family dynasty. Such a clear English monarchical symbol would have readily signaled to Elizabeth that the giver of the gift, Parry, acknowledged the queen's authority and wanted to help Elizabeth construct her queenly authority. Elizabeth, by giving the jewel as a gift to Howard, would remind the privy chamberer of her loyalty to the queen and that her queen rewarded such fidelity. In 1573, Elizabeth received a gold pelican jewel that contained rubies, diamonds, and a pearl pendant that she subsequently gave away to "the younge Countyes of Huntingdone."[27] It is unlikely that Elizabeth gave away her jewels because she was displeased with them, because they were the symbols, in jewel-form, that Elizabeth used to bolster her monarchical image. Instead, the queen's action testifies to the larger purpose of the courtly system of gift exchange that often centered on dress and its accessories. Just as courtiers could use symbolic jewelry or colored garments to signal to Elizabeth that they would be useful allies in the creation of her public personae, Elizabeth could further reinforce the notion that she needed her subjects to help her in this enterprise. This circulation of "majestic capital" mutually bound givers and receivers, creating a sense that both were invested in the well-being of the other. The New Year's gift rolls testify that both men and women participated in this system and that the queen recognized and encouraged equally her female and her male subjects in this collaborative enterprise of fashioning the royal image, which allowed courtiers to provide more than the audience, but also the actors and the props needed for the monarch's display of his or her sovereignty.

The System of Courtly Gift Giving

The tools with which Elizabeth I fashioned her monarchical image often came in the form of fashionable accessories, and her supply of these tools were annually restocked. Every year on the first of January, a list was made that recorded, on one side, who gave what to the queen and, on the other side, what the queen gave in return. Not all of the gift rolls from Elizabeth's forty-five year reign have survived, but the twenty-four extant rolls range from 1559 to 1603, thereby revealing the trends over the entire course of her reign.[28] On both sides of the rolls, the gift givers and recipients are grouped by social status: first, either people with close familial connections to the queen or in high court positions, then dukes, marquesses, earls, and viscounts, followed by bishops, then duchesses, countesses, and viscountesses, followed by lords, then ladies, then knights, then chaplains, then gentlewomen, and finally gentlemen.[29] The second-to-last section lists the "free gifts"—gifts given to servants of the royal household who had not given the queen anything in exchange. Finally, the category of gifts recorded on the New Year's gift rolls were labeled as, "Guiftes gyuen by her Matie and delyuered at sundry tymes in manno^r & forme followinge." This section listed the gifts given by the queen to courtiers and foreign ambassadors for special occasions such as the christening of a child, a diplomatic visit, or the induction into a noble order.

Typically, the queen gave gifts of gilt plate in the form of cups and bowls with or without covers, drinking flagons, and spoons. Although the type of gifts the queen gave did not change, what the queen received from her subjects changed dramatically over the course of her reign.[30] One of the earliest extant rolls, for 1562, records that Elizabeth received eighty-one gifts of some type of coin; forty-six gifts relating to cloth, clothes and their maintenance, jewelry, and personal grooming; and thirty-two noncash non-dress-related gifts such as Sergeant of the Pastry John Betts's gift of "oone pye of Quinces."[31] By 1577, Elizabeth received sixty-two monetary gifts, ninety-five gifts related to dress, and twenty-four noncash non-dress-related gifts.[32] In the last year of her reign, monetary gifts were dramatically reduced to only thirty-six purses, as opposed to the one hundred and thirty-three items related to dress and twenty-one noncash non-dress-related gifts. Over the course of the entire reign, cash gifts were gradually reduced by more than half, whereas presents of clothes nearly tripled.[33]

The giving of gifts appears to be gendered and tied to occupation. Although the number of earls, lords, and knights who gave gifts of jewels and garments increased throughout the reign, as a group, the majority gave purses filled with coins. From the mid-1570s onward, the majority of women within the categories of countess, baroness, and lady shifted from offering gifts of money to gifts of dress. Gentlewomen as a group consistently gave gifts related to dress from the very start of the reign just as the gentlemen as a category almost always gave the gifts that were neither cash nor dress, but were related to their court occupation. It makes sense that the gentlewomen, many of whom worked in the privy chamber, chose to give gifts of cloth, clothes, and fashion accessories because they spent most of their waking hours with the queen, giving them the opportunity to observe what the queen liked in terms of dress and jewelry. More important, these women were involved in dressing the queen, giving them intimate knowledge of the queen's taste, size, and wardrobe needs.

Gift giving at court was not a simple matter. For the gift to fulfill its function of winning the recipient's favor or ensuring his or her loyalty, the gift had to be chosen with care. Unlike the queen, who did not have to worry as much if her gift satisfied the recipient since the honor of receiving a royal present was so great, subjects had to make sure they chose a gift that pleased the queen. The best sources for such information were courtiers, people who saw what the queen wore and could relay the queen's taste. In the system of courtly gift exchange, one level of participation was as a gift advisor to friends and family who did not live at court. When they left court, many courtiers maintained connections to help them from afar. Elizabeth Talbot, Countess of Shrewsbury, who had been a member of the privy chamber at the beginning of Elizabeth I's reign, used her court connections to help her continue to choose presents for the queen. From 1569 until 1584, the Countess of Shrewsbury and her husband were in charge of Elizabeth I's prisoner, Mary, queen of Scots. During this period, the countess's relationship with the queen was often strained as rumors circulated at court questioning whether the countess was loyal to Elizabeth or Mary. The countess wrote numerous letters to her main contacts, Elizabeth and Anthony Wingfield, her half-sister and brother-in-law, for advice to choose a gift that pleased Elizabeth and would reassure her of the countess's fidelity.[34] Although the year is not given, one letter dated December 4 probably relates to a New Year's gift. In it Mrs. Wingfield tells the countess, "I went to my l[ady] cobham and we longe confarde of the matter. I se by her she was muche against you l[ady] giving money mr W and I founde her so muche against the same . . . truly if you l[ady] had geven money I feare yt would have bene ell liked."[35]

Here the countess was able to use her court connections to choose the correct type of gift for the queen. However, it took more than just one person to help the countess; her official contacts were the Wingfields, who in turn sought the council of Lady Cobham, another privy chamberer. Women and men worked together so that courtiers and noncourtiers presented the queen with appropriate gifts. These networks of people kept the system of clothing exchange moving smoothly and extended it to people not living at court.

Not only did women and men help each other in choosing gifts, they also reported the queen's reaction to these gifts. Sir William More was able to find out that his choice of gift had been a successful one from his daughter, who wrote, "Since my coming to the Court, I have had many gratious words of her Majestie . . . yesterday she wore the gown you gave her, and thereby took occasion to speak of you with many gracious speeches of yourself and my brother."[36] This excerpt from an undated letter from a daughter to her father demonstrates exactly how gifts of clothes functioned. By choosing to wear a particular dress given to her by a particular courtier, the queen acknowledged her pleasure with the gift giver. Elizabeth doubly reinforced the ties between her and Sir William More's family by speaking about him and his son to his daughter who was at court. Relating the queen's reaction to a gift was not confined to letters between family and friends, but was even a topic of international diplomacy and politics. While her cousin's prisoner, Mary Stuart, queen of Scots, tried to improve her position with Elizabeth with a sartorial gift. On the queen of Scots' request, the French ambassador presented Elizabeth with a skirt of crimson satin that Mary had sewn herself.[37] The French ambassador reported Elizabeth's reaction to the French king: "The queen of Scots . . . is very well, and yesterday I presented on her behalf a skirt of crimson satin, worked with silver, very fine and all worked with her own hand, to the Queen of England, to whom the present was very agreeable, for she found it very nice and has prized it much; and she [Elizabeth] seemed to me that I found her much softened towards her [Mary]."[38] Although the queen of Scots' attempt to strengthen her bond with Elizabeth, her cousin and fellow monarch, ultimately failed, it nevertheless illustrates that the courtly system of sartorial gift exchange took place not only between the queen and her subjects, but also between Elizabeth and other European royalty. Clothes and jewels were tools of statecraft both at the domestic and the international levels.

Because cloth, clothes, and clothing accessories were tools of government, taking care of these items was an important job and one in which women dominated. Court women placed in charge over the jewels and clothes had an important position because they looked after items of immense monetary value as well as diplomatic importance. A book survives from Elizabeth's reign that recorded the items the queen lost from her wardrobe, items given as gifts to courtiers, deliveries of cloth to Elizabeth's ladies-in-waiting to make small garments such as mufflers, and deliveries of new and old materials to the queen's tailors to make garments for her use. This book also reveals that these women had the authority to sign out and deliver royal sartorial gifts. There are multiple entries where privy chamber women signed out items to be given to other courtiers or subjects. In 1577, Dorothy Stafford and Mary Scudamore signed for "one gown of purple velvet cut all over and snipped the snipes edged w/ purled gold lined w/ cloth of silver" that was given to Rauf Hope, Yeoman of the Wardrobe of the Robe.[39] Besides being able to sign out these gifts, the privy chamber women could also deliver them. In the same year, the book records "item delivered to Mrs Mary Scudamore the vth of december . . . 1577 One Brouche of golde . . . Geoven by her Majestie to Mr. Pagginlanne." Scudamore also signed out the jewel.[40] A 1581 entry states that these women were following the dictates of their queen, "Given to the Lady Sheffilde and delivered by Mrs Skydamores commaundement from the Queens Matie . . . one fore part. . . ."[41] In February 1576, the queen commanded that Mary Scudamore receive material to make a gown intended for her aunt, Mrs. Anne Shelton.[42] These women were the intermediaries that kept the sartorial gift exchange flowing smoothly. At times, these women advised their friends and relatives on what to give, and at other times, they delivered the gifts to the queen and accepted the responsibility for distributing the queen's gifts of favor to her subjects. Moreover, it is important to keep in mind the larger framework in which these gifts functioned. Because gifts of clothes functioned as capital in the political economy of the court, these women were conducting state affairs, not merely domestic tasks whenever they signed out, delivered, or received deliveries of jewels, clothes, and cloth.

The women involved in the system of gift exchange at court were actively participating in building and maintaining the network of support Queen Elizabeth I required to survive on the throne. Scholars who depict the Elizabethan privy chamber as an apolitical, domestic space devoid of any political maneuvering ignore the political implications of clothes, their meanings, and their circulation. These items were more than just passive props used to impress subjects and foreign princes, rather they were kept, worn, and distributed to forge and perpetuate connections between the queen and her subjects and to bind England's monarchy to other European rulers. Subjects and monarchs understood the courtly system of sartorial gift giving as a means of earning favor to further family, individual, or other group interests. By dressing the queen, subjects played a significant role in fashioning the monarchy.

Notes

1. The National Archive (TNA), London, LC 2/4/3 is the account book for Elizabeth I's coronation, and TNA, LC 2/4/4 is her funeral account book.

2. TNA, LC 2/4/3 f.57a v.

3. The exchange of gifts at the New Year was practiced on a wide scale in early modern Europe, as Natalie Zemon Davis demonstrates in *The Gift in Sixteenth-Century France* (Madison: University of Wisconsin Press, 2000), 23–24.

4. Marcel Mauss, *The Gift: The Form and Reason for Exchange in Archaic Societies*, trans. W. D. Halls (New York: Norton, 1950; rpt. 1990). J. L. Nevinson, "New Year's Gifts to Queen Elizabeth I, 1584," *Costume* 9 (1975), 27, states that gifts were given to the queen "in lively expectation of favors to come."

5. Lisa M. Klein, "Your Humble Handmaid: Elizabethan Gifts of Needlework," *Renaissance Quarterly* 50, no. 2 (1997): 464–65. Klein incorporates Annette Weiner's work on gift exchange, which "identifies a feature of gift-giving even more fundamental than reciprocity: namely, the paradox of giving-while-keeping," where people exchange "alienable possessions" to keep "inalienable possessions" such as landholdings. See also Susan Frye, "Sewing Connections: Elizabeth Tudor, Mary Stuart, Elizabeth Talbot and Seventeenth-Century Anonymous Needleworkers," *Maids and Mistresses, Cousins and Queens: Women's Alliances in Early Modern England*, ed. Susan Frye and Karen Robertson (New York: Oxford University Press, 1999), 167–69.

6. Klein, "Your Humble Handmaid," 471. More generally Ann Rosalind Jones and Peter Stallybrass, *Renaissance Clothing and the Materials of Memory* (New York: Cambridge University Press, 2000), 19, argue that gifts of dress were more binding than gifts of money.

7. Klein, "Your Humble Handmaid," 485; Frye, "Sewing Connections," 166; Jones and Stallybrass, *Renaissance Clothing*, 153–54.

8. Klein, "Your Humble Handmaid," 466, 474, also gives an example of the queen exchanging gifts so that both she and the recipient of her gift would remember each other.

9. For example, Natalie Mears, "Politics in the Elizabethan Privy Chamber: Lady Mary Sidney and Kat Ashley," *Women and Politics in Early Modern England, 1450–1700*, ed. James Daybell (Aldershot, UK: Ashgate, 2004), 77, argues that the privy chamber women were not "confined to the domestic roles of delivering cloth and clothing, checking fabric receipts and keeping account of Elizabeth's personal jewels." Although Mears convincingly demonstrates that privy chamber women played important political roles in the dissemination of news, she consigns the duties of taking care of the queen's clothes and jewels to a domestic space devoid of politics. Klein, "Your Humble Handmaid," 484–85, argues that gifts of clothes enabled women to participate in court politics by offering gifts to the queen to build personal and political relationships, which in turn allowed women "to fashion themselves as subjects." My essay will show other ways in which dress and dress accessories connected women to Elizabethan politics.

10. David Starkey first worked out his model of the Henrician privy chamber in "The King's Privy Chamber, 1485–1547" (Ph.D. dissertation, Cambridge University, 1973). Starkey also addressed the rise of the early Tudor privy chamber in "Intimacy and Innovation: The Rise of the Privy Chamber, 1485–1547," *The English Court: From the Wars of the Roses to the Civil War*, ed. David Starkey (New York: Longman Inc., 1987), 71–118; and "Court,

Council, and Nobility in Tudor England," *Princes, Patronage and Nobility: The Court at the Beginning of the Modern Age c. 1450–1650,* ed. Ronald G. Asch and Adolf M. Birke (New York: Oxford University Press, 1991), 175–203.

11. Pam Wright, "A Change in Direction: The Ramifications of a Female Household, 1558–1603," *The English Court: From the Wars of the Roses to the Civil War,* ed. David Starkey (New York: Longman, 1987), 150, 152, argues that the removal of the privy purse from the control of the privy chamber was indicative of the depoliticization of Elizabeth's privy chamber. Scholars who have sought to revise this view are Charlotte Merton, "The Women Who Served Queen Mary and Queen Elizabeth: Ladies, Gentlewomen and Maids of the Privy Chamber, 1553–1603" (Ph.D. dissertation, Cambridge University, 1992); Elizabeth A. Brown, "'Companion Me With My Mistress': Cleopatra, Elizabeth I, and Their Waiting Women," *Maids and Mistresses,* 131–45; and Mears, "Politics in the Elizabethan Privy Chamber," 67–82.

12. TNA, LC 2/4/3 f.61v.

13. The first scholar to question the identity of the portrait's sitter by analyzing the clothing was Janet Arnold, *Queen Elizabeth's Wardrobe Unlock'd* (Leeds: W. S. Maney, 1988), 56–57.

14. The coronation account book, TNA, LC 2/4/3 f.59v, only records that the duchess received "Velvet Crimsin xvj yards/Clothe of golde, yelowe Playne}ij yards." Another manuscript source TNA, E 101/429/3 f.8v states that for the coronation the duchess also received cloth of gold for the "turning up the sleeves."

15. Arnold, *Queen Elizabeth's Wardrobe Unlock'd,* 57. For a general overview of the evolution of sixteenth-century English fashion, see Jane Ashelford, *A Visual History of Costume: The Sixteenth Century* (London: B. T. Batsford, 1983; rpt. 1993).

16. There is an extensive bibliography concerning the monarchical display of power through pageantry; see, for example, Sydney Anglo, *Spectacle, Pageantry and Early Tudor Policy* (Oxford: Clarendon Press, 1969); Roy Strong, *Splendor at Court: Renaissance Spectacle and the Theater of Power* (Boston: Houghton Mifflin, 1973); R. Malcolm Smuts, *Court Culture and The Origins of a Royalist Tradition in Early Stuart England* (Philadelphia: University of Pennsylvania Press, 1987); and David Howarth, *Images of Rule: Art and Politics in the English Renaissance, 1485–1649* (Berkeley: University of California Press, 1997).

17. *The Passage of Our Most Drad Soueraigne Lady Elyzabeth Through the Citie of London to Westminster the Day Before Her Coronacion* (London: Richard Totull, 1558/59). This pamphlet was published shortly after Elizabeth's January 1559 coronation, but under the old calendar, which was used at the time, it was still 1558.

18. R. Malcolm Smuts, "Public Ceremony and Royal Charisma: The English Royal Entry in London, 1485–1642," *The First Modern Society: Essays in English History in Honor of Lawrence Stone,* eds. A. L. Beier, David Cannadine, and James M. Rosenheim (Cambridge: Cambridge University Press, 1989), 66–67, 71.

19. The case of the Duke and Duchess of Norfolk proves that although links could be forged, the chains did not always hold. The duke, after burying three wives, would be executed for treason when he tried to marry Mary Stuart, queen of Scots.

20. The pelican symbolized Christian charity in the early modern period, because the pelican was believed to strip her own flesh in order to feed her young. This symbol was useful for Elizabeth to portray herself as a good motherly monarch who would willingly sacrifice herself for her subjects' well-being. See Roy Strong, *Gloriana: The Portraits of*

Queen Elizabeth I (London: Thames and Hudson, 1987; rpt. Pimlico, 2003), 83; Diana Scarisbrick, *Tudor and Jacobean Jewelry* (London: Tate Publishing, 1995), 65; and *Elizabeth: The Exhibition at the National Maritime Museum,* ed. Susan Doran (London: Chatto & Windus in association with The National Maritime Museum, London: 2003), 192–93.

21. "New-Yere's Gifts Charged Upon Lady Howarde, 1573–4," in John Nichols, *The Progresses and Public Processions of Queen Elizabeth* (London: n.p., 1823), 1: 380. The New Year's gift roll to which this list refers I do not believe has survived, so no cross-checking can be done.

22. Susan Frye, *The Competition for Representation* (New York: Oxford University Press, 1993).

23. For further discussion of the various meanings of the phoenix symbol, see Scarisbrick, *Tudor and Jacobean Jewelry,* 62–66, and Strong, *Gloriana,* 82–83; Susan Doran, entry for "item 203 A Choice of Emblems and Other Devises, 1586" in *Elizabeth: Exhibition at the National Maritime Museum,* 199–200; and Tarnya Cooper, "The Queen's Visual Presence," in *Elizabeth: Exhibition at the National Maritime Museum,* 179.

24. British Library (B.L.), Additional MS 4827. In Nichols, *The Progresses and Public Processions of Queen Elizabeth,* 2: 2, for the same year there is a list of all the jewels given at New Year's placed in the charge of Lady Howard. The list describes Mrs. Townsend's gift as "Item, a smale ring of gold, with a phenex of ophall, and a rose of VIII smale rubyes."

25. Maria Hayward states in "Gift-Giving at the Court of Henry VIII: The 1539 New Year's Gift Roll," *Antiquaries Journal* 85 (2005), 128, that Henry VIII also circulated his New Year's gifts. In 1539, Henry VIII gave one of his gifts, a standing cup, to the Duchess of Norfolk.

26. Merton, "The Women Who Served Queen Mary and Queen Elizabeth," "Appendix 1: Membership of the Privy Chamber," 262, only found documents listing her for 1577/8, but the records Merton cites often do not reflect the full tenure of a privy chamberer's career. I would argue that Elizabeth gave one of her jewels to Elizabeth Howard, because she was at court serving the queen at this time.

27. Nichols, *Progresses and Public Processions of Queen Elizabeth,* 1: 324. In that same year, she gave away four other jewels to three people, but Elizabeth often put gifts back into circulation at court.

28. Jane A. Lawson, "This Remembrance of the New Year: Books Given to Queen Elizabeth as New Year's Gifts," *Elizabeth I and the Culture of Writing,* ed. P. Beal and G. Ioppolo (London: British Library, 2007), 133. My analysis of Elizabeth's New Year's gift rolls is based on my examination of twenty of those twenty-four surviving rolls.

29. The list of names of who gave and who received gifts on New Year's Day are not exactly the same. Although the maids of honor, the six to eight young unmarried women who served the queen as her personal attendants, received gifts of gilt plate, they are not recorded as having presented gifts to the queen. The maids of honor are not listed in the free gifts section either. At this time, I am not sure why the maids of honor were exempt from giving the queen a gift while still receiving one from Elizabeth.

30. The bishops who always gave money and the chaplains who gave money or prayer books were notable exceptions. These two groups are not included in my analysis of New Year's gift giving for the rest of this essay.

31. B. L. Harleian Roll V.18. One of the gifts counted as cash was a "round pece of siluer."

32. TNA C47/3/39.

33. Klein, "Your Humble Handmaid," 459 n. 2, compares the gifts given to Elizabeth in 1562 and 1589.

34. Klein, "Your Humble Handmaid," 469–61, also argues that Elizabeth Talbot, countess of Shrewsbury needed to have a successful New Year's gift in order to mend her relationship to the queen which had been strained over the course of the year when her daughter had secretly married the son of the Countess of Lennox, mother-in-law to Mary, queen of Scots, and gave birth to a daughter who had claims to the throne of both England and Scotland. The marriage incurred the queen's wrath, not only because it was done in secret and could affect the line of succession to the English and the Scottish thrones, but it meant that Mary, queen of Scots, who was under house arrest and in the custodianship of the Earl and Countess of Shrewsbury, was in contact with the Countess of Lennox, which Elizabeth I had also forbidden. Mary S. Lovell in her biography of the Countess of Shrewsbury, *Bess of Hardwick: Empire Builder* (New York: Norton, 2006), 240–58, also recounts the countess's machinations to marry her daughter to royalty and her use of gifts to mend her relationship with Elizabeth I.

35. Folger Shakespeare Library, Washington D.C., Cavendish-Talbot Letters, X.d.428 (131), Elizabeth Wingfield to Elizabeth Talbot, Countess of Shrewsbury, 9 December no year given, but the Folger online guide to the Cavendish-Talbot letters <http://shakespeare.folger.edu/other/html/dfocavendish.html>, suggests the year 1585 as a possibility. Janet Arnold in *The Queen's Wardrobe Unlock'd*, 97, has transcribed the letter slightly differently than I have. Arnold's version is this: "I went to my lady cobham and we longe confarde of the matter. I se[e] by her she was muche againste yow honour givinge money. mr. W and I founde her so muche agannst the same that . . . truly if yow honour had geven money I feare yt woulde have bene ell liked."

36. Nichols, *The Progresses and Public Processions of Queen Elizabeth*, 3: 82–83.

37. Arnold, *The Queen's Wardrobe Unlock'd*, 94; Margaret Swain, *The Needlework of Mary, Queen of Scots* (New York: Van Nostrand Reinhold, 1973), 82–83.

38. Swain, *The Needlework of Mary, Queen of Scots*, 83.

39. TNA, C 115/91 f.56; Janet Arnold, "*Lost from Her Majesties Back*" *Items of Clothing and Jewels Lost or Given Away by Queen Elizabeth I Between 1561 and 1585, Entered in One of the Day Books Kept for the Records of the Wardrobe of the Robes*, Costume Society Extra Series 7 (Wisbech, Cambridgeshire, UK: Daedalus Press, 1980), 59.

40. TNA, C 115/91 f.56; Arnold, "*Lost from Her Majesties Back*," 59.

41. TNA, C 115/91 f.76; Arnold, "*Lost from Her Majesties Back*," 72. Nor was this an isolated case. In 1585, the daybook records, "Itm deliuered by the Commaundement of Mrs Blaunch and Mrs Skidmore to Mr. Jhones the j of Maye j rownd kirtle of white tuft taffeta with ij pere of bodyes layd with a narrow lase of golde and silver to make a gowne for Mr. Harvey his daughter," TNA C 115/91 f.86, Arnold, "*Lost from Her Majesties Back*," 80.

42. TNA, C 115/91f. 51; Arnold, "*Lost from Her Majesties Back*," 54.

9. Thrice Royal Queen

Katherine de Valois and the Tudor Monarchy in Henry V *and* Englands Heroicall Epistles

SANDRA LOGAN

The sixteenth-century English chronicles are recognized as a centrally formative resource for conceptualizing English national identity, influencing the work of later Elizabethan writers of epic poetry, chorography, drama, and short prose histories.[1] Yet, later writers *reshaped* their source materials in significant and creative ways, constructing versions of history that offered different perspectives and foregrounded different problems from those addressed obliquely in the *longue durée* historical accounts. The historical figure I shall attend to in this essay first caught my attention as I made my way through the Tudor Room of London's Royal Portrait Gallery, for she was conspicuous in her absence from the depictions of the roots and branches of the Tudor royal line. Next to the portrait of Henry VII, the gallery notes read: "Henry VII was the son of Edmund Tudor and head of the house of Lancaster. He defeated and killed the Yorkist Richard III at the battle of Bosworth Field in 1485, establishing the Tudor monarchy." The failure to mention women in this note is not unusual, and it perpetuates a patriarchal view of identity, succession, and agency.[2] The missing figure in these gallery notes is Henry's mother Margaret, from whom he could tenuously claim his Lancastrian heritage, but my interest in the present analysis is the *real* founder of the Tudor monarchy, Henry's grandmother, Katherine de Valois. Katherine was the daughter of Charles VI of France and Isabeau of Bavaria, sister to the dauphin who eventually ruled as Charles VII, wife of Henry V of England as a result of the Treaty of Troyes between France and England, queen of England and of Northern France after the death of her father in 1422 through this marriage to Henry V, mother to Henry VI of England, and grandmother to Henry Tudor, who became Henry VII of England.

Katherine represented a matrix of royal interconnections that fulfilled all possible women's roles with relation to monarchical and patriarchal order: daughter, sister, wife, widow, and mother of kings, she epitomized the potential for women's influence at the apex of the hierarchical gender order of medieval England and Europe. It is ironic, then, that her presence is so frequently absent from history as it is told by charts of succession and as described by the rhetoric of English national development. She is almost entirely disassociated from representations of the Tudor line that literally emerged from her royal body and that gained a portion of its legitimacy through her.

Katherine is perhaps best known to modern audiences, as she no doubt was to late-Elizabethan ones, through her representation as the "irresistible object of affection" in Shakespeare's *Henry V*, and as King Henry's "capital demand" in the submission of France to English conquest after the battle of Agincourt.[3] She is also featured in Michael Drayton's *Englands Heroicall Epistles,* written a few years before Shakespeare's play, as a widow exchanging letters with her future lover or husband Owen Tudor.[4] It is there, even more than in Shakespeare's vexed dramatization, that her most interesting representation emerges, as Drayton strives to encapsulate the cultural value and royal validity of the French/Welsh Tudor line, emphasizing the complex heritage that other historical accounts tended to elide. In the context of the succession debates of the entire Elizabethan period, as England sought to regain its last French holding, Calais, and strove to lay claim to the peripheral realms of Scotland and Ireland, writers of history in its various forms argued through an array of militaristic, legalistic, and naturalistic means for the English right to make such claims.[5] Wales, more effectively subdued than the other British territories since the reign of Edward II, came to serve as the touchstone and repository of true Britishness in the imagination and self-representations of sixteenth-century writers and politicians, despite the only tangentially British identity of the nation's kings. Thus, erasures such as the one I address here signal not only gendered readings of history, but also anxious reinscriptions of cultural and political heritage in the pursuit of national legitimation and imperialist justification.

Representations of Katherine in the Chronicle Histories

Edward Hall, who dedicates his *Chronicle* to the third Tudor monarch, child-king Edward VI, traces Edward's monarchical heritage to one female ancestor—Margaret—and erases another—Katherine de Valois.[6] Margaret, Edward's great-grandmother, hailed from the illegitimate offspring of John of Gaunt, a line that had been actively excluded from the succession by both Henry IV and Henry VI. Katherine, although she was French by heritage and place of birth, was the royal mother of Henry VI as well as of Edward's great-grandfather, Edmund Tudor. Neither Hall nor Raphael Holinshed includes an account of Katherine's years as dowager queen following the death and funeral of her first English husband, Henry V, while her young son ruled under a powerful and self-serving protectorate. Further, both Hall and Holinshed attend in careful detail to the earlier marriage of Henry V to Katherine de Valois, which was the linchpin of the Treaty of Troyes, and Hall is explicit about the value of marriage as a diplomatic tool when referring to the marital binding of the houses of Lancaster and York after the succession of Henry VII. Yet, Katherine's legally prohibited marriage to Owen Teuther [Tudor] after Henry V's death receives no mention in either chronicle at its moment of occurrence.

Katherine's historical presence is invoked only to report her death, at which point Hall briefly notes the actual emergence of the Tudor line. Having commented that she "departed out of this transitory life, & was buried by her husband, in the minster of Westmynster" (184), Hall explains the later years of her life as follows: "Katheryne queen and mother to [Henry VI] the king of England . . . after the death of king Henry the fifth her husband, being young and lusty, following more her own appetite, then friendly counsel, and regarding more her private affection than her open honor, took to husband privily, a goodly gentleman, and a beautiful person, garnished with many Godly gifts, both of nature and of grace, called Owen Teuther, a man brought forth and come of the noble lineage, and ancient line of Cadwalader, the last king of the Britons" (184–85). Although Hall leaves Katherine's years with Tudor entirely out of his history, he does mention here that through this legally proscribed marriage Katherine produced a daughter and three sons, one of whom would become king of England (185).[7] Both Owen and Katherine disappear at this point, although an additional note later in the troubled reign of Henry VI reveals the discovery of their grandson, the future Henry VII, who Hall reports had been kept essentially captive in Wales. Only then, ten years after the actual chronological moment of Henry's birth, does Hall reveal that this first Tudor king was born to Katherine's son Edmund and to Margaret, quasi-legitimate heir to the Lancastrian line, three months after the death of Edmund, and when Margaret was not yet thirteen.

Hall, working to legitimate the Tudor claim by undoing the vexing problems of the Beaufort line's post-birth legitimacy and their exclusion from the succession, reports Henry VI's acknowledgment of the inherent quality and inevitable rise of Henry Tudor, his half-brother's son, as "he, to whom both wee and our adversaries levyng [leaving] the possession of all thynges, shall hereafter geve rome and place" (287). Thus, the troubling aspects of the past are rewritten through Hall's assertion of Henry VI's monarchical pronouncement and Margaret's Lancastrian ancestry as the basis for Henry's claim to the throne. Katherine, in whom royalty unquestionably resided, is excluded in an apparent attempt to "English" the royal succession.

Katherine's most important moment in history as told by Hall and by Holinshed, the later sixteenth-century chronicler, is the moment of her marriage to Henry V, a condition of the Treaty of Troyes negotiated in 1420. In the context of this discussion of Katherine's erasure, however, it is significant that both accounts depict the English proclamation of peace as establishing a familial bond that extends beyond the linking mechanism of the marriage vows. Both redefine Henry as the *legitimate son and heir of his wife's parents,* in effect circumventing the princess's linking role. The proclamation, circulated throughout England after the treaty was signed, and included in full in both Hall and Holinshed, asserts in Henry's voice: "it is accorded betweene *our father* and us, that forsomuch as by the bond of matrimonie made for the good of the peace betweene us and our most deere beloved Katherine, daughter of *our said father, & of our most deere moother Isabel his wife; the same Charles and Isabel beene made our father and moother: therefore them as our father and moother we shall have and worship,* as it fitteth and seemeth so worthie a prince and princesse to be worshipped, principallie before all other temporall persons of the world" (Holinshed, 3.115, Proclamation Article 1, emphasis added).[8] In effect, while the marriage ceremony transforms the social identities of husband and wife, the oaths of allegiance, peace treaty, and proclamation transform the social (and inevitably the political) relationship between Henry and his in-laws, creating a legalistic, textual confluence of their disjunctive bloodlines that is reliant on neither birth nor marriage.

In article twenty-five of this proclamation, we find the "familial bond" reinforced by a formal declaration of Henry's proper titular form during King Charles's lifetime: in French, *"Nostre treschier filz, Henry roy d'Engleterre heretere de France"*; and in Latin, *"Praeclarissimus filius noster Henricus rex Anglae & haeres Franciae"*—a formula that makes Charles the verbal conduit of his own legitimate son's ongoing delegitimation.[9] Finally, Hall records in its entirety a speech delivered by Henry establishing his right to the French throne through the female line, in which Henry asserts that "the childe followeth the womb," and adds "although the one part be Englishe yet the surer side is French" (101). Hall's inclusion of the whole speech emphasizes that Henry's right to France was inhered in his natural body through his lineage, traceable through Isabel, his great-great-grandmother, while Holinshed, by briefly paraphrasing this speech, downplays this blood right in order to foreground the importance of the treaty. Holinshed thereby foregrounds the treaty's reconfiguration of Henry's social relationship to the French royal line, and its associated transformation of Henry's political rights.[10]

Like Hall, Holinshed falls very nearly silent on Katherine's presence and role in England once the marriage is accomplished. After her husband's death and her return to court with her young son Henry VI, she disappears until her death in 1437 is recorded. Only at that point does Holinshed reveal her marriage, exactly replicating Hall's depiction of her lust and desire for Owen Tudor as impediments to her judgment, his description of Tudor's excellent qualities, and his assertion of Owen's position as founder of the Tudor monarchical line (3.190). Neither Hall nor Holinshed reveals the machinations of the protectorate through which the English nobility attempted to rein in and deactivate the threatening presence of the dowager queen, although both refer in passing to the pertinent statute, issued in the sixth year of her son's reign, which proscribed the queen's marriage except by the permission of her son once he reached his majority. In effect, both Henry VI and her other offspring are "Englished" through this erasure of her presence and significance throughout the first 13 years of her son's reign, as the "bastard" of Orleans (the French dauphin) waged successful war against the English claimant and as the English monarchy dissolved in civil war.

Shakespeare's Recalcitrant Princess

In Shakespeare's *Henry V*, Henry is persuaded that the divisions and conflicts within his realm and associated with his monarchy might be mitigated or resolved through a reclaiming of French territory conquered by earlier monarchs. The legitimacy of his claim to France is established by an explicitly self-serving clergy, through the legalistic and historical precedent of inheritance through the female line—an argument that foregrounds the significance of women in the legitimation of lines of succession, though perhaps ironically. In this assertion of Henry's right, Shakespeare aligns more with Hall than Holinshed. He also works up, from Hall's bare hint of affection between the royal couple, the scenes in which Henry—in actuality absent from Troyes while the details of the treaty were worked out—attempts to convince the "irresistible" Katherine to agree to become his queen. The play, however, repeatedly links violence and desire, situating Katherine as the figure whose royal body stands in for and displaces the bodies of French subjects and the unconquered French towns that Henry effectually threatens to ravage if he she does not submit to him.

She becomes the means through which peace is procured, and in consecrating their marriage at the end of the play, Charles, king of France, declares,

> Take her, fair son, and from her blood raise up
> Issue to me, that the contending kingdoms
> Of France and England, whose very shores look pale
> With envy of each other's happiness,
> May cease their hatred, and this dear conjunction
> Plant neighborhood and Christian-like accord
> In their sweet bosoms, that never war advance
> His bleeding sword 'twixt England and fair France. (5.2.348–55)[11]

Here the play invokes an early modern commonplace, that the exchange of women through diplomatic marriage ensures amity and peace between contentious realms, calling attention to women's significance in mediating the relationships between competing state projects and agendas. In particular, it is the capacity to produce heirs who unite the blood of two monarchical lines that figures centrally in the play's projection of future peace achieved through diplomatic matrimonial exchange. Indeed, it is only through such reproduction, Charles's speech suggests, that such peace can be made permanent.

Yet, Shakespeare seems acutely aware that this projection is fallacious, for the play's projected future of unity is displaced by the Elizabethan retrospective awareness of the collapse of this unity under the reign of the happy couple's issue, Henry VI. In the context of this awareness, it is perhaps not so surprising that Katherine is depicted in this play as ambiguous in her responses to Henry's propositions, knowing he seeks her hand as a means of cementing his dominance over the newly conquered French territory.[12] As Henry attempts to persuade Katherine to pledge her love for him, Shakespeare's deft handling of their interactions brings into sharp relief the vulnerability of women in such circumstances, obliged to marry out of political and filial duty, and stages the impossibility of forcing women's affection despite the male desire to rhetorically transform martial conquest into marital harmony.

In the unfolding drama of the play, Katherine resists Henry's advances and retains her autonomy from him despite the male characters' assertions that women's will is easily overcome once they enter the marriage bed. In the context of assurances that she will become pliant, Katherine herself offers only noncommittal responses to Henry's propositions and assertions, repeating various permutations of "I cannot tell wat is dat" (5.2.177). Resisting his demand that she confess her love for him and commit to the marriage, she asks, "Is it possible that I sould love de ennemie of France?" (5.2.169–70), and later tells him that it is for her father to decide—what contents him will content her (5.2.247–50). She thereby acknowledges that she has no voice in the negotiations, but insists on her fealty to her father, resisting the offer to realign her loyalties and reasserting her national allegiance. In depicting her as a tool of male power mongering, the play's attention to the unwillingness of the princess to express or enact feelings of affection suggests that resistant agency remains viable in the face of political inevitabilities. Indeed, we might ask whether perhaps Shakespeare intended to represent the failure of the diplomatic methods enacted here—which neither transform Katherine's perceptions nor produce the long-term stability so optimistically predicted by the male monarchical figures.

Shakespeare's ambivalent representation of male conquest has suffered from scholarly misreading and from filmic alteration, both because we have a soft spot for the notion that "love conquers all," and because we still believe, in some fundamental way, that women gain power through their sexual appeal—a belief that reinforces gender stereotypes and limits the ways in which we can recognize and understand challenges to those stereotypes. In Shakespeare's depiction of Katherine, her refusal to succumb to Henry's blandishments, and her later explicit recognition of the performativity of Henry's passion ("Your majesty 'ave fausse French enough to deceive de most sage demoiselle dat is en France" [5.2.218–19]) allow her to retain a sense of autonomy and resistance to Henry's scripted attempts to exact a pledge of love. In fact, the play reverberates with the reality of martial/marital conflict. When Henry turns to the Duke of Burgundy for advice on how to win Katherine over, Burgundy characterizes "maids" as needing to become accustomed to the notion of "handling" (5.2.306–11), suggesting a parallel between the recalcitrance of Katherine and of France, and indicating that the resistance Henry has encountered immediately following his conquest will naturally dissipate in time. The French king puts this relationship in more strikingly martial terms, stating that his cities, like his daughter, are "girdled with maiden walls" but are now subject to the will of their conqueror, thereby emphasizing the symbolic nature of the diplomatic marriage (5.2.21–22). However, in the context of this play's invocation of England's unsuccessful future anterior [Chorus/Epilogue following Act 5, 1–14], Shakespeare suggests that Henry stands to gain neither her love nor France's, despite the characters' articulations of masculine certainty about the power of the "sword."

This suggestion resonates with the actual unfolding of history, in that diplomatic marriages had historically done little to mitigate the long-term imperialist tensions between nations. Shakespeare's play is saturated, in these closing scenes, with the realities of such failure, and despite its apparent romanticization of the royal marriage, the play not only leaves the tension between Katherine and Henry unresolved, but retrospectively projects a dire future for their son, King Henry VI of England and France. This future was part of the contentious past that was reshaped and in effect resolved, not by this marriage, but by Katherine's *remarriage* after the death of her first English husband, against the will of the protectorate that had actively attempted to render her reproductive royal body politically unavailable.

The Desiring Dowager Queen

This same Katherine is featured in Michael Drayton's 1597 *Englands Heroicall Epistles,* a series of pairs of fictive letters between historically important lovers. In this pair of letters, Katherine writes to the clerk of the wardrobe in her son's court, Owen Teuther or Tudor, expressing her passion for him and inviting him to woo her despite the difference in their social positions. Introducing her exchange with Owen, Drayton describes Katherine as "*the dowager of England and Fraunce, daughter to* Charles *the French king, holding her estate with* Henrie *her son*ne . . . [who] falleth in love with Owen Tudor, a Welshman, a brave and gallant Gentleman of the Wardrobe to the young King her son . . ." ("The Argument"). Drayton is thus acutely sensitive to the complexities of the relative sites of power associated with Katherine.

In Katherine's letter to Owen, as Drayton scripts it, love is the impetus to her rational action, through which the trajectory of royal succession is transformed, and the divisions of the royal family overcome. His version of the story offers an alternative to the chronicles' negative representation of Katherine's physical and emotional desires and redeems passion as a positive aspect of human agency, overturning the simplistic view of passion as a feminine weakness and the negative opposite of male rational capability. Drayton also calls attention to the question of national memory, reminding his readers that France has been centrally a part of English history—a history consistently rewritten in the period as patriarchal and purely English. When Drayton wrote this epistolary exchange, the Tudor line depicted in these accounts was on the wane and the succession remained unresolved. Drayton seems ironic in his handling of the history of English succession, suggesting through this series of letters that there is little virtue or purity in the English line, and that the myth of continuity is fallacious.[13] Katherine's role helps to elucidate this irony.[14]

Written a few years before Shakespeare's play, Drayton's *Heroicall Epistles* picks up Katherine's story several years after the play ends, and after the death of Henry V, with the widowed queen Katherine attempting to retain her autonomy despite the strictures imposed on her by the protectorate who effectually ruled England in the name of her son, the boy-king Henry VI. In her own historical moment, as the widow of the powerful Henry, and with her many connections to European royalty, Katherine was not considered innocuous. Because Katherine was still of reproductive age, there was a fear among the controlling members of the nobility that she might marry again and establish an alternate line of succession. To mitigate this threat, a bill was passed in the Parliament of 1427–28, prohibiting a queen dowager from marrying *without the king's consent,* with the restrictive additional caveat that the king's permission could only be granted *once he had reached his majority.*[15] Since the bill was written when the king was only six years old, Katherine would be past child-bearing age by the time she could gain permission to wed.

The legal mechanisms through which her disruptive potential was reined in signal a sharp awareness of the value of royal women's reproductive capability as a vector through which male members of the nobility might imagine and enact their fantasies of upward mobility and political self-promotion. In this case, while Hall and Holinshed attribute the marriage to Katherine's self-interest and lack of self-control, Drayton identifies both personal passion and political ambition as elements of Katherine's desire. These desires were realized when, despite the statute prohibiting this action, Katherine did remarry in secret, some time in 1431 or 1432. Her husband was Owen Tudor, as Hall and Holinshed note, and she bore him three sons—Jasper, one unnamed, and Edmond, who would marry Margaret Beaufort and produce Henry Tudor, who became Henry VII and the first Tudor king. This marriage between the French royal heir and a Welsh mercenary soldier restored the ancient British bloodline by linking it to the French royal line, and reconfigured the English succession, producing a branch of heirs who returned to the main branch through subsequent marriages.

Drayton's invocation of blood-right, passion, and resistance to royal decrees had a significant sixteenth-century analogue in John Dudley's failed attempt to circumvent Henry VIII's will determining the succession, supplant the claim of Mary Tudor (Henry's daughter), and secure the throne for the descendents of the Seymour line, Lady Jane Grey and her husband Guildford Dudley. He commemorates this attempt to reconfigure the succession through "heroical epistles" between Lady Jane and Guildford. Drayton was writing in the late years of Elizabeth's reign, fully aware that in the first decade of that reign a second attempt had been made to lay claim to the succession through marriage into the Seymour line. When Jane's sister Catherine wed Edward Seymour, Earl of Hereford, early in Elizabeth's reign, Catherine could readily be configured as a viable vessel for masculine political desire, and this is how Elizabeth I read Catherine's and Edward's unapproved marriage.[16] Although he was perhaps not bold enough to create a pair of letters between the still-living Edward Seymour and the deceased Catherine, Drayton's inclusion of letters between Charles Brandon and Mary Tudor and between Guildford Dudley and Jane Grey emphasizes the legitimacy of the Seymour line and its viability for the Elizabethan succession, despite the queen's draconian exclusion of them from the line of succession in direct opposition to her father's will.

Drayton's epistolary tract calls attention to this legitimacy, not only through expositions on lineage and equivocations about the role of human law and action in the face of providential determinism, but also through resonances between these other pairs of letters and those of Katherine de Valois and Owen Tudor. As the late-Tudor political world surely knew, the 1536 Act of Parliament that prohibited marriage without monarchical approval, which Elizabeth invoked to deny the legitimacy of the marriage between Catherine Grey and Edward Seymour, had a parallel in the statute passed in the sixth year of the reign of Henry VI, explicitly prohibiting Katherine's marriage. If the offspring of the Grey-Seymour marriage were illegitimate under this act, as Elizabeth insisted, then she herself and all of the Tudors were also illegitimate, descendants of a monarch (Henry VII) whose own father was born of a marriage that was legally proscribed. Drayton's epistolary reiterations of these parallels render his *Heroicall Epistles* a pointed critique of Elizabethan succession policy and a reconfiguration of the relationship between female desire and political intervention.

Drayton exonerates Lady Jane of any political motives in her marriage, and Elizabeth I had similarly presumed that Catherine Grey was merely a pawn in the political machinations of her husband and his family. However, in representing Katherine de Valois's resistance to the protectorate's attempt to control her reproductive potential, Drayton chooses to portray her as driven by passion *and* personal political ambition. These desires are *hers,* not Tudor's. As she communicates her desires to Tudor, she lays claim to three kingdoms (presumably France, England, and Scotland) and invokes her royal connections, asserting their ongoing viability and value: "Nor these great titles vainely will I bring, / Wife, daughter, mother, sister to a King" (65–66). Yet, she privileges Owen above all these relations, assuring him that "Of Grandsire, Father, Husband, Sonne, and Brother, / More thou alone to mee, then all the other" (67–68). As Drayton represents her, Katherine assures Owen that their marriage will not constitute a transgression against the "Gaunt-borne great Lancastrian line" (70), an assurance that relies on the historical memory of her son's resuscitation of the Lancastrian claim through Edmund's marriage to Margaret. While both the Stuart and the Seymour lines were traceable back to this Welsh-French alliance, the living issue of the Seymour union, disenfranchised and disinherited by Elizabeth, retained the relatively pure heritage of this line, less "diluted" by Scottish and even additional French blood, and thus more directly traceable back to this French-Welsh alliance and to the militaristic potential it represented. Drayton's fictive letters thus offer a pointed commentary on Elizabethan politics drawn from the very grounding union of the Tudor line.

In reasserting the Seymour claim, Drayton differs significantly from the earlier Tudor chroniclers. Praising both Owen's "nature and . . . grace," but more importantly identifying him as "a man brought forth and come of the noble lineage, and ancient line of Cadwalader, the last king of the Britons" (185), Hall attributes to Katherine's Welshman ancestral British royalty and identifies him with the Welsh mythic tradition that foretells of a heroic son of Cadwalader who would return again to rule. By locating both the royalty of the Tudor line and its ancestral virtues in the person of Owen Tudor, mercenary soldier and household clerk, Hall effectively effaces Katherine from the royal line, despite her validity. He also negates her value as a woman—that is, he negates her *chastity*—by attributing this marriage to her lust and suggesting that because it was done out of "private" interest it constituted a blow to her honor. He does so, however, in the context of making a distinction between *her* failure to heed the advice of others or to adhere to the legal prohibitions against her marriage, on the one hand, and her selection of a mere household clerk who turns out to be the mythic descendant of the Briton's last true king, on the other. For Hall, she is thus wed by her own choice to a man whose natural nobility overrides the taint of her unrestrained desire and collapsed chastity, and we can see the mythical inevitability of the "return of the king" in this depiction of their union.

Finally, we see in Hall the conflicted sixteenth-century view of usurpation. He depicts Henry IV's usurpation of the throne as ultimately fruitless and centrally the cause of a vastly destructive and disruptive battle for power among the lines of the English nobility, calling him "the first aucthor of this division" (title page). However, there was always the recognition of a providential hand at work, even in the overthrow of a legitimate monarch. In this case, Henry IV's divisive claim is also the means through which England gained access to Katherine through Henry's son, bringing her into England and making her available to Owen, the bearer of the true, if suppressed, royalty of the ancient Britons. Such histories emphasize the indecipherability of the overarching "divine plan," relying for comfort on the notion that "god works in mysterious ways." Hall in effect offers a revisionary history in which Welsh purity and nobility rectify the wandering line of succession, returning England to its proper course.

In Drayton's *Heroicall Epistles,* we find a very different depiction of this marriage, but there are resonances with Hall's interest in Wales. Emphasizing Katherine's French heritage and legitimate association with England through Henry V and Henry VI, Drayton presents her as a queen in love "*with . . . a Welshman, a brave and gallant Gentleman of the Wardrobe to the young King her sonne*" ("The Argument"). Where Hall and Holinshed see a woman succumbing to her baser nature, falling through her unchaste desire into the arms of an heir to the ancient royalty of Britain, Drayton sees a royal widow, daughter, and mother to kings, in love with a gentleman of virtue—but only a gentleman nonetheless. The widowed queen is, according to Drayton's introduction, driven to broach the subject of love by fears that the nobility will try to thwart her, and that without assurances of his success, the man she has selected will be reluctant to take the initiative. Katherine must overcome three kinds of patriarchal resistance—that of the French royal family, who would wish her to marry an equal, that of the English nobility who wish to keep her in check, and that of her lover, who might be discouraged by his social inferiority to her. Owen's lack of nobility is thus a central issue for Drayton.

Drayton's epistle acknowledges Katherine's powerful agency and determination in the context of her attempted subjugation by the nobility and implies that, seen retrospectively, she is a more significant tool in the trajectory of history than the men who tried to control her. Even more importantly, her passion is the mechanism through which history fulfills itself, so that her active pursuit of love can be understood not merely as a form of lost control and failed rationality, as in the chronicles, but as a deliberate enactment of will and reason. His depiction of her works in direct contradiction of the chronicle depictions—where they see a destabilizing force reined in by the power of a mythically predicated, inevitable trajectory, he sees a self-controlled and rational agent of historical development, whose will is vitally important in shaping events. As Drayton tells it, the French line remains vital and active, centrally a part of English monarchical identity.

Thus, although Drayton's introduction describes Katherine as denying her superiority to Owen, in the letter she repeatedly insists on it, and in the context of claiming to approach him as a supplicant, she asserts her inherent and bequeathed authority over him, thereby retaining her political potency in the pursuit of the match. For instance, she admonishes him not to

> think less virtue in this royal hand,
> Which now entreats, that wonted to command,
> For in this sort, though humbly now it woo,
> The day hath been, thou would have kneeled unto. (3–6)

She cautions him, "Nor thinke that this submission of my state, / Proceeds from frailtie, (rather judge it fate)" (7–8). She parallels her condition of self-abasement to that of Alcides, Phoebus, and Jove, all of whom submit to love by disguising their greatness, and in the process either retain or gain power. Moreover, in the context of this empowerment through submission, she reasserts her power over Owen, reminding him, "He was thy King, that sued for love to mee, / Shee is thy Queene that sues for love to thee" (15–16). She then draws explicit parallels between the strength of her affection for Owen and for her deceased husband, suggesting the exchangeability of men in an emotional economy geared to the preservation of her own royal value.

That value is also predicated on her claims to fidelity to her first husband, voiced through her references to her emotional commitment in that marriage, thereby highlighting her chastity. As she tells Owen, "When *Henry* was, what's *Tudors* now, was his; / Whilst yet thou art, what's *Henries, Tudors* is" (17–18). This depiction of "successive" love refutes other writers' suggestions that she is given over to lust and unchaste desire. It legitimates her passion by arguing that her love, which was once Henry's, is bequeathed to Owen by her deceased husband himself, and that in effect she is experiencing a revival of her earlier love, not a change of affection: "My love to Owen, him my Henry giveth, / My love to Henry, in my Owen liveth" (19–20). In effect, Drayton draws on the theory of the "king's two bodies" to establish an analogy between the eternal nature of monarchical power and the eternal nature of love, both of which transcend the limitations of the mortal body of the monarch. Katherine then extends this self-legitimating assertion, legitimating *Owen* through her love, by suggesting that the two of them have always been linked through Henry: "Onely in Henry, was my Tudor then, / Onely in Tudor, Henry now agen" (21–22). Here, Drayton works to rewrite Katherine as a woman of constancy and devotion and as the figure who serves as a link between the past and the future. He thereby suggests that she is the vector through which the glory of the conquering heroic King Henry V is reborn in the adult Owen, in effect circumventing her own son, Henry VI.

Drayton, acutely aware of Katherine's negative value in the chronicles, labors to establish her chastity and purity, her constancy, and her rational passion. He asserts her French heritage as equal to English heritage in value, as she argues that the French, as much as the English, are descendants of the gods (73–74) and proclaims herself to be "Not onely *Henries* Queene, but boast aswell, / To be the childe of *Charles* and *Isabell*" (83–84). He also gives her an argument that links French and Welsh martial power and poses it against England's claims, as she insists, "Our famous Grandsires (as their owne) bestrid, / That horse of fame, that *Jove*-begotten steed" (79–80).

Despite his attention to the importance of Katherine's French heritage in English monarchical succession, however, Drayton also explicitly situates her as the reviver of Welshness, which is in effect a revival of the bloodline and power of ancient Britain. She insists on the royal viability of Owen's line, given legitimacy through the marriages of daughters of King John and Edmund Longshanks to Welshmen of princely descent.[17] Drayton also asserts other elements of the ancient connection, arguing in Katherine's voice,

> And Wales as well as haughty England boasts,
> Of Camilot, and all her Penticosts;
> A nephews room in great *Pendragons* race,
> At *Arthurs* Table held a princely place,
> . . .
> If these our auncient Chronicles be true,
> They altogether are not free from you. (91–98)

For Drayton, as for the chroniclers, Katherine's love and wooing of Owen lead the way to a return of the kings of Wales, to whom England legitimately belongs, but the assurances of Welsh legitimacy come at the expense of the exclusivity of mythic English claims. In the context of the sixteenth-century collapse of England's claims in France, Drayton uses Katherine's mythological invocations to establish the martial force of Wales, and to suggest that if England could temporarily conquer France ("If of the often conquests of our Land, / They reare the spoyles of their victorious hand" [95–96]), Wales nevertheless retained the power to conquer England. She then recounts the history of Welsh victories over the English:

> When bloody *Rufus* sought your utter sack,
> Twice entring Wales, yet twice was beaten back.
> When famous Cambria wash'd her in the flood,
> Made by th' effusion of the English blood;
> And oft return'd with glorious victorie,
> From Worster, Herford, Chester, Shrewsbury,
> Whose power, in every conquest so prevails,
> As once expuls'd the English out of Wales. (99–106)

Drayton thereby suggests that martial conquest alone has not suppressed the royal right of Wales or implicitly of France, and that both hold the potential to return to their former positions of dominance. In short, the linking of the French line, which embodies royal greatness parallel to that of the gods, with the Welsh, which embodies the pure blood of ancient Britain, offers a foundation for English monarchy that is more powerful than that of mere royal legitimacy. For Drayton, Katherine's legitimacy as a French and an English queen authorizes her pursuit of Owen Tudor, through which she resuscitates the ancient British line.

While Drayton's epistle privileges Wales as the root of English identity, and works on one level to undo the "foreign" national identity of Henry VII, the French elements of the Tudor line remain active in this account. Through this means, the purity of English royal lines is called into question, as the tensions between French, English, and Welsh are made visible. Drayton's view of historical development is chaotic and competitive, suggesting that all outcomes are transitory and all futures possible. For Drayton, without passion as the impetus to action—chaste, virtuous, and pursued through logical, reasoned means—the Tudor era would not have occurred. If the invocation of Katherine's "passion and lust" in the chronicles serves to negate her value and legitimacy as a royal figure, Drayton foregrounds her heritage and agency, depicting a moment of history in which passion supports a resistance to patriarchy, serves as the basis of new alliances, and instigates political transformation. Given the poem's invocation of Welsh and French martial potential, Drayton also cautions that no conquest, treaty, or succession can be understood as the "end of history."

Notes

1. The most important study of these processes is Richard Helgerson, *Forms of Nationhood: The Elizabethan Writing of England* (Chicago and London: University of Chicago Press, 1992).

2. A return to the gallery in 2006 reveals that the notes have been altered since my previous visit in 2004 and now include mention of Margaret.

3. The wooing scene between Henry and Katherine was also included in the earlier *The Famous Victories of Henry the Fifth* (London: printed by Thomas Creede, 1598).

4. I take the earliest possible date of Henry V as 1599, given recent analyses of the play's topical references. Drayton's *Englands Heroicall Epistles* were first published in 1597, expanded and republished in 1598 and in numerous subsequent editions. I have referred to the Bodleian Library copy from *Early English Books Online: Englands Heroicall Epistles*, 1597, printed at London by James Roberts for N. Ling, STC (2nd ed.) / 7193. SCT/218. 10. Hereafter, Drayton is cited in text by line numbers where applicable. Drayton's own alterations of the text for some later editions appear to reflect concerns about the reception of what I take to be his sympathies with the Seymour faction, after the accession to

the English throne of James I. Drayton is frequently depicted as a supporter of the Stuart succession, but I mean to suggest here that this apparent support was a late and strategic development.

5. An important analysis of the place of Calais in Elizabeth's marriage negotiations can be found in Jonathan Baldo, "Wars of Memory in *Henry V*," *Shakespeare Quarterly* 47, No. 2 (Summer, 1996): 132–59.

6. Edward Hall, *Hall's Chronicle* [1548, 1550] (London: n.p., 1809; rpt. New York: AMS Press Inc., 1965). Hereafter, Hall is cited in text.

7. This marriage is not confirmed by any documentation, but to my knowledge was not challenged in English materials of the period.

8. All references to Holinshed are taken from Raphael Holinshed's *Chronicles of England, Scotland, and Ireland*, ed. Henry Ellis (6 vols. 1807–8; rpt., New York: AMS Press Inc., 1965).

9. A final official transformation took the form of the redesign of the great seal to include Henry's new status and titles (Holinshed, 3.119).

10. Hall offers an extended refutation of those French writers who sought to negate Henry V's claim to France established by the treaty and the marriage, and then produces in full the speech delivered after the banquet, pp. 100–104. Also resonant here are concerns over demonstrable legitimacy and the uncertainty of the paternal line. Hall seems especially aware that the original Tudor claim to the throne was only tenuously legitimate, whereas Holinshed had the additional legitimacy problems of the Stuart and Seymour lines to deal with. Both, of course, were aware that Mary I and Elizabeth had been declared bastards and only later returned to the succession by statute. For an extended commentary on the problem of bastardy in Elizabethan literature and culture, see Michael Neill's *Putting History to the Question: Power, Politics, and Society in English Renaissance Drama* (New York: Columbia University Press, 2000), esp. chs. 5 and 6.

11. All references to *King Henry V* are from The Riverside Shakespeare, 2nd ed., ed. Herschel Baker et al. (Boston: Houghton Mifflin, 1997).

12. These issues are addressed in two important contemporary sources: Jean E. Howard and Phyllis Rackin, *Engendering a Nation: A Feminist Account of Shakespeare's English Histories* (London; New York: Routledge, 1997); and Katherine Eggert, "Nostalgia and the Not Yet Late Queen: Refusing Female Rule in *Henry V, English Literary History* 61, No. 3 (Autumn, 1994): 523–50.

13. Drayton may be following Holinshed here. Holinshed consistently refutes the notion of a continuous chain of English succession, and although he promotes monarchy as the "natural" form of government in England, he negates the notion of the three realms' inherent continuity, referring repeatedly to conquest and treaty as the mechanisms of "unity."

14. Richard F. Hardin offers a historicized reading of Drayton's historical verse in *Michael Drayton and the Passing of Elizabethan England* (Lawrence, Manhattan, Wichita: University of Kansas Press, 1973), 31–59.

15. This is the bill referred to only in passing in Hall and Holinshed.

16. Hertford was the great-grandson of Mary Tudor (Henry VIII's younger sister) and Charles Brandon, Duke of Suffolk. Jane was the eldest daughter, Catherine a younger daughter of Henry Grey and Francis Brandon, Mary and Charles's eldest daughter. Jane and Catherine were Mary Tudor's granddaughters, then, and the Catherine-Edward match

joined the granddaughter and great-grandson of Mary, whose heirs were designated successors to the throne by Henry VIII should his own line fail. Curtis Breight addresses Elizabeth's handling of the Hertford affair in "Realpolitik and Elizabethan Ceremony: The Earl of Hertford's Entertainment of Elizabeth at Elvetham, 1591," *Renaissance Quarterly* 45 (1992): 20–48. See also Jean R. Brink's *Michael Drayton Revisited* (Boston: G. K. Hall, 1990), 38–65.

17. Drayton's historical note explains that "*Lhewellin,* or *Leolin ap Iorwerth,* married *Ioan,* daughter to King *Iohn*" and "*Lhewellin ap Grypheth* married *Ellinor,* daughter to *Simon Mountfort* Earle of Leicester, and Cosin to *Edward Longshankes,* both which *Lhewellins* were Princes of Wales" (39).

10. Warning Elizabeth with Catherine de' Medici's Example

Anne Dowriche's French Historie *and the Politics of Counsel*

MIHOKO SUZUKI

Anne Dowriche's *The French Historie* (1589), a verse adaptation and elaboration of three episodes from a French prose chronicle by Jean de Serres, translated into English by Thomas Timme, was published during a period that saw many publications of English translations of French pamphlets, such as Michel Hurault's *A Discourse Upon the Present State of France* (1588), *The Contre Guyse* (1589), and Philippe de Mornay's *A Letter Written by a French Catholicke Gentleman* (1589).[1] J. H. M. Salmon has demonstrated the pervasive influence of the French religious wars on political thought in England during the Elizabethan period and throughout the seventeenth century.[2] Perhaps because of the gender of its author, Salmon does not include Dowriche's work in his 1959 list of twenty-seven texts published during 1589; yet it clearly participates in the conversation concerning the French political situation, with implications for England and its relationship to Catholic France. Published when the accession of Henri de Navarre in France encouraged hope for the Protestant cause, the year after the English defeat of the Armada, two years after the execution of Mary Queen of Scots, and three years after the death of Philip Sidney in battle against the Spanish in the Netherlands, *The French Historie,* I suggest, asks to be read as a work of political commentary.[3]

Dowriche was born into a family whose members were prominent landowners and Members of Parliament (MPs) in southwest England, beginning with her great-grandfather Sir Richard Edgecombe, who was Henry VII's controller of the household as well as a personal friend of the monarch. Her grandfather Sir Peter, a knight and sheriff, accompanied Henry VIII against

France, and was an associate of Cardinal Cromwell. Her father, another Sir Richard, who was, according to the Oxford *DNB,* "one of the most respected figures in the southwest," earned a reputation as a poet. Her brother, Pearse, to whom she dedicated *The French Historie,* was an active puritan MP who was returned to eight Parliaments from 1555 to 1593. During Pearse's lifetime, the family suffered financial decline; even so, his son, Anne's nephew, served as an MP well into the seventeenth century. Anne derived from her birth family a sense of entitlement to be involved in public life fostered over many generations, as well as an interest in poetry that her father cultivated. And the fact that the will of her grandfather, Sir Peter Edgecombe, granted his two younger sons £100 each and his daughter Anne £300, perhaps indicates that Dowriche's birth family did not value sons at the expense of daughters.[4]

Anne married Hugh Dowriche, a puritan preacher, and contributed to her husband's work, *The Iaylors Conversion* (1596); Micheline White discusses Anne and Hugh Dowriche's collaboration in their efforts to "promote Protestant doctrine and prevent political upheaval," noting correspondences between their works and arguing for the importance of the support of her husband for Dowriche's literary production.[5] I suggest, however, that because the publication of Anne's work preceded her husband's by seven years, and because she dedicated her *French Historie* to her brother, Pearse, asking for his "patronage" and "protection,"[6] she joins other contemporary women writers such as Isabella Whitney, who also dedicated *A Sweet Nosgay* (1573) to her brother Geoffrey, and Mary Sidney, whose most important literary relationship was with her brother, Philip. In these examples, brothers appear to have been enabling figures for the woman writer's authorial identity and practices. The appeal to and invocation of the brother at once marks the woman's place in an appropriately domestic relationship while gesturing toward the public world inhabited by the male sibling who functions as alter ego. Although the political theorist Carole Pateman and seventeenth-century English writers, both male and female, such as John Webster and Aphra Behn, have shown how "fraternal patriarchy" can be as strict and controlling of the lives of women as conventional patriarchy, these writers invoke brothers as enabling surrogates.[7] Shakespeare's *Twelfth Night* indicates a similar understanding of how sisters can benefit from the presence (and absence) of brothers: Viola cross-dresses as a young man and seeks service in Duke Orsino's household when she believes her twin brother Sebastian to have been shipwrecked. Shakespeare underscores their similarity by having Olivia, who initially falls in love with the cross-dressed Viola, happily accept Sebastian as her beloved.

In the case of Dowriche, whose brother was an MP, her dedication to him brings her work into the public realm, while affirming her own propriety as a sister under a brother's protection. The close identification of Dowriche with her brother is indicated in the way she includes her own name and her brother's in the couplet that introduces Dowriche's moral counsel to her brother to establish her own virtue and thus the legitimacy of her political counsel: "*The sharpest* EDGE *will soonest* PEARSE *and* COME *vnto* AN end. / Yet DOWT not, *but be* RICHE *in hope, and take that I doo send*" (A3). In what follows, the first letter of each line read vertically spells out his name (fig. 10.1). Moreover, the copy of *The French Historie* held by the Huntington Library includes on its title page a manuscript identification of "AD" as "Ann Dowriche," linking her name with "Peirse Edgcombe," thereby indicating that Dowriche's brother did indeed provide the impetus for the circulation of her work (fig. 10.2).

Elaine Beilin, the scholar most responsible for calling attention to the importance of Dowriche's work, has argued that the *French Historie* is concerned with the parliamentary controversy concerning free speech, juxtaposing Dowriche's text to parliamentary texts from the 1570s and 1580s.[8] I will suggest in this chapter that Dowriche participates in what John Guy called the "rhetoric of counsel in early modern England."[9] While Elizabeth stressed the limits of Parliament's authority to counsel in order to protect her sovereignty, the idioms of "counsel" that occur in More's *Utopia*, Elyot's *The Book Named the Governor*, and Book VIII of Richard Hooker's *Of the Laws of Ecclesiastical Polity* "underpin parliamentary debates of the 1560s, 1570s and 1580s concerning the queen's marriage and the Protestant succession of the throne."[10] The question of who is entitled to counsel and how was a vexed and volatile one during these years. Thomas Nicholls, "Citezeine and Goldesmyth of London," presented his 1550 folio translation of Thucydides to Edward VI as useful counsel for the monarch;[11] yet John Stubbs met the gruesome punishment of having his hand severed for arrogating to himself the right to advise the queen against the French match, and Philip Sidney was rusticated as a result of his letter to the queen containing the same advice. Elizabeth was shrewd and perspicacious in her own choice of counselors, elevating to that position both William Cecil, whose grandfather David Cecil came from a minor gentry family to become a burgess in parliament for Stamford, and William's son Robert Cecil (*DNB*, s.v.). Pierre Bourdieu states that gender and class contribute to the "status-linked right to politics," according to which an individual is authorized or called upon to acquire and express political competence.[12] I suggest that Dowriche, a granddaughter, daughter, and sister of MPs, uses strategic indirection to proffer counsel to Elizabeth through her authorship of the *French Historie*.[13]

PEARSE EDGECOMBE.

The ſharpeſt EDGE *will ſooneſt* PEARSE *and* COME *vnto* AN *end,*
Yet DOWT *not, but be* RICHE *in hope, and take that I doo ſend.*
A. D.

P PVt not your truſt in fading earth puft vp with fainting ſtaies;
Poſſeſſe the Lord, ſo ſhall you ſtill perſiſt in godlie waies.
E Exalt your eies from common ſhapes, eſteeme not of this pelfe;
Expreſſe in deeds what faith you haue, examine wel your ſelfe.
A As windes diſperſe the wau'ring chaffe, and toſſe it quite away;
All worldlie pompe ſhall ſo conſume, and paſſe without delay.
R Repleated oft with wandring change recount your life to be;
Remember wel, no bleſſed fruite remaines on curſed tree.
S So ſhal you trace the perfect path ſaluation to attaine;
So ſhal you ſee this glittering gloſe ſet out to be but vaine.

E EXtinguiſh then the carnal courſe exempted from aboue;
Expell the qualmes of fond delights, excell in godlie loue.
D Depart not from the liuing Lord, delight to read his word;
Delaie no time, for he doth ſtill defend vs with the ſword.
G Giue to your God your ſoule & life, good gain inſues thereby;
Grieue not the Spirit that warneth you great dangers for to flie.
C Caſt all your care on him alone, care for no other praie,
Conſidering he your greateſt griefes can quicklie take awaie.
O Of all things lent vnto this life one thing accompt the beſt,
Onelie the truth & feare of God, on which our ſouls muſt reſt.
M Make no accompt of truſtles traſh, moleſting miſers minde;
Mark how theſe maskers oftẽtimes much care & ſorow finde.
B Beware betimes of had I wiſt; be not theſe pleaſures vaine?
Beleeue in Chriſt, and ſo you ſhall be ſure to liue againe.

A 3 To

Figure 10.1. From Anne Dowriche, *The French Historie,* 1589, RB 31353. This item is reproduced by permission of The Huntington Library, San Marino, California.

Only later in the seventeenth century do women such as Elinor James, a printer's widow who published many petitions to the Parliament and the monarchs of her day—Charles II, James II, William and Mary, Anne, and George I—explicitly construct themselves as counselors intervening publicly in political affairs.[14] Literary representation of women as counselors, however, can be found earlier in the century, in Aemilia Lanyer's calling atten-

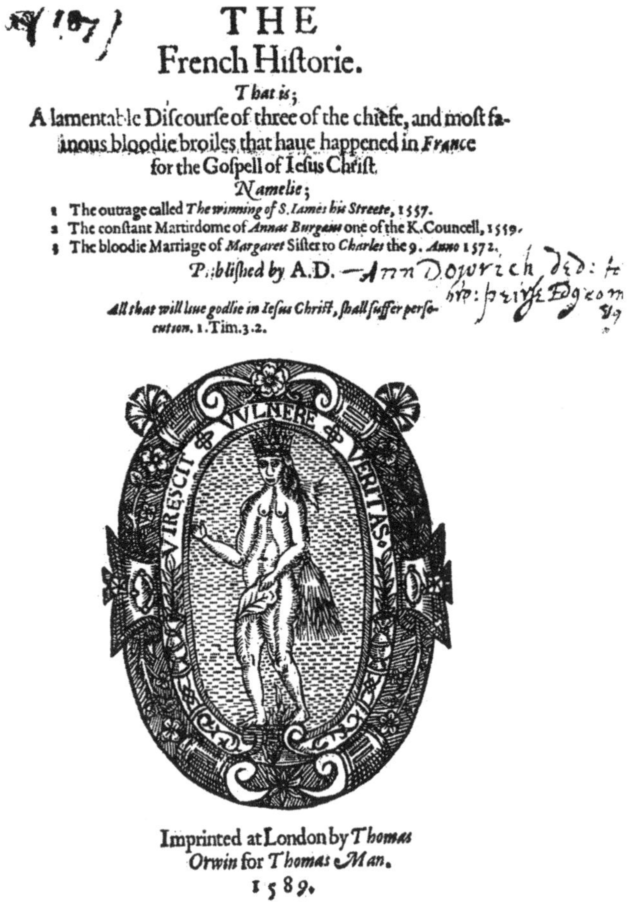

THE
French Hiſtorie.
That is;
A lamentable Diſcourſe of three of the chiefe, and moſt famous bloodie broiles that haue happened in *France* for the Goſpell of Ieſus Chriſt.
Namelie;
1 The outrage called *The winning of S. Iames his Streete*, 1557.
2 The conſtant Martirdome of *Annas Burgaus* one of the K. Councell, 1559.
3 The bloodie Marriage of *Margaret* Siſter to *Charles* the 9. *Anno* 1572.
Publiſhed by A.D.
All that will liue godlie in Ieſus Christ, ſhall ſuffer perſecution. 1.Tim.3.2.

VIRESCIT VULNERE VERITAS

Imprinted at London by *Thomas Orwin* for *Thomas Man.*
1589.

Figure 10.2. From Anne Dowriche, *The French Historie,* 1589, RB 31353. This item is reproduced by permission of The Huntington Library, San Marino, California.

tion in *Salve Deus Rex Judaeorum* (1611) to Pilate's wife as a wise counselor whose advice concerning the disposition of Christ Pilate failed to heed, and in Elizabeth Cary's representation in *Tragedie of Mariam* (1613) of Salome as an evil counselor to her brother Herod, one who exhorts him to execute his innocent wife Mariam. In *A Mouzell for Melastomus* (1617), Rachel Speght claims that one of the duties of women is "to give good councell unto her husband, the which he must not despise," giving the examples of Abraham and Sarah, Pilate and his wife, and others.[15]

Although Dowriche was writing before these examples of literary and actual female counselors, she could have been familiar with the example of Christine de Pizan, whose *Book of Faytes and Arms and of Chyvalrye* was translated and published by William Caxton in 1489. In the epilogue, Caxton indicates that Henry VII commissioned him to translate and publish the work so that "euery gentylman born to armes & all manere men of werre . . . captayns / souldiours / . . . & all other shold haue knowlege how they ought to behaue theym in the fayttes of warre & of bataylles / . . . for certayn in myn oppinyon it is as necessary a boke & as requysite / as ony may be for euery estate hye & lowe that entende to the fayttes of werre."[16] Although the title pages of these works do not carry Christine's name, the texts prominently include references by Christine to herself as author, references that call attention to her gender. If Dowriche's great-grandfather was a close associate of Henry VII and her grandfather accompanied Henry VIII on his military expeditions, it is reasonable to expect that this work by Christine might have been available and known to Dowriche.

Dowriche's interest in counselors is evident in her focus on the courageous speech of Annas Burgaeus as a counselor to Henri II, though he was condemned to death for it. Beilin has pointed out the homology between the names of the protagonist and author, Annas and Anne (the French version of Annas's name is Anne; and in fact at the conclusion of her poem, Dowriche signs herself as "Anna"). Gaspard de Coligny, also featured in the *French Historie* as a prominent victim of the St. Bartholomew's Day Massacre, was a counselor to Charles IX who advised him to intervene in the Netherlands but was murdered by Guise with the connivance of the king. In the *French Historie,* even after he has been wounded he gives counsel to the king:

> For though that I doo lie heere wounded as you see,
> The chiefest treason they intend is not alone to me:
> But to your noble Grace, whose death they daily craue,
> Whose life by treason long ere this, & now desire to haue.
> . . .
> God grant you see in time your frends from fleeting foe,
> That still in safetie you may reigne deuoide of griefe and woe. (22v)

Jean de Serres's *Lyfe* of Coligny also emphasizes Coligny's wisdom in counseling the king on matters both domestic and diplomatic.[17] He notes that Coligny was of a "noble and renowmed howse" that possessed "right of souereintie" (Aiiv–Aiii). Dowriche's own family could be described in these terms, and her focus on these counselors suggests that Dowriche, despite her gender, is signaling her intent to proffer counsel to Elizabeth.

Yet she avoids the fate of Annas and Coligny (or the fate of John Stubbs and his printer) by refracting her political writing through the subject matter of her work, the French history, and by basing it on a chronicle by Serres, translated by Timme. Although Dowriche's work is not, strictly speaking, a translation, she aimed at the protection that many publishers sought by publishing translations.[18] In addition, by deploying the literary device of channeling her discourse through two male speakers, she succeeded in avoiding both censorship and punishment.

I have elsewhere discussed the ways in which the example of Elizabeth appears to have enabled female authors and women's political intervention during the Jacobean period and throughout the seventeenth century.[19] Previous scholars of Dowriche have apparently been reluctant to acknowledge her critique of Elizabeth due, perhaps, to the proximity of the categories of "woman writer" and "female monarch." In fact, the striking device on the title and final pages—the figure of naked truth wearing a crown with "scourges at her back" (38), surrounded by the Latin motto "virescit vulnere veritas" (truth grows strong at the wound; truth flourishes through injury)—can be read as an emblematic conflation of female monarch and female writer (figs. 10.2 and 10.3). Yet this emblem can also be read as indicating the superiority of persecuted truth over the censoring authority, especially given the recent terrible punishment of Stubbs. The verse commentary accompanying the emblem on the final page calls attention to the difference in social hierarchy and power between Truth and her adversaries, contrasting Truth "devoid of worldlie weeds" and those "who thinke they swim in wealth," though in fact they are "wretched, poore & vile." Dowriche ends the poem and her work itself with the defiant couplet: "Yet no despite or paine can cause hir cease; / She wounded, springs; bedecks with crown of Peace," recalling Annas Burgaeus' rhetorical question to Henri II: "If *Truth* do conquere Kings; if *Truth* do conquere al?" (11v). In keeping with both readings of the emblem, Dowriche is critical of Elizabeth because she contested Elizabeth's policies, yet her critique is complicated by her gendered authorial identity and her identification with Elizabeth as a female monarch. Her ambivalent representation of Catherine de' Medici as an effective architect of the St. Bartholomew Day's Massacre functions as a demonized double of Elizabeth as a female monarch.

Randall Martin has shown that Dowriche used Innocent Gentillet's *Contra Machiavell* to represent Catherine de' Medici as a Machiavellian ruler.[20] Significantly, the English translation of Henri Estienne's *A Mervaylovs Discourse Vpon the Lyfe, Deedes, and Behauiours of Katherine de Medicis, Queene Mother* (1575) presents not only an indictment of Catherine but also an ex-

Veritie purtraied by the French Pilgrime.

FRom Seate ſupernall of cœleſtiall Icue
Deſcended Truth, *deuoid of worldlie weed;*
And with the brightneſſe of her beames ſhe ſtroue
Gainſt Sathan, Sinne, & Adams *fleſhlie Seed;*
Reproouing wrongs, bewailing worldlings need;
Who thinke they ſwim in wealth (blinded by guile):
Yet wanting Truth; *are wretched, poore & vile.*

The World reproou'd; in rage attempts hir wracke,
Sathan aſsiſts, malicious Men deuiſe
Torments for Truth, *binde ſcourges at hir backe,*
Exclaime againſt hir with blaſphemous cries;
Condemning hir, exalting earthlie lies:
Yet no deſpite or paine can cauſe hir ceaſe;
She wounded, ſprings; bedeckt with crowne of Peace.

FINIS.

Figure 10.3. From Anne Dowriche, *The French Historie,* 1589, RB 31353. This item is reproduced by permission of The Huntington Library, San Marino, California.

tended diatribe against women's rule. The French original was used to indict the female rule of Marie de Medicis in the seventeenth century and Marie Antoinette in the eighteenth century.[21] While François Hotman's political treatise *Francogallia* (1573, 1576, 1583), which includes a more dispassionately presented chapter on "Whether under Francogallican law women are not as much excluded from the government of the kingdome as they are from inheriting it," was not translated in its entirety until the eighteenth century, Estienne's *Mervaylovs Discourse,* which purports to be about Catherine, had been translated and published, despite the lengthy disquisition against gynocracy and its implications for Elizabeth's rule.[22]

Estienne's tract exemplifies the use of Catherine to warn against the ills of woman's rule in general, but Dowriche, in her work, which represents the male sovereigns Henry and Charles as far from ideal, clearly does not intend her representation of Catherine to indicate a disapproval of female rule. Rather, Catherine very effectively exhorts "the King and other of her bloodie counsaile" (23v) to launch the massacre, so that she is cast in the role of an evil counselor, manipulated by Satan and following the tenets of Machiavelli, rather than a ruler in her own right. At the same time, the similarities between Catherine's speech and Elizabeth's addresses to Parliament and to her troops on the eve of the Armada only the year before are inescapable:

> Plucke vp therefore your sprites, and play your manlie parts,
> Let neither feare nor faith preuaile to dant your warlike harts.
> What shame is this that I (a woman by my kinde)
> Neede thus to speake, or passe you men in valure of the mind?
> For heere I doo protest, if I had bene a man;
> I had my selfe before this time this murder long began. (24)

Thomas Deloney's 1588 ballad, *The Queenes Visiting of the Campe at Tilsburie With Her Entertainment There* attests to the currency of Elizabeth's speech to the troops.[23] Geoffrey Fenton's 1569 *Discourse* on the French civil wars had included a very similar account of Catherine addressing the soldiers in Limoges: "she visited the battels & squadrons of his horsmen one after an other, perswading them to omitte no duetie, to continue their seruice to his maiesty."[24]

Catherine, like Elizabeth, who emphasized her woman's body but also her "heart and stomach of a king" in addressing her troops at Tilbury, calls attention to her female gender in appealing to their masculine courage. Yet unlike Elizabeth who vowed to lead and protect her people, Catherine, like Lady Macbeth, taunts the king and his "trustie mates" (23) for being less manly than she is. In having Catherine recall Elizabeth in this way, while representing her as an emasculating "woman on top," Dowriche represents Catherine as one who oversteps her role as counselor as well as transgresses gender boundaries.[25]

Despite these distinctions between Catherine and Elizabeth that would appear to contrast them as anti-types, it is nevertheless difficult to escape the similarities between them, especially in light of the similarity of their effectiveness as orators. As in the cases of Shakespeare's Joan of Arc and Spenser's Radigund, characters created by contemporaries of Dowriche and apparent anti-types to Elizabeth, the distinction between type and anti-type becomes difficult to maintain. The proximity in the representations of Elizabeth and Catherine points also to a political proximity of which Dowriche would be critical: Elizabeth's government sought to preserve an alliance with the Catholic monarchy of France, engaging in lengthy negotiations over the proposed match with Alençon, which began in 1572, the year of the St. Bartholomew's Day Massacre and the general persecution of the Protestants, and continued until 1579.[26] Maurice Wilkinson states that Elizabeth personally was not sympathetic to the Huguenots nor did she approve of rebellious subjects; in order to counterbalance the danger from Spain, she was determined to pursue an alliance with France, against popular sentiment in England, especially in the wake of St. Bartholomew. In this she was "aided by the influence of Catherine on the French side."[27]

In fact, Dowriche notably refrains from extensively praising or celebrating Elizabeth by contrast with the French monarchs; rather, in her conclusion, which immediately follows the extended and graphic description of the "bloodie and periuered" (33) Charles IX's horrible death, she indicates that she intends her *French Historie* as a monitory example, perhaps recalling the horrible way in which Herod's body disintegrates—literally rotting apart—in the Chester cycle.[28] Indeed, these lines from near the conclusion of Dowriche's *French Historie* closely resemble a passage of admonition from Stubbs's *Gaping Gulf*:

> The Lord grant *England* peace and mercie from aboue,
> That from the *Truth* no trouble may their fixed heart remoue
> With wished life and health Lord long preserue and keepe
> That Noble Queene *Elizabeth* chiefe Pastor of thy sheepe:
> And that she maie finde out, and hunt with perfect hate
> The Popish hearts of fained friends before it be too late:
> And that in wofull *France* the troubles that we see,
> To *England* for to shun the like, may now a warning be. (37v)

Here is the passage from Stubbs: "For the Lord's namesake, therefore, O Christian Queen Elizabeth, take heed to yourself and to the Church of Jesus Christ for which he shed his blood, and which he hath shielded under your royal defense; show yourself a zealous prince for God's gospel to the end; foresee, in a tender love to this people committed to your government, the continuance of the truth among them and their posterity."[29]

Dowriche casts the admonition as a prayer, but she strikingly interpellates Elizabeth as a shepherd and hence protector of her people and a determined "hunter" of Catholics. The urgency ("before it be too late") of her "warning" is in keeping with Donald Kelley's observation that the massacre had a traumatic effect, "haunt[ing] an entire generation of Protestants," causing them to suspect that it might be renewed at any time.[30]

As I indicated earlier, these lines are preceded by an account of Charles's gruesome death, where Dowriche explicitly inserts herself as speaker: "I briefely will repeate / The sentence of mightie God / gainst murder and deceate," and places the French king's death as an example of God's striking against "bloodie tyrants" from the Old Testament: "I read also of one *Aristobolus* by name, / Who hath for murder left behinde a blacke & bloodie fame" (35v). This page where Dowriche's biblical glosses multiply and surround the text (fig. 10.4) generalizes her point concerning the fate of evil rulers and gives her license to dilate on their destruction. Given the gender of the author, perhaps most notable is the case of Abimelech, who met his end when "from a womans hand a milstone downe was sent / From off a wall: which with the weight his brain pan al to rent" (35). Dowriche's representation of symbolic violence against the bodies of tyrants participates in what Natalie Zemon Davis has called the "rites of violence" of religious rioters who assumed the roles of "priest, pastor, and magistrate" and resorted to a "repertory of actions, derived from the Bible" because religious and/or political authorities were perceived to be failing in their duties.[31] Here the religious impulse combines with a political one; the violence works to purge the body politic of tyrannical surfeit and disease. These lines that immediately precede the address to Elizabeth follow accounts of tyrants and heroically resisting subjects—including the nameless "common hangman" of Lyon who refuses the king's directive to "defile [his] hands with guiltlesse blood" (32) and the soldiers who refuse orders to kill innocent prisoners. They thereby indicate the damage to the institution and prestige of the monarchy that the French civil wars have accomplished.[32]

The prospect of the French connection is precisely what led Philip Sidney and others to fear the rise of tyranny in England.[33] From Dowriche's own perspective and that of many of her contemporaries, the fate of Stubbs already inscribes the tyrant's wrath on the body of the subject. Yet as Michel Foucault has argued, the exercise of the monarch's overwhelming power can have unintended effects, eliciting sympathy for its victim.[34] The general support of Stubbs's position is indicated by the fact that the jury refused to convict him and the judge was imprisoned for refusing to charge him with conspiring to excite sedition. Stubbs was moreover vindicated by his continued and active presence in public life: he was returned as an MP serving on various parliamentary committees. Dowriche represents the rending of the subject's body by tyrants as a synecdoche for the dismemberment of the body politic

The French Hiſtorie.

Iudg.9.53.54 And after by his Page was thruſt vnto the heart
With ſword, leſt that a womãs ſtroke his glory ſhuld ſubuert.
As [a] *Triphon* did intrap with face of frendlie cheere
Good *Ionathan*, to whom he did a faithfull frend appeare:
So did he quicklie feele the weight of falſed word,
Who ſhortlie was by *Simon* [b] ſlaine, and iuſtlie put to ſword.
I read alſo of one [c] *Ariſtobolus* by name,
Who hath for murder left behinde a blacke & bloodie fame.
For firſt he did conſent with famine for to pine
His mother, for becauſe ſhe would the kingdome not reſigne.
And alſo was content by death to make away
Antigonus his brother deere, which was his owne decaie.
For when the deed was done, he felt a preſent griefe
In conſcience for ſo cruell act; which then without reliefe
Did dailie ſo torment his ſore afflicted hart,
That freſh remorſe did often giue new cauſe of greater ſmart.
At length from [d] griſlie corſe his blood by peacemeale came;
For brothers blood frõ earth did call his blood to quit the ſame
And thus in fearfull wiſe he yeelded vp his breath:
So was his fierce & wicked life repaide with worthie death.
Our [e] *Charles* like vnto this from Gods reuenging hand
By bloodie death, repaies the blood he ſhed within his land.
From eares, from noſe, frõ mouth, from hart that was ſo ſtout,
Frõ euery part his blood was ſeen, wher blood might iſſue out.
The man that would not yeeld when men did mercie craue,
For mercie cries vnto the Lord but mercie none can haue.

[a] Triphon beeing Tutor and chief counſellor vnto yong king Antiochus, and hauing deuiſed with himſelf a plot of conſpiracie to kill his maſter, thoght that Ionathan being hie preſt of the Iewes, would be a hinderance vnto this attempt, being a frend vnto Antiochus. Therfore Triphon feining great frẽdſhip vnto Ionathan, with flattering words ſo trained him by truſt, that hee perſwaded him of 40. thouſand men which Ionathan broght with him, that he ſhould ſende awaie all ſauing one thouſand: with which ſmall companie when he was entered into the Citie Ptolemais vnder truſt of aſſured promiſe to haue the Citie deliuered vnto him by Triphon: and being come within the gates, hee was by Triphon taken priſoner, and all his men ſlaine. 1. Maccab. 12. 41. Ioſephus Antiquit. Iud. lib. 13. cap. 10. [b] *But Triphon inioyed not this trecherie long: for he was ſtill cruellie purſued by Simon the brother of Ionathan, & at laſt in Apania was taken & put to the ſword. Whoſe trecherie was a right picture of K. Charles his villanie.* [c] *Ariſtobolus after he had put his mother & brother to death, greeued in conſcience, fell into ſuch horrible extremitie, that blood came from him both by vomit & otherwiſe til it brought him to his end.* [d] *The Image of K. Charles his iudgment.* [e] *Charles the 9 by the iuſt ſtroke of Gods reuenge, died of bleeding at al parts of his bodie where was anie iſſue.*

For

Figure 10.4. From Anne Dowriche, *The French Historie*, 1589, RB 31353. This item is reproduced by permission of The Huntington Library, San Marino, California.

in civil war. Elizabeth's rhetoric of compassion, mercy, and maternal concern for her subjects was belied by her cruelty, as her promises of aid to the Protestants were not backed up by her actions: her violence and hypocrisy resemble those of Charles, whom Dowriche indicts in her poem. Through her celebration of Burgaeus and others who refused to obey tyrants, even at the cost of their lives, Dowriche counters the dominant ideology of passive obedience and articulates a stance that is indebted to resistance theory, which in England was closely identified with Catholics rather than Protestants.[35]

Although at the conclusion of *French Historie* Dowriche returns to the device of a French pilgrim speaking to the Englishman, she firmly claims her poem itself as "this worke of mine" in asking Christ to bless her creation and affixing her name as "Anna Dowriche," using the form of her name that most directly recalls the outspoken counselor Annas Borgaeus (37v). Although she declines to base her evaluation of Elizabeth on gender solidarity, and is by no means uncritically celebratory of her, the gender of her sovereign (as well as that of Catherine de' Medici) appears to have emboldened Dowriche to take the role of a female counselor, modelling herself after male counselors such as Coligny and Burgaeus. In addition, she found legitimation for taking on this role through her family's longstanding involvement in counsel as Members of Parliament, the sense of urgency arising from what was perceived as the continuing Catholic threat in England and Elizabeth's tyrannical disregard of her Protestant subjects, as well as Dowriche's own learning and ability as a writer. Moreover, she establishes her virtue and moral authority through her counsel to Pearse, implicitly contrasting her legitimacy as a counselor to that of Catherine de' Medici whom she represents as being manipulated, like Eve, by Satan.[36]

In the dedication to Pearse, she refers to Erasmus's adage, "Sileni Alcibiades," which was referred to by Thomas More in his *Utopia:* "if you consider the matter, I assure you it is most excellent and well worth the reading: but if you weigh the manner, I confesse it is base & scarce worth the seeing. This is therefore my desire; that the simple attire of this outward forme, maie not discourage you from seeking the comfortable tast of the inward substance" (A2). In calling attention to the discrepancy and contradiction between the outside and the inside, and in deliberately deploying poetical devices such as the dream vision to frame her work and the *ubi sunt* topos (O noble *France* . . . / . . . / Where is thy vernant hiew? Thy fresh and flowring fame? [1]), Dowriche translates Timm's history into literature, a genre that may have ceded history's "truth-claim" but was more useful for Dowriche who took cover under literature's indirection. Sir Thomas Elyot's *The Book Named the Governor,* excuses Homer's "leasings"—fiction or lies—for its value in advancing counsel, by contrast to the "leasings" he condemned when excoriating fraud and deceit perpetrated by rulers.[37] Dowriche, too, distinguishes the imaginative amplification of history as advancing the aim of counsel from the unscrupulous fraud practiced by tyrannical rulers such as the French kings, and even Elizabeth herself, against their unsuspecting and vulnerable subjects.

Enabled by the presence of strong female monarchs on both sides of the channel, Dowriche writes as a female counselor in the tradition of Christine de Pizan, and contemporaneously with the higher-born Mary Sidney, who also wrote to counsel Elizabeth. Mary Sidney's *Antonius* (1592), published a year after Dowriche's text, is a translation from French magistrate, playwright, and royal counselor Robert Garnier's *Marc Antoine* (1578), whose work calls attention to the monarch's responsibility in allowing the country to fall into disorder. Sidney alters Garnier's original to make the Cleopatra in her work more explicitly a figure for Elizabeth; this representation is more critical of the still-reigning Elizabeth than later Jacobean representations (most notably Shakespeare's) because it indicates that her rule was marred by passion. Both Dowriche and Sidney, unprecedented in venturing to address political subjects explicitly, appropriate the tradition of earlier male counselors such as Sir John Fortescue (*De Laudibus Legum Angliae* [composed 1468–71]) and Sir Thomas Smith (*De Republica Anglorum* [composed 1562–65; published 1583]), whose political writings compared England to France. These women writers use the French subject (in Dowriche's case) and translation from a French text (in Sidney's case) to enable their intervention in the prestigious but hitherto exclusively male domain of political writing.

A generation later, Elizabeth Cary, having represented an evil counselor Salome in *Mariam,* herself wrote *The Historie of Edward II* (published 1680), to counsel Henrietta Maria, through the negative example of Isabel, the French queen of Henry VI—using a strategy strikingly similar to that of Dowriche, who exhorts Elizabeth through the negative example of Catherine de' Medici.[38] These works indicate that women saw themselves as capable of acting as counselors, especially to female monarchs or consorts. Examples later in the century such as Margaret Fell Fox, Elizabeth Cellier, Elinor James, and Joan Whitrowe continue this heretofore unacknowledged tradition of women who sought to contribute to public and political discourse through counsel.[39] Although Cellier's proposal to James II to institute foundling hospitals and establish a professional society of midwives remained in manuscript, the other writers published their works. Thus they were able to reach a wider public through their participation in print culture, as did Dowriche, one of the earliest examples of women who produced political commentary by assuming the role of counselor in early modern England.

Notes

I thank the Folger Shakespeare Library for granting me a fellowship to conduct research on this project, and Jason Peacey and Lois Schwoerer for helpful advice during my tenure there. I also acknowledge with thanks the suggestions offered by members of the writing group on early modern studies at the University of Miami. An earlier version of this chapter was presented at the Modern Language Association for the Division on English Renaissance Literature.

1. Jean de Serres, *The Three Partes of Commentaries Containing the Whole and Perfect Discourse of the Ciuill Warres of Fraunce, Vnder the Raignes of Henry the Second, Frances the Second, and of Charles the Ninth: With an Addition of the Cruell Murther of the Admirall Chastilion, and Diuers Other Nobles, Committed the 24 Daye of August, anno 1572,* trans. *Thomas Timme* (1574).

2. See J. H. M. Salmon, *The French Religious Wars in English Political Thought* (Oxford: Clarendon, 1959), Appendix, "A List of French Works Published in England 1560–98," 175–77. A. G. Dickens, "The Elizabethans and St. Bartholomew," *The Massacre of St. Bartholomew: Reappraisals and Documents* (Hague, the Netherlands: Martinus Nijhoff, 1974), 54, states that there were seventy books translated from French in the years 1589–90. The Folger Shakespeare Library holds two volumes that are contemporary compilations of French pamphlets from 1588–89: shelf number 14004, copies 1 and 2.

3. For a different recent view of Dowriche's work as providential narrative seeking to inculcate moral lessons, see Megan Matchinske, "Moral, Method, and History in Anne Dowriche's *The French Historie,*" *English Literary Renaissance* 34 (2004): 176–200.

4. *Oxford Dictionary of National Biography* (cited as *DNB* in text), s.v.; S. T. Bindoff, ed., *House of Commons 1509–1558,* History of Parliament Trust (London: Secker and Warburg, 1982); P. W. Hasler, ed., *The House of Commons 1558–1603,* History of Parliament Trust (London: Her Majesty's Stationery Office, 1981), s.v.

5. Micheline White, "Power Couples and Women Writers in Elizabethan England: The Public Voices of Dorcas and Richard Martin and Anne and Hugh Dowriche," *Framing the Family: Narrative and Representation in the Medieval and Early Modern Periods,* ed. Rosalynn Voaden and Diane Wolfthal (Tempe: Arizona Center for Medieval and Renaissance Studies, 2005), 121, 119–38.

6. Anne Dowriche, *The French Historie* (1589), A2v. Further references are included parenthetically in the text.

7. On "fraternal patriarchy," see Carole Pateman, *The Sexual Contract* (Stanford, Calif.: Stanford University Press, 1988), 3. Webster's *The Duchess of Malfi* (1614; Q1 1623) centers on the destruction of the duchess by her two brothers because she married without their consent; in Aphra Behn's *The Rover, Part I* (1677), the brother of the female protagonists asserts his prerogative to arrange matches for his sisters in competition with his own father. See also Juliet Flower MacCannell, *The Regime of the Brother: After the Patriarchy* (New York: Routledge, 1991).

8. Elaine Beilin, "'Some Freely Spake Their Minde': Resistance in Anne Dowriche's *French Historie,*" *Women, Writing, and the Reproduction of Culture,* ed. Mary E. Burke, Jane Donawerth, Linda L. Dove, and Karen Nelson (Syracuse, N.Y.: Syracuse University Press, 2000), 119–40. See also Beilin's *Redeeming Eve: Women Writers of the English Renaissance* (Princeton, N.J.: Princeton University Press, 1987), 101–7; "Writing Public Poetry: Humanism and the Woman Writer," *Modern Language Quarterly* 51.2 (June 1990): 249–71, esp. 258–67.

9. In "The Rhetoric of Counsel in Early Modern England," *Tudor Political Culture,* ed. Dale Hoak (Cambridge: Cambridge University Press, 1995), 292–310, Guy argues that "the term 'counsel' . . . underpinned not only the assumptions, but also some of the most important practices and political structures of the Tudor and early-Stuart policy . . . 'counsel' ranked high among the paradigms and traditions which informed public discourse and shaped political institutions" (292). Elizabeth stressed the limits of Parlia-

ment's authority to counsel to protect her sovereignty (302). But see Michael Mendle, "The Great Council of Parliament and the First Ordinances: The Constitutional Theory of the Civil War," *Journal of British Studies* 31 (April 1992): 133–62, on the history and precedent of "the claim that the two houses of Parliament constituted the king's 'great council'" (134). Mendle points out that a 1630 anonymous treatise, "A True Presentation of Fore-Past Parliaments to the View of Present Times and Posteritie" connected the parliamentary–great council identification with the parliamentary liberty of freedom of speech and goes on to discuss the 1576 case of Peter Wentworth (136–37).

10. John Guy, *Politics, Law and Counsel in Tudor and Stuart England* (Aldershot, UK: Ashgate, 2000), ix. In addition to the texts listed above, Guy cites *Pasquil the Playne* and *Of the Knowledge That Maketh a Wise Man,* Thomas Starkey's *Dialogue Between Reginald Pole and Thomas Lupset,* Foxe's *Acts and Monuments,* and John Hooker's *Order and Usage of the Keeping of a Parliament in England.* On counsel in Sidney's *Arcadia* and his "Letter" to Elizabeth concerning the French match, see Blair Worden, *The Sound of Virtue: Philip Sidney's Arcadia and Elizabethan Politics* (New Haven, Conn.: Yale University Press, 1996), chapter 8, "Three Crises of Counsel." See also Margaret P. Hannay, "Princes You as Men Must Dy: Genevan Advice to Monarchs in the Psalms of Mary Sidney," *English Literary Renaissance* 19 (1989): 22–41.

11. *The Hystory Writtone by Thucidides the Athenyan of the Warre, Whiche Was Between the Peloponesians and the Athenyans, Translated Oute of Frenche Into the Englysh Language by Thomas Nicolls Citezeine and Goldsmyth of London* (1550). The dedicatory poem praising Edward VI refers to "his highe Counsailles deliberation." Nicolls also translates the dedication by James Colyn to the French original, addressed "to the right Illustryous and right high excellency of Princes, and to the right noble magnificence of Lordes and nobilitie of Fraunce," presenting "the knowledge of hystoryes" and its description of "deliberacions, counsels and exploytes" as "teachying us to rule and gouerne, in thinges present and to comme, by Iudgement and remembrance of thinges passed" (v–vi).

12. Pierre Bourdieu, *Distinction: A Social Critique of the Judgement of Taste,* trans. Richard Nice (Cambridge, Mass.: Harvard University Press, 1984), 409.

13. On counsel and consent, see Michael Graves, *The Parliaments of Early Modern Europe* (London: Longman, 2001), chapter 8. Graves argues that the importance of counsel was fading for early modern monarchs so that the function of parliaments became limited to approving taxation, and all but three of Elizabeth's parliaments were called to raise money (1572 and 1586–87 to consider the threat of Mary Stuart). He concludes, "generally, she sought *auxilium* and not *consilium*" (106); "In brief, Elizabeth did not welcome advice" (219).

14. On James, see Suzuki, *Subordinate Subjects: Gender, the Political Nation, and Literary Form in England, 1588–1688* (Aldershot, UK: Ashgate, 2003), 267–75.

15. *The Polemics and Poems of Rachel Speght,* ed. Barbara Kiefer Lewalski (New York: Oxford University Press, 1996), 21.

16. William Caxton, *Fayttes of Armes and of Chevalrie,* ed. A. T. P. Byles, Early English Text Society (London: Oxford University Press, 1937), 291.

17. Jean de Serres, *The Lyfe of the Most Godly, Valeant and Noble Capteine and Maintener of the Trew Christian Religion in Fraunce, Iasper Colignie Shatilion, Sometime Greate Admirall of Fraunce,* trans. Arthur Golding (1576), Hiiv–Hiii.

18. Dickens, "The Elizabethans and St. Bartholomew," states that "if a Frenchman had written a thing first, an English publisher could anticipate a good chance of avoiding trouble with the censor" (54) and that the translations reveal "little sympathy with the fence-sitting so long practiced by Elizabeth in regard to the struggle in France and the Netherlands" (58). Archbishop Parker in a letter to Burghley called the queen's government "this neutral government" and "this Machiavel government" (quoted in Dickens, 64), thus indicating that some did voice, albeit privately, criticism of Elizabeth's lack of zeal in following a Protestant policy. Dowriche was not the only writer to use the format of a French history to counsel monarchs. Timme's *Second Booke* includes an oration of the Bishop of Vienna with passages marked in the margin as "the office of a king" and its corruption as "a Tyrant": "The king reigneth and ruleth with the good will, loue, and consent of the people: but the Tyrant ruleth by violence and force" (88–89), an exhortation to call a Parliament (90), as well as specific counsel on policies, marked "a lesson for Kinges and Queenes" with a manuscript annotation "ag. Taxes & polling" in the Folger copy (22242.2): "let him consider that whatsoeuer he spendeth more than his ordinarie reuenewes, tribute, custome and tallage, is as it were the substance and bloud of the people whome hee is set to gouerne by Gods appointment" (100). J. E. Neale sees the rise of a radical Protestant (puritan) opposition with an alternative parliamentary program of its own, and a growing influx of educated, self-confident gentlemen, who were versed in the study of law and rhetoric as resulting in the increasing capacity and willingness to challenge the monarchical government. See Neale, *Elizabeth I and her Parliaments* (1953–57; rpt. New York: St. Martin's Press, 1958), I: 28; and *The Elizabethan House of Commons* (New Haven, Conn.: Yale University Press, 1950), 302–8.

19. Mihoko Suzuki, "Elizabeth, Gender, and the Political Imaginary in Seventeenth-Century England," *Debating Gender in Early Modern England 1500–1700*, ed. Cristina Malcolmson and Mihoko Suzuki (New York: Palgrave, 2002), 231–53.

20. Randall Martin, "Anne Dowriche's *The French History,* Christopher Marlowe, and Machiavellian Agency," *SEL: Studies in English Literature, 1500–1700* 39, no. 1 (winter 1999): 69–87.

21. R. J. Knecht, *Catherine de' Medici* (London and New York: Longman, 1998), 165. While Salmon assigns the text to Estienne (19), Knecht maintains that the author is anonymous but describes him as "not . . . a Huguenot, but someone who wished to promote an alliance between the Huguenots and malcontant Catholics against the house of Valois" (164). The French text, *Discours merveilleux de la vie, actions & deportemens de Catherine de Medicis, Royne-mere* (1578), has been edited by Nicole Cazauran (Geneva: Droz, 1995). See also Elaine Kruse, "The Woman in Black: The Image of Catherine de Medici from Marlowe to Queen Margot," in *"High and Mighty Queens" of Early Modern England: Realities and Representations,* ed. Carole Levin, Jo Eldridge Carney, and Debra Barrett-Graves (New York: Palgrave, 2003), 223–37.

22. François Hotman, *Francogallia,* Latin text by Ralph E. Giesey, translated by J. H. M. Salmon (Cambridge: Cambridge University Press, 1972), 123–24. The English translator was Robert Molesworth, a disciple of Algernon Sidney; it appeared in 1711 and again, revised, in 1721. On Hotman, see Donald Kelley, *François Hotman: A Revolutionary's Ordeal* (Princeton, N.J.: Princeton University Press, 1973).

23. Although Susan Frye in "The Myth of Elizabeth at Tilsbury," *Sixteenth Century Journal* 23 (1992): 95–114, has shown that the Armada speech was not published until James's reign to protest the Spanish match, Deloney's contemporary ballad includes a brief speech of Elizabeth to her troops:

And then bespake our noble Queene,
My loving friends and countriemen:
I hope this day the worst is seene,
That in our wars ye shall sustaine.
But if our enimies doe assaile you,
Never let your stomackes faile you.
For in the midst of all your troupe
we ourselves will be in place:
To be your joy, your guide and comfort,
even before our enimies face.

24. Geoffrey Fenton, *A Discourse of the Ciuile Warres and Late Troubles in Fraunce, Drawn into Englishe* (1569), 88.

25. I take the term "woman on top" from Natalie Zemon Davis, "Women on Top," *Society and Culture in Early Modern France* (Stanford, Calif.: Stanford University Press, 1975), 124–51.

26. It is noteworthy that aspects of Catherine's "black legend" were transferred to later Catholic and anti-Protestant accounts of Elizabeth. Dowriche's *French Historie* includes the accusation that the queen of Navarre, Jeanne d'Albret, was poisoned by perfumed gloves, a charge first reported in *Discours merveilleux* and repeated in Hotman and de Serres. (For an account of Jeanne's death from natural causes—tuberculosis and an abscess in the right breast—see Nancy Lyman Roelker, *Queen of Navarre Jeanne d'Albret 1528–1572* [Cambridge, Mass.: Harvard University Press, 1968], 387–92.) Elizabeth was accused of using this same method in eliminating her rival for the affections of Alençon in *The Secret History of Alancon and Queen Elizabeth: A True History* (1691). On this and other "secret histories" of Elizabeth, see John Watkins, *Representing Elizabeth in Stuart England: Literature, History, Sovereignty* (Cambridge: Cambridge University Press, 2002), chapter 7. Salmon makes this connection between the two rulers: "Interest of state, and not religious idealism, dominated the statecraft of Catherine de' Medici as much as it did that of Elizabeth of England." *Society in Crisis,* 190. Maurice Wilkinson similarly states: "Doubtless the religion of Catherine and Elizabeth was of the same nature, pure formalism, but . . . [Elizabeth] could assume an enthusiasm for Protestantism which she never felt—and some forms of it she heartily hated—which Catherine could not put on for Catholicism" *A History of the League or Sainte Union 1576–1595* (Glasgow: Jackson, Wylie and Co., 1929), 8. On Elizabeth's "matchless duplicity," see Wilkinson, 28. Even after the Armada, Elizabeth continued to pursue a pro-French policy, sending Thomas Bodley on a special mission to Henry III, offering her assistance (62).

27. Wilkinson, *A History of the League,* 22, 26–27.

28. Rebecca Bushnell, *Tragedies of Tyrants: Political Thought and Theater in the Renaissance* (Ithaca, N.Y.: Cornell University Press, 1990), 87.

29. John Stubbs, *The Discovery of a Gaping Gulf*, ed. Lloyd E. Berry (Charlottesville: University Press of Virginia, 1968), 29.

30. Donald R. Kelley, "Martyrs, Myths and Massacre: The Background of St. Bartholomew," *The Massacre of St. Bartholomew*, 202.

31. Natalie Zemon Davis, "The Rites of Violence," *Society and Culture in Early Modern France*, 152–89.

32. Dickens, "The Elizabethans and St. Bartholomew," suggests that Elizabeth's persistence in the Alençon match gave the massacre far more domestic significance than it could otherwise have acquired, and "promoted early politico-religious dissent and opposition in England." The massacre harked back to the resistance to Marian persecution: the 1576 edition of Fox alludes to the massacre; the version of 1583 gives a three-page account of the massacre. Moreover, the situation in England recalled the reign of Mary in bringing the specter of the marriage of an English queen to a foreigner, a Catholic, and absolutist prince, which revived religious partisanship and the fearful prospect of the loss of national identity. "So the Massacre and the match not only damaged the credit of French monarchy but began the erosion of English monarchy." Further, the massacre promoted "a disillusion with authoritarian monarchy in general, a disillusion which started to rub off the shining surface of the Tudor monarchy" (61–62, 67–69). Kelley, "Martyrs, Myths and Massacre," 201, argues that the massacre brought about "a growing quantity of polemic and theorizing about the problem of war guilt . . . about ideas of political resistance, constitutional government, sovereignty, and the structure of society in general."

33. See Worden, *Sound of Virtue*, 8, 100, and *passim*. Robert P. Adams, "Despotism, Censorship, and Mirrors of Power Politics in Late Elizabethan Times," *Sixteenth Century Journal* 10, no. 3 (1979): 5–16, argues that in the 1590s, Englishmen "experienced . . . occasional and sometimes intense despotism . . . under Elizabeth" (5), and that "the establishment came almost morbidly to fear the printed word whenever it might seem hostile" (7).

34. Michel Foucault, *Discipline and Punish: The Birth of the Prison*, trans. Alan Sheridan (New York: Pantheon, 1977).

35. See, for example, *Leicesters Commonwealth* (1584) and Robert Parsons, *A Conference About the Next Succession to the Crowne of Ingland* (1594). See also Peter Holmes, *Resistance and Compromise: The Political Thought of the English Catholics* (Cambridge: Cambridge University Press, 1982).

36. Susan Wiseman, *Conspiracy and Virtue: Women, Writing, and Politics in Seventeenth-Century England* (Oxford: Oxford University Press, 2006), 332, remarks on the "vital connection between personal and political virtue" for Anne Halklett and other writers on conspiracy in late seventeenth-century England.

37. Elyot, "Of Fraude and Deceipt, Which Is Against Iustice," Book III, chapter 4: "Wherefore of all iniuryes, that which is done by fraude, is most horrible and detestable, not in the opinion of man onely, but also in the sight and iudgement of God. . . . And the diuel is called a lyar, and the father of leasings . . ." (150v).

38. For this reading, see Suzuki, "'Fortune is a Stepmother': Gender and Political Discourse in Elizabeth Cary's *Historie of Edward II*," *The Literary Career and Legacy of Elizabeth Cary, 1621–1680*, ed. Heather Wolfe (New York: Palgrave, 2006), 89–105.

39. See, for example, Margaret Fell Fox, *Letter to the King from M.F.* (1666); Elizabeth Cellier, *A Scheme for the Foundation of the Royal Hospital* (composed 1687); Elinor James, *May It Please Your Majesty, to Accept My Thanks* (1688); *To the Right Honourable the House of Lords* (1688); Joan Whitrowe, *The Humble Address of the Widow Whitrow to King William* (1689); *To Queen Mary: The Humble Salutation and Faithful Greeting of Widow Whitrowe With a Warning to the Rulers of the Earth* (1690). These texts are available in volume 3 of *Women's Political Writings 1610–1725*, ed. Hilda L. Smith, Mihoko Suzuki, and Susan Wiseman, 4 vols. (London: Pickering and Chatto, 2007).

11. History, Power, and the Representation of Elizabeth I in *La Princesse de Clèves*

ELIZABETH KETNER

In *La Princesse de Clèves,* Mme de Lafayette inscribes her heroine's story in a greater political and historic context, the court of Henri II of France. Although her heroine, Mme de Clèves, is fictional, Lafayette portrays the princess's love affair with the Duc de Nemours as part of a private and personal reality that falls into the realm of historical possibility: she suggests that a relationship such as theirs might have occurred, but it also would have gone unnoticed in traditional historic accounts. Lafayette thus privileges personal and private love relationships, amorous intrigues, rivalries, and quarrels, showing that they are often responsible for events that take place in the public realm.[1] In other words, treaties, alliances, wars, and allegiances, whose motivations remain only superficially or inadequately explained in the official historical record, become comprehensible when the interpersonal relationships between members of this court, as well as those with other European rulers and aristocrats, are revealed. In commingling fiction with history, Lafayette underscores women's roles, which have traditionally been neglected, in shaping a particular historical moment.

Hovering at the margins of Lafayette's reconstruction of history is Elizabeth I of England. Though she does not figure as a character in the text, she nevertheless maintains an implicitly central position. She plays a significant role in both Mme de Clèves's love relationships with the Duc de Nemours and the political intrigues taking place at Henri II's French court, and her portrait and the story of her past are circulated there. Lafayette not only explicitly links the English queen to Mme de Clèves, she also accounts for Elizabeth's famous reign as the virgin queen who never married as a multilayered love story, creating an ambivalent and, at times, conflicting image of Europe's most famous and most powerful monarch. The specific details of Elizabeth's past that Lafayette incorporates into the narrative are quite sparse; nevertheless, although little is said, much is implied (especially when the facts of Elizabeth's well-known reign and other literary representations of her are taken into account). It is therefore necessary to read between the gaps in Lafayette's telling of Elizabeth's story to understand the greater implications about her representation and about the working of history in general in this novel.[2] Through Elizabeth's inscription, Lafayette privileges the relationship between the *vie privée* and history while critiquing autonomous monarchal power.

In this chapter, I explore the way in which Lafayette links Elizabeth's decision not to marry to the princess's renunciation of marriage to the Duc de Nemours at the novel's conclusion. The feminist readings that examine this text have proven insightful, but they fail to account fully for the representation of Elizabeth. It is perhaps therefore more fruitful to investigate how the resulting image of the English queen changes when the implications surrounding her later history are taken into account. Finally, I explore the extratextual implications of Elizabeth to the historic context in which the novel was published, Louis XIV's reign. Ultimately, I argue that Lafayette creates an ambivalent portrait of Elizabeth, which can be read as a commentary on and warning about the dangers of absolute monarchy.

The novel's narrator implicates Elizabeth in the princess's love relationship with Duc de Nemours before it even begins to unfold, and the heroine is closely linked to Elizabeth throughout the first half of the novel, but the similarities between them are nuanced. Because Lafayette is clearly preoccupied with representing courtly politics in *La Princesse de Clèves,* Elizabeth's representation must be read in different terms than that of the novel's heroine: as a monarch, Elizabeth's motivations, actions, and choices have much more profound political and public consequences than do those of the princess, a relatively minor courtier and subject to the French king. Though the two figures are clearly linked, their differences are important and the text resists allowing readers to view them as foils. It is therefore useful to examine both how they are linked and differentiated from each other in order to appreciate what Lafayette suggests about Elizabeth, monarchical power, and history.

The first mention of Elizabeth ties her to Mme de Clèves and the goings-on in the French court, for both women share a fascination with the Duc de Nemours based on his reputation alone. Mme de Clèves's "curiosité, et même l'impatience de le voir" (curiosity and even impatience to see him) bears a striking resemblance to the fascination that the French Ambassador Radan attributes to Elizabeth (261). Lafayette further underscores Elizabeth's connection to Mme de Clèves through her role in the princess's love affair with the Duc de Nemours: the text presents a marital alliance between Elizabeth and the duc as a viable possibility, but Nemours abandons his plans to go to England, despite his ambition and Henri's clear urging him to pursue the English crown, after he meets and falls in love with Mme de Clèves. The heroine's love affair determines Elizabeth and England's fates.

Lafayette, however, links Elizabeth to the novel's heroine most clearly through their similar decisions to renounce marriage. Although the Princesse de Clèves rejects marriage to the man she loves out of loyalty to her dead husband (whom she does not love, but greatly esteems), it is suggested that Elizabeth refuses marriage altogether out of loyalty to a man she once loved, Courtenay. Just as Mme de Clèves attains a certain amount of independence by rejecting marriage, Elizabeth achieves autonomy by remaining faithful to Courtenay. Although the princess's decision gives her very limited control over her fate, and as Nancy Miller and Joan DeJean suggest, allows her to preserve her love relationship as fantasy while she distances herself from the public realm, Elizabeth's autonomy has greater and farther-reaching political and historical implications, for it allows her to rule as a single monarch and grants her complete control over her kingdom. Lafayette establishes Elizabeth's autonomous power most particularly by invoking the Courtenay story.

The Courtenay love story is the only episode concerning Elizabeth that is described in detail in *La Princesse de Clèves,* and while its historical accuracy is doubtful, it nevertheless plays an important role in the text.[3] This story certainly reinforces the prominent position that Lafayette gives to amorous relationships in political decision-making at court and the shaping of history. Its inclusion, however, has even greater implications: through it Lafayette most closely aligns Elizabeth with the Princesse de Clèves. She also uses it to establish the autonomy of Elizabeth's rule, and when coupled with the narrator's implicit allusion to Elizabeth's future execution of Mary Stuart later in the novel, the flattering portrait of the English queen becomes metaphorically stained with the blood of her beautiful, young cousin. As the novel progresses, the narrator associates Elizabeth ever more closely with her murdering father and implicitly with Louis XIV, and she is ultimately established as a monarch whose autonomous, unchallenged, and unchecked power poses even more of a danger than that of Diane de Poitiers, the usurping mistress of Henri II at the French court.[4] This opens up a space for Lafayette to comment on the dangers of absolute monarchy.

Rumor of Elizabeth's supposed love affair with Courtenay is narrated by the Duc de Nemours, who manipulates the tale as an excuse to forego his plan to travel to England to woo Elizabeth and pursue the English crown. When pressed by the French king to make a decision once and for all, the Duc de Nemours claims that Elizabeth certainly would not marry a stranger like himself when she could pursue a life with the man she loves:

> Il y a apparence qu'elle voudra se rendre heureuse par l'amour. Elle a aimé le milord Courtenay, il y a déjà quelques années; il était aussi aimé de la reine Marie, que l'aurait épousé, du consentement de toute l'Angleterre, sans qu'elle connût que la jeunesse et la beauté de sa soeur Elisabeth le touchaient davantage que l'espérance de régner . . . les violentes jalousies qu'elle en eut la portèrent à les mettre l'un et l'autre en prison, à exiler ensuite le milord Courtenay, et la déterminèrent enfin à épouser le roi d'Espagne. Je crois qu'Elisabeth qui est présentement sur le trône, rapellera bientôt ce milord, et qu'elle choisira un homme qu'elle a aimé, qui est fort aimable, qui a tant souffert pour elle, plutôt qu'un autre qu'elle n'a jamais vu. (290–91)

> [It seems that she would like to please herself in love. She did love milord Courtenay years ago now; he was also loved by Queen Mary, who would have married him with the consent of all of England, without knowing that the youth and beauty of her sister Elizabeth already touched him more than the desire to rule. The violent jealousy that she bore toward them led her to throw them both in prison, and later send Courtenay into exile, and finally caused her to marry the king of Spain. I believe that Elizabeth who presently sits on the throne, will soon recall this milord, and that she will choose a man she loves, who is truly lovable, and who has suffered so much for her, rather than another whom she has never seen.]

All of the details about Elizabeth in this passage result in a rather sympathetic portrait of the young queen. Elizabeth is a woman, like Mme de Clèves, for whom a man would give up the English throne. It is further implied that only the appealing beauty and youth of women as incomparable and singular as Princess Elizabeth and Mme de Clèves could inspire such a sacrifice on the part of their lovers. In this description, moreover, Lafayette removes agency from Elizabeth, as she appears to have been more acted upon than active. It is well documented that Elizabeth's sister Mary Tudor, the Bloody Mary whose reputation for merciless violence is so well known, accused Elizabeth of plotting to marry Courtenay. Lafayette, however, suggests that the young Princess Elizabeth was innocent in the whole affair and unwittingly became embroiled in one of the many amorous intrigues at court: according to the rumor that Nemours reports, Elizabeth did not choose to antagonize her sister Mary, and she was powerless to escape imprisonment after Mary decreed it. The young Princess Elizabeth appears the victim of Mary's caprice and jealousy.

In light of the sympathetic portrait offered in the interpolated story of Elizabeth's past and the ways that she is linked to Mme de Clèves, it may superficially appear that Lafayette offers a wholly positive view of Elizabeth as a powerful female monarch and historic figure. This reading is particularly tempting in light of Lafayette's desire to recuperate women's roles in shaping history in the text. Her representation is far more complex, however, and it cannot be so easily summarized. Can the feminist reading suggested by Nancy Miller and Joan DeJean, which posits that Lafayette challenges conventional roles available to women in fiction, also be applied to Elizabeth's depiction in *La Princesse de Clèves*? Miller and DeJean argue that Lafayette revises traditional plot conventions open to the heroines of novels in Mme de Clèves's decision to reject the Duc de Nemour's marriage proposal and to leave the court, dividing her time between her country estate and the convent. This decision gives the princess limited control over her fate, but it also makes her story unnarratable, for the range of options available to women in novel plots is limited and her choice does not conform neatly to the accepted available story lines.[5] DeJean further identifies the princess's renunciation of love as part of a political and historical subtext in the novel that has traditionally gone ignored in literary scholarship. She asserts that through the depiction of marriage, Lafayette explores "an issue that was perhaps the final political fallout of the Fronde: the public confrontation between Church and State, doubled by the more private struggle between husband-family and wife, for control over marriage, and therefore over property."[6] The princess "recreates herself as the owner of a family plot, in the double sense of an ancestral estate and of a family romance" by refusing to marry Nemours.[7] These readings are compelling in that they are some of the first to account for the princess's dual residence at the novel's end. Furthermore, they effectively place the work in a greater context of women's writing in seventeenth-century France and reevaluate the historico-political content of the work by locating a form of resistance to traditional novel plots in the princess's refusal to be possessed by a husband in marriage.

Miller and DeJean's readings, however, fail to account for the profound ambivalence surrounding Lafayette's depiction of Elizabeth and do not fully explain the scope and breadth of Lafayette's exploration of politics and power in *La Princesse de Clèves*. The brief details offered in Elizabeth's representation paint a contradictory and dark image of her. Although Elizabeth's inscription, similar to the Princesse de Cleves's representation, is clouded by silence and gaps, it is equally important to read into what is implied about Elizabeth to understand how Lafayette is rescripting her history. Elizabeth achieves autonomy in refusing marriage after Nemours gives up his ambition for the English throne, but the control that she wields has significantly different implications for her, a monarch, whose power is nearly absolute, than they do for Mme de Clèves, a naive, young aristocrat, whose options are quite restricted.

When some of the darker and more ominous aspects of Elizabeth's future decisions that Lafayette evokes in the novel, as well as the extratextual implications that the representation of Elizabeth's power might have are considered, Lafayette's seemingly sympathetic portrait of Elizabeth shifts even in the same passage in which she generates sympathy for her. At the end of the Duc de Nemours's narration, he calls attention to Elizabeth's recent ascension and the relative autonomy that she has as the head of the English state, mentioning both her position as monarch and her freedom to recall Courtenay at will. Her autonomy, moreover, is further underscored by Henri II when he informs the Duc de Nemours that Courtenay is dead, thus leaving her single and marriageable. When Lafayette maintains that Elizabeth decides to renounce marriage and with it all other love relationships after Courtenay dies and Nemours decides to remain in France, she also removes Elizabeth from love's influence, and the English queen is established as an autonomous ruler whose judgment is unclouded by passion. Lafayette represents both Mme de Clèves and Elizabeth as singular, "fully conscious of the fact that [they] are not like other women . . . ruled by passions instead of being mistress[es] of [themselves]."[8]

Nonetheless, if Elizabeth's refusal of marriage aligns her with Mme de Clèves because of her similar rejection of the Duc de Nemours's proposal, her position of authority distances her from Lafayette's heroine. Mme de Clèves withdraws from the court and lives out her final days in solitude, exercising only limited control over her fate, but Elizabeth contrastingly stays at court so that she may rule England alone. Her power and authority remain unchecked by king, lover, court, or courtiers, in contrast to Mme de Clèves who is continually constrained by social roles and expectations. In a text that so clearly underscores the drastic difference between the social rules and expectations for rulers and those of the other members of the court, it becomes clear that Elizabeth's position allows her much more autonomy and control than that of the novel's heroine.

The ambivalence surrounding Elizabeth is established even more firmly in the inscription of the historical future in the novel. Lafayette, for instance, depicts the unfolding of history in the prediction and fruition of Henri II's death. As this event precipitates Diane de Poitier's fall from influence and authority, resulting from Catherine de' Medici's vengeful animosity, it is perhaps the best example of the way in which Lafayette illustrates the power of interpersonal relationships to shape and determine political decisions and history. It also helps to place all of the action represented in the novel in a clearer relationship to future historical events, for the fortune-telling scene dramatically foreshadows the king's death at the tournament and catapults Lafayette's readers into a heightened awareness of the way in which the events of the narrative's present shape the extratextual historical future. An awareness of the historical future in a novel in which the French Dauphine Mary Stuart, Elizabeth's cousin and future rival to the throne, figures so prominently cannot but recall Elizabeth's future imprisonment of her. Although the official historical record clears Elizabeth of any wrongdoing in her cousin's death, Lafayette links her to this event.

Lafayette marks her narrative with a specific consciousness about the execution of Elizabeth's cousin Mary Stuart when it is subtly, but ominously evoked in the dauphine's articulation of her "fears of a sad fate."[9] The passage in which Mary tells the young Mlle de Chartres about her worries over her future is important in establishing the complex interplay of the historical past to the narrative's present and the narrative's present to the historical future, for in it Lafayette connects hereditary relationships, past animosities, and love relationships with the shaping of history in far-reaching and profound ways. The dauphine begins her narration by first explaining why she has such limited influence at the French court: "Vous voyez que . . . j'ai un médiocre pouvoir; je suis si haïe de la reine et de la duchesse de Valentinois qu'il est difficile que, par elles ou par ceux qui sont dans leurs dépendance, elles ne traversent toujours toutes les choses que je désire" (You can see . . . that my power here is modest; I am so hated by the queen and the Duchesse de Valentinois that they cross me in everything, either by themselves or through those who depend on their favor) (255). Yet, she insists that the present can only be understood with knowledge of the past: the dauphine exclaims, "elles ne me haïssent qu'à cause de la reine ma mère, qui leur a donné autrefois de l'inquiétude et de la jalousie" (they hate me only because the queen my mother once caused them such uneasiness and jealousy) (255–56). Her mother, she explains, was equally loved by Henri II, the king of Scotland, and Henry VIII, and they all once vied for her hand. Temporal distance does not diminish the role of the past in shaping the present, for Mary Stuart's position at court is completely determined by not only her own, but also her mother's, history. She concludes her history by further linking herself and her fate to that of her mother: "On dit que je lui ressemble; je crains de lui ressembler aussi par sa malheureuse destinée, et quelque bonheur qui semble se préparer pour moi, je ne saurais croire que j'en jouisse" (They say that I resemble [my mother]; I fear that I resemble her, too, in her unfortunate destiny, and whatever happiness seems designed for me, I cannot believe I shall ever enjoy it) (256). Though the dauphine has no concrete reason to believe that she will share her mother's fate, her prediction, as the extratextual historical record informs us, holds true. Lafayette's speculation that Elizabeth played a much more active role in Mary Stuart's execution than the historical record allows anticipates the more explicit explorations of Elizabeth as a figure of tyranny in the French secret histories, such as *The Secret History of Alancon and Queen Elizabeth,* that postdate the novel's publication.[10]

The dauphine does not name Elizabeth as the guarantor of her tragic destiny, but the mention of Henry VIII, Elizabeth's tyrannical father, evokes her prolonged imprisonment of her cousin and clearly links her to the dauphine's destruction. Henry VIII's name can scarcely be mentioned without evoking the slaying of his wives, and the yoking of Elizabeth to her father is thus quite significant. Hereditary ties appear to determine the fates of both Mary Stuart and Elizabeth, and it thus becomes impossible to overlook Elizabeth's cruelty to her cousin in spite of the sympathetic portrait offered in Nemours's narration. Lafayette goes to great lengths to account for Elizabeth's monarchical autonomy and control, and she links her in subtle, yet precise ways to both a violent heritage and future atrocities; when the future is taken into account and in light of certain French perceptions of the Virgin Queen, Elizabeth's image resembles that of an absolute monarch whose reign borders on tyranny.

Lafayette embeds a disguised critique of the kind of absolute power that Louis XIV wielded throughout her novel, and the portrait of Elizabeth is a significant part of her discourse on the threat posed by royal absolutism to the aristocracy. Louis XIV's close scrutiny of all writings published during his reign makes Lafayette's avoidance of transparent commentary understandable. In disguising her critique of absolute monarchy by locating it in the historical past, in a different country, and in a female ruler, Lafayette masks criticism of her king. Nonetheless, while she displaces her commentary on Louis XIV in the representation of an English queen, she also continually links Elizabeth to the French court. Moreover, she reveals the real and serious threats to the autonomy and power of the nobility that accompany the kinds of absolute authority that Elizabeth wields: those members of the aristocracy who threaten her authority are banished, imprisoned, or even put to death. The drastic measures that Elizabeth takes to preserve her power resemble the tight control that Louis XIV exerted over the remaining members of the aristocracy. In the aftermath of the Fronde uprisings that took place between

1648 and 1653, DeJean explains, Louis XIV sent "its leaders . . . into exile" and set the "royal propaganda machine . . . into motion to stamp out any trace of the recent events."[11] He then moved to Versailles, where he kept the remaining members of the aristocracy in lockdown: the palace in fact was "designed to keep the French aristocracy together in one community and under one roof, and to keep its principal members permanently under the king's surveillance."[12] While Lafayette appears to lament a past in which she and the other members of the aristocracy had significantly more control in *La Princesse de Clèves,* as certain critics suggest, she also documents the kind of violence, tyranny, and tight control that characterized Louis XIV's absolutist rule in her representation of Elizabeth I.[13]

Continued critical interest in *La Princesse de Clèves* can be attributed perhaps to its mystifying complexity, for it is a difficult novel to pin down. In temporally distancing the events described in the novel to the historical past and in implying that she is telling the private story of her heroine, Mme de Lafayette creates the illusion that the novel is distanced from any extratextual political commentary about her own time. This has allowed critics and scholars to label the work as a bildungsroman that details the psychological journey of a solitary, fictional character and ignore the novel's political subtext. The novel, however, continually resists this kind of reading, for, ultimately, it is as much about history and politics as it is about the education and evolution of its heroine, and the centrality given to courtly politics in the first half of the novel cannot be ignored. Although feminist critics have begun to reevaluate the extent of Lafayette's commentary, they have not yet fully explored the critique of absolute monarchy that she embeds in her representation of courtly politics and historic events and figures. The implicitly central position given to Elizabeth in the text is one of the ways that Lafayette opens a space in which to comment on monarchical absolutism and the diminishing power of the nobility in Louis XIV's France.

Notes

1. The events that take place in the novel are determined to a large extent by the courtly context. Henri II's court, like Versailles, is the center of the social and political world. The court's harmonious appearance disguises its underlying social tensions: "l'ambition et la galanterie étaient l'âme de cette court . . . les dames y avaient tant de part que l'amour était toujours mêlé aux affaires et les affaires à l'amour. Personne n'était tranquille, ni indifférent . . . on était toujours occupé des plaisirs ou des intrigues" (ambition and gallantry were the soul of this court . . . women had such a part there that love was always mixed with politics and politics with love. No one was tranquil or indifferent . . . everyone was always preoccupied with personal pleasures and political plots). Marie Madeleine Pioche de La Vergne, Comtesse de Lafayette, *La Princesse de Clèves,* in *Romans et nouvelles,* ed. Émile

Magne (Paris: Garnier Frères, 1965), 252. Further references will appear parenthetically in the text. With ambition and love affairs being the preoccupation of every person, the demarcation between the public and private disappears. Love is politicized and politics are eroticized, so that it becomes impossible to distinguish between "des plaisirs [et] des intrigues" (252).

2. I borrow the notion of reading into "the unsaid" (that is to say, reading into what is omitted from the narrative) from Joan DeJean, who insists that we must read through the silence that characterizes so many of the protagonists' responses, for it is in the unsaid and "unsayable" that Lafayette rescripts her heroine's story; see "Lafayette's Ellipses: The Privileges of Anonymity," *PMLA* 99, no. 5 (1984): 884–902.

3. Though it has been documented that the rebels responsible for Wyatt's Revolt in 1554 had a marriage between Elizabeth and Courtenay in mind if they were to succeed in overthrowing Mary Tudor's regime, there is apparently very little, if any, evidence to suggest that a love affair of the nature that Lafayette describes in *La Princesse de Clèves* ever existed between them. See, for example, David Starkey, *Elizabeth: Apprenticeship* (London: Chatto & Windus, 2000) and Susan Doran, *Monarchy and Matrimony: The Courtships of Elizabeth I* (London: Routlege, 1996). Starkey asserts that the rebellion "led to the most dangerous and difficult time of [Elizabeth's] life when she often feared imminent execution or murder" (129). He concludes that Wyatt's Revolt, which "threatened both Mary's throne and her life," provoked a "rage against Elizabeth [that] was . . . deep and long-lasting" (129). Interestingly, Lafayette ignores Elizabeth's many subsequent courtships as well as her well-known and well-documented relationship with Robert Dudley.

4. Lafayette also levels a disguised critique of absolute monarchy in her representation of Henri II's mistress Diane de Poitiers. At the French court, King Henri II is weak, effeminate, and ineffectual, while Diane wields his political power for him and controls the realm: Diane in fact "est maîtresse absolue de toutes choses" (is absolute mistress of everything) (268). Lafayette's representation of the unchecked nature of Diane's power suggests that the king is conversely powerless, and her description of Diane and the king's relationship is couched in misogynistic discourse. For instance, when Henri learns of her infidelities, his reaction is weak and effeminate: it is "douce et modérée . . . par l'extrême respect qu'il a pour sa maîtresse" (soft and moderated . . . by the extreme respect he had for his mistress) (268). In Diane, we see how Lafayette masks her commentary beneath the glittering façade of the court and further embeds it in the kind of misogynistic discourse that Barbara Weissberger identifies and discusses in "'¡A tierra, puto!': Alfonso de Palencia's Discourse of Effeminacy," in *Queer Iberia: Sexualities, Cultures, and Crossings from the Middle Ages to the Renaissance,* ed. Josiah Blackmore and Gregory S. Hutcheson (Durham, N.C.: Duke University Press, 1999), 291–324. It is not, however, Diane's gender that is at issue, but rather, the nearly monolithic nature of her power, for she is a despot who ruins everyone who crosses her. I suggest that the use of misogynistic discourse can be explained by Lafayette's desire to disguise her criticism of the monarchy from Louis XIV's scrutinizing gaze.

5. I am referring specifically to the analysis that Joan DeJean presents in her article "Lafayette's Ellipses: The Privileges of Anonymity," cited above, as well as her book *Tender Geographies: Women and the Origins of the Novel in France* (New York: Columbia University Press, 1991), and the argument presented by Nancy Miller in her article "Emphasis

Added: Plots and Plausibilities in Women's Fiction," in *An Inimitable Example: The Case for the Princesse de Clèves,* ed. Patrick Henry (Washington, D.C.: The Catholic University of America Press, 1992), 15–38.

6. DeJean, *Tender Geographies,* 109–10.

7. Ibid., 123.

8. Marie-Odile Sweseter, "In Search of Selfhood: The Itinerary of the Princesse de Clèves," in *An Inimitable Example: The Case for the Princesse de Clèves,* 217.

9. Janet Letts, *Legendary Lives in La Princesse de Clèves* (Charlottesville, Va.: Rookwood Press, 1998), 14.

10. In *Representing Elizabeth in Stuart England: Literature, History, Sovereignty* (Cambridge: Cambridge University Press, 2002), 158–69, John Watkins explores seventeenth-century French images of Elizabeth's private life, focusing on both Lafayette's image of Elizabeth and later French literary representations from secret history novels. He shows the continuity between Lafayette's image of Elizabeth I and the tyrannical and blood-thirsty images of Elizabeth that are so much a part of the French secret histories that her novel anticipates. In some of the secret histories, the image of Elizabeth shifts dramatically: writers revise the historical record, sometimes arguing for Elizabeth's full responsibility for Mary Stuart's death. Watkins points out that *The Secret History of Alancon and Queen Elizabeth,* an English translation of the original French text, features perhaps the most exaggerated negative image of Elizabeth, for there she "becomes a solitary agent of evil" (167).

11. DeJean, *Tender Geographies,* 41.

12. Ibid., 63.

13. See, for example, Ralph Albanese, Jr., "Aristocratic Ethos and Ideological Codes in *La Princesse de Clèves,*" in *An Inimitable Example: The Case for the Princesse de Clèves,* 87–103.

Selected Bibliography

Adams, Robert P. "Despotism, Censorship, and Mirrors of Power Politics in Late Elizabethan Times." *Sixteenth Century Journal* 10, no. 3 (1979): 5–16.

Agrippa, Henricus Cornelius. *Declamation on the Nobility and Preeminence of the Female Sex.* Ed. Albert Rabil, Jr. Chicago: University of Chicago Press, 1996.

Arcona, Tarsicio de. *Isabel la Católica: Estudio crítico de su vida y su reinado.* 1964. Madrid: Editorial Católica, 1992.

Arnold, Janet. *"Lost From Her Majesties Back": Items of Clothing and Jewels Lost or Given Away by Queen Elizabeth I Between 1561 and 1585, Entered in One of the Day Books Kept for the Records of the Wardrobe of the Robes.* Costume Society Extra Series No. 7. Wisbech, Cambridgeshire, UK: Daedalus Press, 1980.

———. *Queen Elizabeth's Wardrobe Unlock'd.* Leeds, UK: W. S. Maney, 1988.

Bak, János. "Scapegoats in Medieval Hungary." In *Queens and Queenship in Medieval Europe.* Ed. Duggan. 224–33.

———. "Roles and Functions of Queens in Árpádian and Angevin Hungary (1000–1386 A.D.)." In *Medieval Queenship.* Ed. Parsons. 13–24.

Baker, Richard. *A Chronicle of the Kings of England From the Time of the Romans Government Unto the Death of King James, Containing all Passages of State and Church, With All Other Observations Proper for a Chronicle.* London: n.p., 1643.

Beem, Charles. *The Lioness Roared: The Problem of Female Rule in English History.* New York: Palgrave Macmillan, 2006.

Betegón Díez, Ruth. *Isabel Clara Eugenia: Infanta de España y soberana de Flandes.* Barcelona: Plaza Janés, 2004.

Boccaccio, Giovanni. *Famous Women.* Ed. and trans. Virginia Brown. The I Tatti Renaissance Library. Cambridge, Mass.: Harvard University Press, 2001.

Boruchoff, David A., ed. *Isabel la Católica, Queen of Castile: Critical Essays.* New York: Palgrave, 2002.

Bouza, Fernando. "María 'Planeta de Lusitania,' Felipe II y Portugal." In *Felipe II.* 105–15.

Brants, Victor. *La Belgique au XVIIe siècle, Albert et Isabelle: Études d'histoire politique et sociale.* Louvain: Ch. Peeters, 1910.

Breight, Curtis. "Realpolitik and Elizabethan Ceremony: The Earl of Hertford's Entertainment of Elizabeth at Elvetham, 1591." *Renaissance Quarterly* 45 (1992): 20–48.

Brown, Christopher. "Rubens and the Archdukes." In *Albert and Isabella.* Ed. Thomas and Duerloo. 121–28.

Brown, Elizabeth A. "'Companion Me With My Mistress': Cleopatra, Elizabeth I, and Their Waiting Women." In *Maids and Mistresses.* Ed. Frye and Robertson. 131–45.

Brown-Grant, Rosalind. *Christine de Pizan and the Moral Defense of Women: Reading Beyond Gender.* Cambridge: Cambridge University Press, 1999.

Bryson, David. *Queen Jeanne and the Promised Land: Dynasty, Homeland, and Violence in Sixteenth-Century France.* Leiden, the Netherlands; Boston; Koln, Germany: Brill, 1999.

Calendar of State Papers, Domestic Series, of the Reign of Elizabeth, 1591–1594. Ed. Mary Anne Everett Green. London: Longmans, Green, Reader, and Dyer, 1867.

Calendar of the Letters and State Papers Relating to English Affairs, Preserved Principally in the Archives of Simancas. Vol. I: Elizabeth, 1558–1567. Ed. Martin A. S. Hume. London: Her Majesty's Stationery Office, 1892.

Campbell, Lorne. *Renaissance Portraits: European Portrait-Painting in the 14th, 15th, and 16th Centuries.* New Haven, Conn.: Yale University Press, 1990.

Cazauran, Nicole, ed. *Discours merveilleux de la vie, actions & deportemens de Catherine de Medicis, Royne-mer.* 1578. Geneva: Droz, 1995.

Cholakian, Patricia Francis, and Rouben C. Cholakian. *Marguerite de Navarre: Mother of the Renaissance.* New York: Columbia University Press, 2005.

Clifford, Henry. *The Life of Jane Dormer, Duchess of Feria.* Ed. Joseph Stevenson. London: Burnes and Oates, 1887.

Cosandey, Fanny. *La reine de France. Symbole et pouvoir.* Paris: Gallimard, 2000.

d'Albret, Jeanne. *Mémoires et poésies.* Ed. A. de Ruble. Geneva: Slatkine Reprints, 1970.

Davey, Richard. *The Sisters of Lady Jane Grey and Their Wicked Grandfather.* New York: E. P. Dutton and Co., 1912.

Davis, Natalie Zemon. "Women in Politics." In *Renaissance and Enlightenment Paradoxes: A History of Women in the West.* Ed. N. Z. Davis and Arlette Farge. Cambridge, Mass.: Harvard University Press, 1993. 3: 167–87.

———. "Women on Top." In *Society and Culture in Early Modern France.* Stanford, Calif.: Stanford University Press, 1975. 124–51.

DeJean, Joan. *Tender Geographies: Women and the Origins of the Novel in France.* New York: Columbia University Press, 1991.

Delorme, Philippe. *Isabeau de Bavière: Epouse de Charles V, Mère de Charles VII.* Paris: Flammarion, 2003.

Dixon, Annette, ed. *Women Who Ruled: Queens, Goddesses, Amazons in Renaissance and Baroque Art.* London: Merrell; Ann Arbor: University of Michigan Museum of Art, 2002.

Domínguez Casas, Rafael. "The Artistic Patronage of Isabel the Catholic: Medieval or Modern?" In *Queen Isabel I of Castile.* Ed. Weissberger. 123–48.

Doran, Susan, ed. *Elizabeth: The Exhibition at the National Maritime Museum.* London: Chatto & Windus in association with The National Maritime Museum, 2003.

———. *Monarchy and Matrimony: The Courtships of Elizabeth I.* London: Routledge, 1996.

Drumond Braga, Paulo. "D. Joana de Áustria (1535–1573): Uma releitura da sua intervenção na vida portuguesa." *Arquivos do Centro Cultural Calouste Gulbenkian* 34 (1996): 231–42.

Duerloo, Luc. "Archducal Piety and Habsburg Power." In *Albert and Isabella.* Ed. Thomas and Duerloo. 267–83.

Duerloo, Luc, and Werner Thomas, eds. *Albert & Isabelle: Catalogue.* Leuven, Belgium: Brepols, 1998.

Duggan, Anne J., ed. *Queens and Queenship in Medieval Europe.* Woodbridge, Suffolk: Boydell Press, 1997.

Earenfight, Theresa. "Absent Kings: Queens as Political Partners in the Medieval Crown of Aragón." In *Queenship and Political Power.* Ed. Earenfight. 33–51.

———. "Two Bodies, One Spirit: Isabel and Fernando's Construction of Monarchical Partnership." In *Queen Isabel I of Castile.* Ed. Weissberger. 3–18.

———, ed. *Queenship and Political Power in Medieval and Early Modern Spain.* Aldershot, UK: Ashgate, 2005.

Eggert, Katherine. "Nostalgia and the Not Yet Late Queen: Refusing Female Rule in *Henry V.*" *English Literary History* 61, no. 3 (Autumn 1994): 523–50.

Elston, Timothy G. "Transformation or Continuity? Sixteenth-Century Education and the Legacy of Catherine of Aragon, Mary I, and Juan Luis Vives." In *High and Mighty Queens.* Ed. Levin, Carney, and Barrett-Graves. 11–26.

Elyot, Sir Thomas. *The Defence of Good Women.* London: n.p., 1545.

Emerson, Kathy Lynn. *Wives and Daughters: The Women of Sixteenth Century England.* Troy, N.Y.: Whitston, 1984.

Felipe II. La Monarquía y su época: La Monarquía Hispánica. Real Monasterio de San Lorenzo de El Escorial: Sociedad Estatal para la Conmemoración de los Centenarios de Felipe II y Carlos V, 1998.

Fernández de Retana, Luis. *Doña Juana de Austria.* Madrid: El Perpetuo Socorro, 1955.

Flores, Juan de. *Crónica incompleta de los Reyes Católicos.* Ed. Julio Puyol. Madrid: Real Academia de la Historia, 1934.

Forhan, Kate Langdon. *The Political Theory of Christine de Pizan.* Aldershot, UK: Ashgate, 2002.

Fradenburg, Louise Olga, ed. *Women and Sovereignty.* Edinburgh: Edinburgh University Press, 1992.

Friedmann, Paul. *Anne Boleyn.* Vol. II. London: Macmillan and Co., 1884.

Frye, Susan. *Elizabeth I: The Competition for Representation.* New York: Oxford University Press, 1993.

———. "The Myth of Elizabeth at Tilbury." *Sixteenth Century Journal* 23 (1992): 95–114.

———. "Sewing Connections: Elizabeth Tudor, Mary Stuart, Elizabeth Talbot and Seventeenth-Century Anonymous Needleworkers." In *Maids and Mistresses.* Ed. Frye and Robertson. 165–82.

Frye, Susan, and Karen Robertson, eds. *Maids and Mistresses, Cousins and Queens: Women's Alliances in Early Modern England.* New York: Oxford University Press, 1999.

Fuller, Thomas. *The Worthies of England.* Ed. John Freeman. 1662. Rpt. London: George Allen & Unwin, 1952.

García García, Bernardo José. "Bruselas y Madrid: Isabel Clara Eugenia y el duque de Lerma." In *Albert and Isabella.* Ed. Thomas and Duerloo. 67–77.

Garlick, Barbara, Suzanne Dixon, and Pauline Allen, eds. *Stereotypes of Women in Power: Historical Perspectives and Revisionist Views.* Westwood, Conn.: Greenwood Press, 1992.

Gauvard, Claude. "Christine de Pizan a-t-elle eu une pensée politique?" *Revue Historique* 250 (1973): 417–30.

———. "Christine de Pizan et ses contemporains: L'engagement politique des écrivains dans le royaume de France aux XIVe et XVe siècles." In *Une femme de lettres au moyen âge: études autour de Christine de Pizan.* Ed. Liliane Dulac and Bernard Ribémont. Orléans, France: Paradigme, 1995. 105–28.

Gibbons, Rachel C. "The Active Queenship of Isabeau of Bavaria, 1392–1417." PhD Dissertation, University of Reading, 1997.

———. "Isabeau of Bavaria, Queen of France (1385–1422): The Creation of an Historical Villainess." *Transactions of the Royal Historical Society* 6, no. 6 (1996a): 51–73.

———. "The Piety of Isabeau of Bavaria." *Courts, Counties and the Capital in the Later Middle Ages.* Ed. Diana Dunn. Stroud, UK: Sutton Publishing, 1996. 205–24.

Goldsmith, Elizabeth. *Publishing Women's Life Stories in France, 1647–1720.* Aldershot, UK: Ashgate, 2001.

Gómez Bedate, Pilar. "Felismena y doña Juana, princesa de Portugal: Una hipótesis para los enigmas de la *Diana* de Jorge de Montemayor." *Revista Salina* 16 (Nov. 2002): 79–90.

González de Amezúa y Mayo, Agustín. *Isabel de Valois Reina de España.* 3 vols. Madrid: Dirección General de Relaciones Culturales, Ministerio de Asuntos Exteriores, 1949.

Halecki, Oscar. *Jadwiga of Anjou and the Rise of East Central Europe.* Boulder, Colo.; Highland Lakes, New Jersey: Atlantic Research and Publications, 1991.

Hall, Edward. *Hall's Chronicle.* [1548, 1550]. London: n.p., 1809. Rpt. New York: AMS Press Inc., 1965.

Hannay, Margaret P. "Princes You as Men Must Dy: Genevan Advice to Monarchs in the Psalms of Mary Sidney," *English Literary Renaissance* 19 (1989): 22–41.

Henderson, Katherine Usher, and Barbara F. McManus, eds. *Half Humankind: Contexts and Texts of the Controversy About Women in England, 1540–1640.* Urbana: University of Illinois Press, 1985.

Howard, Jean E., and Phyllis Rackin. *Engendering a Nation: A Feminist Account of Shakespeare's English Histories.* London and New York: Routledge, 1997.

Howarth, David. *Images of Rule: Art, Politics in the English Renaissance, 1485–1649.* Berkeley: University of California Press, 1997.

Iongh, Jane de. *Mary of Hungary: Second Regent of The Netherlands.* Trans. M. D. Herter Norton. London: Faber & Faber, 1959.

Isabel la Católica: la magnificencia de un reinado. Ed. Sociedad Estatal de Conmemoraciones Culturales. Salamanca, Spain: Ediciones El Viso, 2004.

Ives, Eric W. *Anne Boleyn.* London: Blackwell, 1986.

Jansen, Sharon. *The Monstrous Regiment of Women: Female Rulers in Early Modern Europe.* New York: Palgrave MacMillan, 2002.

Jordan, Constance. *Renaissance Feminism: Literary Texts and Political Models.* Ithaca, N.Y.: Cornell University Press, 1990.

Kamen, Henry. "Anna de Austria." In *Felipe II.* 265–74.

———. "El secreto de Felipe II: Las mujeres que influyeron en su vida." *Torre de los Lujanes: Boletín de la Real Sociedad Económica Matritense de Amigos del País* 32 (1996): 53–64.

Kantorowicz, Ernst. *The King's Two Bodies: A Study in Medieval Political Theology.* Princeton, N.J.: Princeton University Press, 1957.

Kelly-Gadol, Joan. "Did Women Have a Renaissance?" In *Becoming Visible: Women in European History.* Ed. Renate Bridenthal and Claudia Koonz. Boston: Houghton Mifflin, 1977. 137–64.

Kimm, Heidrun. *Isabeau de Bavière, reine de France 1370–1435. Beitrag zur Geschichte einer bayerischen Herzogstochter und des französischen Königshauses.* Munich: Stadtarchiv, 1969.

Klaniczay, Gábor. *Holy Rulers and Blessed Princesses: Dynastic Cults in Medieval Central Europe.* Trans. Éva Pálmai. Cambridge: Cambridge University Press, 2002.

———. "Proving sanctity in the canonization processes (Saint Elizabeth and Saint Margaret of Hungary)." In *Procès de canonisation au Moyen Âge. Aspects juridiques et religieux—Medieval Canonization Processes. Legal and Religious Aspects.* Ed. Gábor Klaniczay. Rome: École française de Rome, 2004. 117–48.

Klein, Lisa M. "Your Humble Handmaid: Elizabethan Gifts of Needlework." *Renaissance Quarterly* 50, no. 2 (1997): 459–93.

Knecht, R. J. *Catherine de' Medici.* London and New York: Longman, 1998.

Knox, John. *The First Blast of the Trumpet Against the Monstruous Regiment of Women.* 1558. Amsterdam: Orbis Terrarum; New York: Da Capo Press, 1972.

Krones, F. R. von. "Katharina von Brandenburg-Preussen als Fürstin Siebenbürgens 1626–1631." *Zeitschrift für Allgemeine Geschichte, Kultur-, Literatur- und Kunstgeschichte* 1 (1884): 334–58.

Krueger, Roberta. "'*Chascune selon son estat*': Women's Education and Social Class in the Conduct Books of Christine de Pizan and Anne de France." *Papers on French Seventeenth Century Literature* 46 (1997): 19–34.

Kruse, Elaine. "The Woman in Black: The Image of Catherine de Medici from Marlowe to Queen Margot." In *"High and Mighty Queens."* Ed. Levin, Carney, and Barrett-Graves. 223–37.

Lehfeldt, Elizabeth. "Ruling Sexuality: The Political Legitimacy of Isabel of Castile." *Renaissance Quarterly* 53, no. 1 (2000): 31–56.

Levin, Carole. *The Heart and Stomach of a King: Elizabeth I and the Politics of Sex and Power.* Philadelphia: University of Pennsylvania Press, 1994.

Levin, Carole, Jo Eldridge Carney, and Debra Barrett-Graves, eds. *"High and Mighty Queens" of Early Modern England: Realities and Representations.* New York: Palgrave MacMillan, 2003.

Levin, Carole, and Patricia Ann Sullivan, eds. *Political Rhetoric, Power, and Renaissance Women.* Albany: State University of New York Press, 1995.

Levin, Carole, and Jeanie Watson, eds. *Ambiguous Realities: Women in the Middle Ages and Renaissance.* Detroit, Mich.: Wayne State University Press, 1987.

Lindorfer, Bianca Maria. "Ana de Austria, La novia de un hijo y la esposa de un padre." In López-Cordón and Franco. 411–25.

Liss, Peggy K. *Isabel the Queen: Life and Times.* 1992. Rev. ed. Philadelphia: University of Pennsylvania Press, 2004.

López-Cordón, María Victoria, and Gloria Franco, eds. *La Reina Isabel y las reinas de España: realidad, modelos e imagen historiográfica.* Madrid: Fundación Española de Historia Moderna, 2005.

Lovell, Mary S. *Bess of Hardwick: Empire Builder.* New York: Norton, 2006.

Lozano, Jorge Sebastián. "Choices and Consequences: The Construction of Isabel de Portugal's Image." In *Queenship and Political Power.* Ed. Earenfight. 145–62.

Luke, Mary. *The Nine Days Queen.* New York: William Morrow, 1986.

Marcus, Leah S., Janel Mueller, and Mary Beth Rose, eds. *Elizabeth I: Collected Works.* Chicago: University of Chicago Press, 2000.

Martínez Millán, José. "Familia real y grupos políticos: la princesa doña Juana de Austria." *La corte de Felipe II.* Ed. José Martínez Millán. Madrid: Alianza Editorial, 1998. 73–105.

Martin-Ulrich, Claudie. "Catherine de Médicis et Jeanne d'Albret, la reine-mère et la reine conteuse." *Devenir Roi: Essais sur la literature addressée au Prince.* Ed. Isabelle Cogitore and Francis Goyet. Grenoble, France: ELLUG, 2001.

Mazarío Coleto, María del Carmen. *Isabel de Portugal: emperatriz y reina de España.* Madrid: Consejo Superior de Investigaciones Científicas, 1951.

McLaren, Ann. *Political Culture in the Reign of Elizabeth I: Queen and Commonwealth 1558–1585.* Cambridge: Cambridge University Press, 1999.

McManus, Clare. *The Courts of the Stuart Queens.* New York: Palgrave, 2003.

Mears, Natalie. "Politics in the Elizabethan Privy Chamber: Lady Mary Sidney and Kat Ashley." *Women and Politics in Early Modern England, 1450–1700.* Ed. James Daybell. Aldershot, UK: Ashgate, 2004. 67–82.

Merton, Charlotte. "The Women Who Served Queen Mary and Queen Elizabeth: Ladies, Gentlewomen and Maids of the Privy Chamber, 1553–1603." Ph.D. dissertation. Cambridge University, 1992.

Mira de Amescua, Antonio. *La Hija de Carlos Quinto.* Ed. Karl-Ludwig Selig. Kassel, Germany: Rechenberger, 2002.

Morgan, Hiram. "'Never Any Realm Worse Governed': Queen Elizabeth and Ireland." *Transactions of the Royal Historical Society* 14 (2004): 295–308.

Mumby, Frank A. *The Girlhood of Queen Elizabeth: A Narrative in Contemporary Letters.* London: Constable and Co., 1909.

Naunton, Robert. *Fragmenta Regalia, or Observations on the Late Queen Elizabeth, Her Times and Favorites.* London: n.p., 1641.

Neale, J. E. *Elizabeth I and Her Parliaments.* 1953–57. Rpt. New York: St. Martin's Press, 1958.

———. *The Elizabethan House of Commons.* New Haven, Conn.: Yale University Press, 1950.

Nederman, Cary J., and Elaine N. Lawson. "The Frivolities of Courtiers Follow the Footprints of Women: Public Women and the Crisis of Virility in John of Salisbury." In *Ambiguous Realities.* Ed. Levin and Watson. 82–95.

Nevinson, J. L. "New Year's Gifts to Queen Elizabeth I, 1584." *Costume* 9 (1975): 27–31.

Nicholas, Karen. "Women as Rulers: Countess Jeanne and Marguerite of Flanders (1212–1278)." In *Queens, Regents and Potentates.* Ed. Vann. 73–89.

Nichols, J. *The Progresses and Public Processions of Queen Elizabeth.* 3 vols. London: n.p., 1823.

Orlin, Lena. "The Fictional Families of Elizabeth I." In *Political Rhetoric, Power, and Renaissance Women.* Ed. Levin and Sullivan. 85–110.

Orr, Clarissa Campbell, ed. *Queenship in Europe, 1660–1815. The Role of the Consort.* Cambridge: Cambridge University Press, 2004.

Padberg, John. "A Woman Jesuit: Secret, Perilous Project." <www.companysj.com/v272secret.html> (Accessed May 18, 2007).

Parsons, John Carmi, ed. *Medieval Queenship.* Stroud, UK: Sutton, 1998.

The Passage of Our Most Drad Soueraigne Lady Elyzabeth Through the Citie of London to Westminster the Day Before Her Coronacion. London: Richard Totull, 1558/59.

Piret, Etienne. *Marie de Hongrie.* Paris: Jourdan Editeur, 2005.

Pizan, Christine de. *The Book of the City of Ladies.* Trans. Earl Jeffrey Richards. Rev. ed. New York: Persea, 1998.

———. *The Epistle of the Prison of Human Life With an Epistle to the Queen of France and Lament on the Evils of the Civil War.* Ed. and trans. Josette Wisman. New York: Garland, 1984.

———. *The Writings of Christine de Pizan.* Ed. Charity Cannon Willard. New York: Persea Books, 1994.

Pulgar, Fernando del. "Crónica de los Reyes Católicos." In *Crónica de los reyes de Castilla.* Ed. Cayetano Rosell. 3 vols. Biblioteca de Autores Españoles 70. Madrid: Atlas, 1953. 1: 223–511.

Quilligan, Maureen. *The Allegory of Female Authority: Christine de Pizan's Cité des Dames.* Ithaca, N.Y.: Cornell University Press, 1991.

Raeymaekers, Dries. "The Court and Household of the Archdukes Albert and Isabella, 1598–1621." Filed under 2006–1, Birgit Houben and Dries Raeymaekers, "Changing Formats: Court and Household in the Habsburg Netherlands, 1598–1641." (Paper for the second Low Countries Conference, Antwerp 2006). <www.lowcountries.nl/workingpapers.html> (Accessed September 28, 2008).

Réthelyi, Orsolya, Beatrix F. Romhányi, Enikő Spekner and András Végh, eds. *Mary of Hungary: The Queen and Her Court 1521–1531.* Budapest, Hungary: Budapesti Történeti Múzeum, 2005.

Reyes y mecenas: Los Reyes Católicos-Maximiliano I y los inicios de la Casa de Austria en España. Ed. Fernando Checa Cremades. Madrid: Ministerio de Cultura, 1992.

Riquer, Martín de. *Heráldica castellana en tiempos de los Reyes Católicos.* Barcelona, Spain: Quaderns Crema, 1986.

Rodríguez Villa, Antonio, ed. *Correspondencia de la Infanta Archiduquesa Doña Isabel Clara Eugenia de Austria con el Duque de Lerma y otros personajes.* Madrid: Fortanet, 1906.

Roelker, Nancy. *Queen of Navarre: Jeanne d'Albret.* Cambridge, Mass.: Harvard University Press, 1968.

Rosales, Luis, and Luis Felipe Vivanco. *La mejor reina de España.* Madrid: Ediciones Jerarquía, 1939.

Sade, Marquis de. *Histoire secrète d'Isabelle de Bavière.* Ed. Gilbert Lély. Paris: Gallimard, 1953.

Sághy, Marianne. "Aspects of Female Rulership in Late Medieval Literature: The Queens' Reign in Angevin Hungary." *East Central Europe—L' Europe du Centre Est* 20–23 (1993–1996): 69–86.

Salvador Esteban, Emilia. "La precaria monarquía hispánica de los Reyes Católicos: reflexiones sobre la participación de Isabel I en el gobierno aragonés." In *Homenaje a J.A. Maravall.* Ed. María Carmen Iglesias, Carlos Moya, Luis Rodríguez Zúñiga. 3 vols. Madrid: Centro de Investigaciones Sociológicas, 1985. 3: 315–27.

Sánchez, Magdalena. *The Empress, the Queen, and the Nun: Women and Power at the Court of Philip III of Spain.* Baltimore: Johns Hopkins University Press, 1998.

Sanz Ayán, Carmen. "La regencia de doña Juana de Austria. Su dimensión humana, intelectual y política." In *Felipe II.* 137–43.

Saring, Toni. "Kurfürstin Anna von Preußen." *Forschungen zur brandenburgischen und preußischen Geschichte* 53 (1941): 248–95.

Scheller, Rita. *Die Frau am preussischen Herzogshof (1550–1625).* Cologne and Berlin: Grote Verlag, 1966.

Schumann, Cordula. "Humble Wife, Charitable Mother and Chaste Widow: Representing the Virtues of the Infanta Isabella Clara Eugenia (1599–1633)." Ph.D. thesis, University of London, Courtauld Institute of Art, 2000.

Schuster, Georg. "Eine brandenburgische Prinzessin auf dem siebenbürgischen Fürstenthrone." *Hohenzollern-Jahrbuch* 5 (1901): 121–36.

The Secret History of the Duke of Alancon and Q. Elizabeth: A True History. London: Will with the Whisp, 1691.

Smith, Hilda L., Mihoko Suzuki, and Susan Wiseman, eds. *Women's Political Writings 1610–1725.* 4 vols. London: Pickering and Chatto, 2007.

Smuts, R. Malcolm. "Public Ceremony and Royal Charisma: The English Royal Entry in London, 1485–1642." In *The First Modern Society: Essays in English History in Honor of Lawrence Stone.* Eds. A. L. Beier, David Cannadine, and James Rosenheim. Cambridge: Cambridge University Press, 1989. 65–93.

Somerset, Anne. *Elizabeth I.* New York: St. Martin's Press, 1992.

Stafford, Pauline. "More Than a Man or Less Than a Woman? Woman Rulers in Early Modern Europe." *Gender and History* 7 (1995): 486–90.

———. *Queens, Concubines and Dowagers: The King's Wife in the Early Middle Ages.* London and Washington, D.C.: Leicester University Press, 1983.

Starkey, David. "Court, Council and Nobility in Tudor England." In *Princes, Patronage and Nobility: The Court at the Beginning of the Modern Age c. 1450–1650.* Ed. Ronald G. Asch and Adolf M. Birke. New York: Oxford University Press, 1991. 175–203.

———. *Elizabeth: Apprenticeship.* London: Chatto & Windus, 2000.

———. "Intimacy and Innovation: The Rise of the Privy Chamber, 1485–1547." *The English Court: From the Wars of the Roses to the Civil War.* Ed. David Starkey. New York: Longman, 1987. 71–118.

Stephenson, Barbara. *The Power and Patronage of Marguerite de Navarre.* Aldershot, UK: Ashgate, 2004.

Straub, Theodor. "Isabeau de Bavière, Legende und Wirklichkeit." *Zeitschrift für Bayerische Landesgeschichte* 44 (1981): 131–55.

Strong, Roy. *Gloriana: The Portraits of Queen Elizabeth I.* London: Thames and Hudson, 1987. Rpt. London: Pimlico, 2003.

———. *Splendor at Court: Renaissance Spectacle and the Theater of Power.* Boston: Houghton Mifflin, 1973.

Suárez Fernández, Luis. *Isabel, mujer y reina.* Madrid: Ediciones Rialp, 1992.

Suzuki, Mihoko. "Elizabeth, Gender, and the Political Imaginary in Seventeenth-Century England." In *Debating Gender in Early Modern England 1500–1700.* Ed. Cristina Malcolmson and Mihoko Suzuki. New York: Palgrave, 2002. 231–53.

———. "'Fortune is a Stepmother': Gender and Political Discourse in Elizabeth Cary's *Historie of Edward II.*" *The Literary Career and Legacy of Elizabeth Cary, 1621–1680.* Ed. Heather Wolfe. New York: Palgrave, 2006. 89–105.

———. *Subordinate Subjects: Gender, the Political Nation, and Literary Form in England, 1588–1688.* Aldershot, UK: Ashgate, 2003.

Swain, Margaret. *The Needlework of Mary, Queen of Scots.* New York: Van Nostrand Reinhold, 1973.

Tate, R. B. "Políticas sexuales: de Enrique el Impotente a Isabel, maestra de engaños (magistra dissimulationum)." In *Actas del Primer Congreso Anglo-hispano.* Tomo III: Historia. Ed. R. Hitchcock and Ralph Penny. Madrid: Castalia, 1994. 165–75.

Thibault, Marcel. *Isabeau de Bavière: Reine de France. La Jeunesse (1370–1405).* Paris: Perrin et Cie, 1903.

Thøfner, Margit. "*Domina & Princeps proprietaria.* The Ideal of Sovereignty in the Joyous Entries of the Archduke Albert and the Infanta Isabella." In *Albert and Isabella.* Ed. Thomas and Duerloo. 55–66.

Thomas, Werner. "Andromeda Unbound: The Reign of Albert and Isabella in the Southern Netherlands, 1598–1621." In *Albert and Isabella.* Ed. Thomas and Duerloo. 1–14.

Thomas, Werner, and Luc Duerloo, eds. *Albert and Isabella: Essays.* Leuven, Belgium: Brepols, 1998.

Tomas, Natalie. "Alfonsina Orsini de' Medici and the 'Problem' of a Female Ruler in Early Sixteenth-Century Florence." *Renaissance Studies* 14, no. 1 (2000): 70–90.

Valera, Diego de. *Memorial de diversas hazañas.* Vol. 3 of *Crónicas de los reyes de Castilla.* Ed. Cayetano Rosell. Biblioteca de Autores Españoles 70. Madrid: Atlas, 1953. 173–202.

Vales Failde, Javier. *La emperatriz Isabel.* Madrid: Revista de Archivos, Bibliotecas y Museos, 1917.

Valois, Marguerite de. *Mémoires et autres écrits (1574–1614).* Ed. Éliane Viennot. Paris: Champion, 1999.

Vann, Theresa M., ed. *Queens, Regents and Potentates.* Dallas, Tex.: Academia, 1993.

Vauvilliers, Mlle. *Histoire de Jeanne d'Albret Reine de Navarre.* 3 vols. Paris: L. Janet et F. Guitel, 1818.

Verberckmoes, Johan. "The Archdukes in Their Humour." In *Albert and Isabella.* Ed. Thomas and Duerloo. 137–44.

Viennot, Éliane. *La France, les femmes et le pouvoir: L'invention de la loi salique Ve-XVIe siècle.* Paris: Perrin, 2006.

Villalpando, Antonio de. *Razonamiento de las reales armas de los serenísimos e muy exclaresçidos príncipes e muy altos e poderosos reyes e señores, los señores don fernando el quinto e doña Ysabel la segunda. In Orígenes de la monarquía hispánica: propaganda y legitimación (ca. 1400–1520).* Ed. José Manuel Nieto Soria. Madrid: Dykinson, 1999. 373–410.

Villermont, Marie H. de. *L'Infante Isabelle: gouvernante des Pays-Bas.* Paris: Librarie S. François, 1912.

Vives, Juan Luis. *The Education of a Christian Woman: A Sixteenth-Century Manual.* Trans. Charles Fantazzi. Chicago: University of Chicago Press, 2000.

———. *The Instruction of a Christen Woman.* Ed. Virginia Walcott Beauchamp, Elizabeth H. Hageman, and Margaret Mikesell. Urbana: University of Illinois Press, 2002.

Walker, Julia. "Re-Politicizing the Book of the Three Virtues." *Au champ des escriptures: actes du colloque international sur Christine de Pizan.* Ed. Eric Hicks, Diego Gonzalez, and Philippe Simon. Paris: Champion, 2000. 533–48.

Warnicke, Retha. *The Rise and Fall of Anne Boleyn.* Cambridge: Cambridge University Press, 1989.

Watkins, John. *Representing Elizabeth in Stuart England: Literature, History, Sovereignty.* Cambridge: Cambridge University Press, 2002.

Weissberger, Barbara F. *Isabel Rules: Constructing Queenship, Wielding Power.* Minneapolis: University of Minnesota Press, 2004.

———. "Isabel's 'Nuevas leyes': Monarchic Law and Justice in *Triunfo de Amor.*" In *Juan de Flores: Four Studies.* Ed. Joseph J. Gwara. Papers of the Medieval Hispanic Research Seminar 49. London: Department of Hispanic Studies, Queen Mary, University of London, 2005. 91–113.

———, ed. *Queen Isabel I of Castile: Power, Patronage, Persona.* Woodbridge, Suffolk: Boydell and Brewer, 2008.

Welzel, Barbara. "*Princeps Vidua, Mater Castrorum.* The Iconography of Archduchess Isabella as Governor of the Netherlands." *Jaarboek Koninklijk Museum voor Schone Kunsten Antwerpen* (1999): 158–75.

Wiesner, Merry E. *Women and Gender in Early Modern Europe.* New York: Cambridge University Press, 1993.

Wiesner-Hanks, Merry. "Women's Authority in the State and Household in Early Modern Europe." In *Women Who Ruled: Queens, Goddesses, Amazons in Renaissance and Baroque Art.* Ed. Annette Dixon. London: Merrell; Ann Arbor: University of Michigan Museum of Art, 2002. 27–59.

Wiseman, Susan. *Conspiracy and Virtue: Women, Writing, and Politics in Seventeenth-Century England.* Oxford: Oxford University Press, 2006.

Wolf, Armin. "Reigning Queens in Medieval Europe: When, Where, and Why." In *Medieval Queenship.* Ed. Parsons. 169–88.

Wood, Charles T. "The First Two Queens Elizabeth, 1464–1503." In *Women and Sovereignty.* Ed. Fradenburg. 121–31.

———. *Joan of Arc and Richard III: Sex, Saints and Government in the Middle Ages.* New York: Oxford University Press, 1988.

Wright, Pam. "A Change in Direction: The Ramifications of a Female Household, 1558–1603." In *The English Court: From the Wars of the Roses to the Civil War.* Ed. David Starkey. New York: Longman, 1987.

Wyhe, Cordula van. "Court and Convent: The Infanta Isabella and Her Franciscan Confessor Andrés de Soto." *Sixteenth Century Journal* 35, no. 2 (2004): 411–45.

———. Critical introduction. Jean Terrier, *Portraicts des S S Vertus de la Vierge contemplées par feue S.A.S.M. Isabelle Clere Eugenie Infante d'Espagne.* Glasgow: Glasgow Emblem Studies, 2002.

Yanko, Aroní. *Juana de Austria: Reina en la sombra.* Barcelona: Balacqva, 2003.

Yarza Luaces, Joaquín. *Los Reyes Católicos: Paisaje artístico de una monarquía.* Madrid: Nerea, 1993.

Index

absolutism, 196–202, 203n4
Actes and Monuments, 135
Adams, Tracy, 4
adultery, 13, 17–19, 47–48, 84–85, 197
Agrippa of Nettesheim, 3
Albert, Archduke, 64–71, 73; authority of, 67, 71; as cosovereign, 64–66; death of, 72; love between Isabel Clara Eugenia and, 68–69; rituals of, 69–70
Alexander the Great, 52
Alfonso, Prince, 47
Althusser, Louis, 46
Ample Declaration on the Joining of Her Arms to Those of the Reformers (Ample déclaration sur la jonction de ses àrmes à celles des Réformés), 30, 32–41. *See also* d'Albret, Jeanne
Andreas II (Hungary), 80, 85
Anglés, Higinio, 113
Anguissola, Sofonisba, 113, *114*
Anna of Austria, 104, 109, *116,* 116–17
Anna of Prussia, 82
Anne of Cleves, 132–33
Antonius, 187
Aristotle, 49
Arras and Troyes. *See* Treaty of Arras; Treaty of Troyes
arts and music, 104–6, 108–9, 112–15
Ashley, Katherine, 131
Asteley, Catherine, 145
authority: absolute, 196–99; cosovereign women and, 67, 70–74; gender and, 43, 49, 168–69; legitimation of, 34. *See also* power
Aylmer, John, 3

The Banquet of Herod and the Decapitation of John the Baptist, 90–91, 91
Barbara of Cilly, 80
Báthory, Sigismund, 82, 85
Bazán, Álvaro de, 106
Beatrix of Naples, 80
Beaufort, Margaret, 165
Bedmar, Marquis de, 72
Behn, Aphra, 175
Béla II (Hungary), 80
Berry, Jean de, 20
Bethlen, Farkas, 81
Bethlen, Gabriel: death of, 86; marriage of, 81–85, 90–91; succession of Catherine and, 87
Bethlen, István, 86, 93
Betts, John, 149
Beza, Theodore, 31
Blanche of Castile, 2, 23
Blount, Elizabeth, 132
Boccaccio, Giovanni, 1–2, 4
Bocskai, Stephen, 82
Bodin, Jean, 34
Boleyn, Anne, 123, 130–32
Boleyn, Mary, 131–35
The Book Named the Governor, 176, 186
Book of Faytes and Arms and of Chyvalrye, 179

The Book of the City of Ladies, 1–2. *See also Le Livre de la cité des dames*
Borja, Francisco de, 107, 116
Bourbon, Antoine de, 30–31, 33, 36–37
Bourbon, Louis de, 32
Bourdieu, Pierre, 176
Brandon, Catherine, 166
Brandon, Charles, 166
Brantôme, Pierre de Bourdeille, 18
Bryson, David, 40
Burgaeus, Annas, 179–80, 185

Cabezón, Antonio, 108
Callot, Jacques, 75
Calvete de Estrella, Juan, 105
Calvin, Jean, 31
Cano, Melchor, 108
Capilla, Alonso de, 113
Cárdenas, Gutierre de, 50
Carey, Henry, 7, 132–34
Carey, Katherine, 7, 132–34
Carey, William, 131–33
Carlos, don (Spain), 104, 109–11, *110,* 115
Carranza, Bartolomé, 108, 119n20
Cary, Elizabeth, 178, 187
Castro, Leonor de, 107
Catalina Micaela (Spain), 115
Catalina of Portugal, 118n6
Catherine of Aragón, 3, 127, 130, 132
Catherine of Brandenburg, 2, 6; letters written by, 96n27; marriage of, 81–85; opposition to, 88–93; portraits of, *90–91,* 91–92, *92;* reign of, 85–93; resignation of, 93; rights as ruler, 85–87; Transylvanian diet and, 85–87; viewed as a foreigner, 92–93
Catholicism: Church of England and, 129; Francisco Franco and, 56–59; National, 56–57, 108; in the Netherlands, 65–66; the Reformation and, 31–32, 37–39; in Transylvania, 87
Caxton, William, 179
Cazalla, Agustín, 108
Cecil, David, 176
Cecil, Mildred, 136
Cecil, William, 176
Cecilia Renata of Habsburg, 82
Cellier, Elizabeth, 187
Charles II (England), 177
Charles V (France), 15
Charles V (Spain), 9, 65, 103–4, 106–7, 113
Charles VI (France), 13, 17–18; children of, 157, 160–62; insanity of, 14–15, 21; Katherine de Valois and, 160–62; power granted to Isabeau of Bavaria by, 15–16
Charles VII (France), 13, 18, 20
Charles IX (France), 9, 35, 65, 103–4, 106–7, 113, 116, 179, 183
Charles Robert of Anjou (Hungary), 80
Chartier, Jean, 17
children, 35, 115; ascending to the throne, 31; legitimacy of, 13–15, 17–18, 48, 123–24, 131–32, 135; memoirs written by women for their, 39–40. *See also* marriage
Christian IV (Denmark), 82
Chronique de Charles VII, roi de France, 17
Church of England, 125–26, 129
cloth and clothing: coronation, 142, 144–46; fashionable, 147–49; gifts of, 142–44; paintings depicting, 145, *145*
coats of arms, 44–46, 51–56, 60n6
Coligny, Gaspard de, 179–80
Concordia de Segovia, 51, 53
Constance, empress of Rome and queen of Sicily, 2
Contra Machiavell, 180
The Contre Guyse, 174
Córdoba, Fray Martín de, 2–3, 49–50
Cornwallis, Thomas, 128
coronation cloth, 142, 144–46
cosovereignty: symbolism and, 68–70; women and, 64–66
courts, royal, 82–83, 90–91, 106, 108–9; gift exchanges within, 142–44, 149–52, 155n29; jewels and, 147–48, 151–52, 153n9
Cranmer, Thomas, Archbishop of Canterbury, 130
Cruz, Anne J., 6–7
Csáky, István, 84
Cueva, Beltrán de la, 47

d'Albret, Henri, 30, 33
d'Albret, Jeanne: Catherine de Medici and, 31, 33–34, 38; children of, 31, 35; historical analysis of, 1, 5; imprisonment of, 37–39; intended audiences for writings of, 34–35; legitimation of authority of, 34; marriages of, 30–31, 36–37; the Reformation and, 31–32, 38–39; self-assertion of, 39–41; writings of, 30, 32–39
Davis, Natalie Zemon, 184
Deák, Éva, 6
Defence of Good Women, 3
DeJean, Joan, 196, 198
Deloney, Thomas, 182

Derrida, Jacques, 34
d'Etaples, Lefèvre, 31
Dickenson, John, 75
diets, 85–87
A Discourse Upon the Present State of France, 174
Domínguez Casas, Rafael, 53–54
Dowriche, Anne, 8, 174; connections to English government, 174–76; as counselor to Elizabeth I, 176–80; criticism of Catherine de Medici, 180–84; criticism of violence, 183–85; siblings of, 175–76
Dowriche, Hugh, 175
Drayton, Michael, 8, 158, 164–71, 171–72n4
dress, royal. *See* cloth and clothing
Dudley, Guildford, 165
Dudley, John, 165
Dürer, Albrecht, 113
du Tillet, Jean, 18–19
Dyngley, Joanna, 137

Edgecombe, Geoffrey, 175
Edgecombe, Pearse, 175, 186
Edgecombe, Richard, 174
Edward II (England), 158
Edward VI (England), 123; birth of, 131; death of, 126–27; John Perrot and, 135; Katherine de Valois and, 158–59; Protestantism and, 125–26; siblings of, 123–25, 130
Ekman, Mary C., 5
Eleonore of Brandenburg, 92
Elizabeth Kotromanic (Hungary), 80
Elizabeth Piast (Hungary), 80
Elizabeth Stuart, 92
Elizabeth the Cuman (Hungary), 80
Elizabeth Tudor (Elizabeth I England), 1–2, 4, 6–8, 88, 111; Anne Dowriche's criticism and counsel of, 180–86; Catherine de' Medici and, 182–83; Church of England and, 125–26, 129; coronation cloth and, 142, 144–46; fashions worn by, 147–49; gift exchanges and, 142–44, 149–52, 155n29; gifts received by, 147–48; half-siblings of, 132–34; jewels worn by, 147–48, 153n9; John Perrot and, 135–38; Mary I and, 126–29, 150–51, 156n34; portraits of, 147–48, 154–55n20; portrayed in *La Princesse de Clèves*, 194–202; portrayed in *The Secret History of Alancon and Queen Elizabeth*, 204n10; religious beliefs of, 126–27; siblings of, 123–25
Elyot, Thomas, 3, 176, 186

Emerson, Kathy Lynn, 131
Englands Heroicall Epistles, 8, 158, 164–71, 171–72n4
Enrique II (Spain), 48–49
Enrique IV (Spain), 47–48, 50
Estienne, Henri, 180–82
Estrada, Diego de, 82
Eworth, Hans, 145

Felipe IV (Spain), 46. *See also* Philip IV (Spain)
Fell Fox, Margaret, 187
Fenton, Geoffrey, 182
Fernández de Córdoba, Gonzalo, 74
Fernando of Aragon: chosen by Isabel I, 48–49; coat of arms of, 44–46, 51–54; shared power of, 43, 51–53, 103
The First Blast of the Trumpet against the Monstrous Regiment of Women, 3
Fitzalan, Mary, *145*
Fitzroy, Henry, 130–31
Fitzwilliam, William, 136–37
Fortescue, John, 187
Foucault, Michel, 184
Foxe, John, 135
Francis Charles of Launenburg, 93
Franco, Francisco, 47, 56–59
Francogallia, 181
François I (France), 30–32, 37
François II (France), 32
Fredegonde, 2
Frederick V of the Palatinate, 82, 92
The French Historie, 174–79, *177*, *178*, 183, *185*. *See also* Dowriche, Anne
Friedmann, Paul, 132
Fuenllana, Miguel de, 108, 113
Fuente, Francisco de la, 113
Fuller, Thomas, 134
Fumaroli, Marc, 33

Gaping Gulf, 183
Garden of Noble Maidens, 3
Gardiner, Stephen, 128, 138
Garnier, Robert, 187
Genio de España: exaltaciones a una resurrección nacional y del mundo, 56
Gentillet, Innocent, 180
George William (Transylvania), 82, 88
Gertrudis of Andechs-Meran, 80
gift exchanges, 142–44, 149–52, 155n29
Gil, Juan, 52
Giménez Caballero, Ernesto, 56

Giselle of Bavaria, 80
Gómez de Silva, Ruy, 107, 117
González de Amezúa y Mayo, Agustín, 112–13
González Iglesias, Juan-Antonio, 53
Gossaert, Jan, 69
Graham, Helen, 57
Granada, Luis de, 108
Greenblatt, Stephen, 32
Grey, Jane, Lady, 3, 125, 127–28, 165
Grey, John, Lord, 134
Grey, Katherine, 134, 165–67
Grey, Mary, 134–35
Gustavus Adolphus (Sweden), 82, 92
Guy, John, 176
Guzmán, Eufrasia de, 111

Hale, John, 132
Hall, Edward, 158–61, 167–68, 172n10
An Harborowe for Faithful and Trewe Subjectes, 3
Harington, John, 137–38
Hastings, Edward, 128
Hatton, Christopher, 135
Helena (queen of Hungarian Kingdom), 80
Henri de Navarre (Henry IV of France), 174
Henri II (France), 8, 179, 194, 196, 199–200
Henri III de Navarre (France), 31, 33
Henri VI (France), 13
Henry III (France), 130. *See also* Henri III de Navarre (France)
Henry IV (England), 159, 167
Henry V (England), 16–17, 20, 157, 165, 172n10
Henry V (Shakespeare), 158, 161–64
Henry VI (England), 159–61, 187; portrayed by Michael Drayton, 165; portrayed by Shakespeare, 158, 161–64
Henry VII (England), 157, 165, 174, 179
Henry VIII (England), 174, 179; children of, 123–29, 131–32, 135; Church of England and, 129; John Harington and, 137–38; literary portrayals of, 200–201; marriages of, 123–24, 130–31; mistresses of, 131–32
Herrera, Melchor de, 113
La hija de Carlos Quinto, 104
Hilliard, Nicholas, 147–48
L'Histoire de nostre temps, 34
The Historie of Edward II, 187
Holinshed, Raphael, 159–61, 168
Holt, Mack P., 32
Holy Roman Empire, 88
Hooker, Richard, 176
Hoskins, Anthony, 132
Hotman, François, 181
Howard, Elizabeth, 148
Howard, William, 128
Howey, Catherine, 6–7
Hughes, Jonathan, 131, 133
Hurault, Michel, 174

The Iaylors Conversion, 175
Ibarra, Francisco de, 71
Ignatius of Loyola, 107
Illescas, Gonzalo, 113
Index of Forbidden Books, 108
The Instruction of a Christen Woman (De Institutione Feminae Christianae), 3
Irene, empress of Constantinople, 2
Isabeau of Bavaria: access to power, 25; alliance with Louis of Orleans, 17–18; authority granted by Charles VII to, 15–16; black legend of, 13, 17–20, 27n2; children of, 13–15, 17–18; Christine de Pizan and, 1–2, 4–5, 14, 17, 20–24; death of Louis, Duke of Burgundy and, 16–17; historical analysis of, 1, 4–5; marriage of, 13–15; as mediator, 15–16, 22–23, 25–26; modern scholarship on, 24–26; scandals surrounding, 13; sources of information about, 19–20
Isabel Clara Eugenia: birth of, 115; cosovereign power of, 64–70; demoted to governor, 67–68, 75; depicted in paintings, 69; duties and authority of, 70–74; historical analysis of, 2, 6, 9; loss of sovereignty after Archduke Albert's death, 72–74; marriage of, 64–69; as mediator, 74–76; rituals of, 68–70; territories ruled by, 65–66
Isabel de Valois (Spain), 6, 65, 111–13, *112*, 115
Isabel I of Castile: coat of arms of, 44–46, 51–54, 60n6; death of, 103–4; Francisco Franco and, 47, 56–59; historical analysis of, 1–6, 9; in the line of succession, 47, 51; marriage of, 43–46, 48–49; national Catholicism and, 56–57; power of, 43, 51–53, 103; propaganda used by, 47–48; texts dedicated to, 54–55
Isabelle of Jagiello, 81
Isabel of Portugal, 6, 103
Ives, Eric, 131–32

James, Elinor, 177, 187
James I (England), 74, 130. *See also* James VI (Scotland)

James II (England), 187
James VI (Scotland), 136
Jardín de nobles doncellas, 3
Jesuits, 107–8
jewels, 147–48, 151–52, 153n9
Joanna, queen of Jerusalem and Sicily, 2
Joan of Arc, 13, 54, 182
John II (Hungary), 81
John the Fearless, duke of Burgundy, 16–18, 20
John the Good (France), 16
Juana of Austria, 2, 7, 9, 47, 67, 103; Anna of Austria and, 116–17; children of, 103–4, 115; court of, 106; crises faced by, 106–8; death of, 117; Isabel de Valois and, 111–13; marriage of, 104, 111; nephew of, 104, 109–11, *110*, 115; participation in plays, 113–15; portraits of, *105*, 109, *114*; religious beliefs of, 107–8; secular interests of, 104–6, 108–9, 112–15; siblings of, 103–4
Juana of Castile, 47–48
Juan Manuel of Portugal, 104
Juan I (Spain), 51
Juan II (Spain), 47, 50
judges, women as, 50–51

Kamen, Henry, 116
Károlyi, Zsuzsanna, 82
Katherine de Valois (England), 8; children of, 164; familial connections to the Tudor monarchy, 157–59; French throne and, 160–61; marriage of, 164–71; portrayed by Michael Drayton, 158, 164–71; portrayed by Shakespeare, 158, 161–64; representations in chronicle histories, 158–61; succession as queen, 164–71
Kelley, Donald, 184
Ketner, Elizabeth, 8
Keyes, Thomas, 134–35
Knollys, Francis, 133
Knox, John, 3
Krauss, Georg, 88
Kusche, Maria, 109

Ladislaus IV (Hungary), 80
Lafayette, Madame de, 8, 194–202
Lanyer, Aemilia, 177–78
Legrand, Jacques, 19
Lerma, Duke of, 68, 70–71
Les six livres de la République, 34
A Letter Written by a French Catholicke Gentleman, 174
Levin, Carole, 6–7
Liss, Peggy, 3, 50
Le Livre de la cité des dames, 22–24. *See also The Book of the City of Ladies*
Logan, Sandra, 8
Longshanks, Edmund, 170
Louis, duke of Orleans, 13, 15–16; Christine de Pizan and, 20–24; rumored affair with Isabeau of Bavaria, 13, 17–20
Louis I of Anjou, 80, 88
Louis II (Hungary), 80
Louis XII (France), 18
Louis XIV (France), 8, 46, 55, 195, 201–2
The Lyfe of the Most Godly, Valeant and Noble Capteine and Maintener of the Trew Christian Religion in Fraunce, Iasper Colignie Shatilion, Sometime Greate Admirall of Fraunce, 179–80

Malte, Ethelreda, 137–38
Malte, John, 137
Marc Antoine, 187
Margaret of Austria, 3, 67–68, 71
Margaret of Parma, 115
Marguerite [Margot] de Valois (France), 40, 116
María, Empress (Spain), 65, 67, 104
Maria Christierna of Habsburg, 81
Maria Teresa (Spain), 46, 55
Marie de Lorraine, 3
Marot, Clément, 31
marriage: adultery and, 13, 17–19, 47–48, 84–85, 197; arranged, 82–84; children and, 13; Church of England and, 129–31; cosovereignty in, 64–67; finances and, 82–83, 90–91; love and, 64, 68–69, 164–71; political reasons for, 30–31, 48–49, 55, 85–86, 92–93, 104, 116, 165, 196; problems in, 36–37; responsibility to produce heirs and, 109–11; rituals, 62n33; symbolism and, 44–46, 51–54; unification of kingdoms through, 48–49. *See also* children
Martin, Randall, 180
Martínez Silíceo, Juan, 103
Martin-Ulrich, Claudie, 34
Mary, Queen of Scots, 3, 32, 109, 130, 150, 156, 174, 200–201; execution of, 6, 8–9, 196, 201, 204n10; imprisonment of, 133, 151
Mary of Habsburg, 80
Mary Stuart. *See* Mary, Queen of Scots
Mary I (England), 3, 6–7, 9, 32, 109, 129–30,

166, 172–73n16, 197, 203n3; claim to throne, 165–66; death of, 129; Edward VI and, 123–24; Elizabeth I and, 126–29, 150–51, 156n34, 197–98; literary portrayals of, 196–97, 200–201; marriage of, 104, 111, 120n39, 128; religious beliefs of, 129; siblings of, 7, 123–30
Mary Tudor: Juana of Austria and, 104, 111, 120n39
Mascarenhas, Leonor de, 103
Matthias Corvinus, 80
Matthias of Habsburg, Archduke, 104
Mauss, Marcel, 143
Maximilian II (Austria), 65, 104
mediators, women as, 15–16, 22–23, 25–26, 74–76
Medici, Catherine de, 2–3, 8, 18, 200; Anne Dowriche on, 180; children of, 111–13; Elizabeth I and, 130, 182–83; Jeanne D'Albret and, 31, 33–34, 38; Juana of Austria and, 109, 115–16; as a Machiavellian ruler, 180–81
Medicis, Marie de, 181
Medina, Pedro de, 113
memoirs. *See* writers, women
Mendoza, Íñigo de, 55–56
A Mervaylovs Discourse Vpon the Lyfe, Deedes, and Behauiours of Katherine de Medicis, Queene Mother, 180–82
Mikó, Ferenc, 87
military actions, 106, 170–71, 182, 191n23
Miller, Nancy, 196, 198
Mira de Amescua, Antonio, 104
Mois, Rolam del, 109
Montaigu, Jean de, 20
Montemayor, Jorge de, 107
More, Thomas, 176, 186
More, William, 151
Morgan, Hiram, 136
Mornay, Charlotte Arbaleste de la Borde de, 39–40
Mornay, Philippe de, 39–40, 174
Moro, Antonio, 109
Moura, Cristóbal de, 117
A Mouzell for Melastomus, 178
De mulieribus claris, 1–2
Murphy, Beverley, 131
Mussolini, Benito, 56

Naunton, Robert, 137, 141n37
Navarre, Marguerite de, 1, 5, 30–31
Navarro, Cristóbal, 113, 121n52
Nebrija, Antonio de, 51
Nemours, Duc de, 194–99
Newton, Judith, 46
Nicholls, Thomas, 176
Nicolaus, Grand Duke (Russia), 82
Niño y Laso, Rodrigo, 68
De nobilitate et praecellentia sexus foeminei, 3

Of the Laws of Ecclesiastical Polity, 176
Of the Nobilitie and Excellencie of Womankynde, 3
On Famous Women, 1–2
Orlin, Lena, 130
O'Roughan, Denis, 137
Ottoman Empire, 81, 88
Owen, George, 128

Palencia, Alfonso de, 50–51
Parker, Geoffrey, 105, 108
Parr, Katherine, 123–24, 138
Parry, Blanche, 148
Parry, Thomas, 131
Pastoralet, 17–18
Pateman, Carole, 175
Paul III, Pope, 107
Peckius, Petrus, 74–75
Pelican Portrait, 147, 154–55n20
Pérez, Joseph, 115
Perrot, John, 135–38
Perrot, Mary Berkeley, 135
Philip, Duke of Burgundy, 15–16, 21
Philip II (Spain), 6–7, 31, 73, 137; Anna of Austria and, 116; Isabel Clara Eugenia and, 64–66; Juana of Austria and, 105, 108; Juana of Castile and, 103–8, 111–12; Mary Tudor and, 111, 120n39; portraits of, 109
Philip III (Spain), 65, 67–68, 71, 116–17
Philip IV (Spain), 67, 72–76
Philip the Good (France), 17
Phoenix Portrait, 148
Pintoin, Michel, 17, 19
Pizan, Christine de, 1, 2, 4–5, 14, 17, 20–26, 179
politics: diets and, 85–87; marriage used in, 48–49, 55, 85–86, 92–93, 104, 116, 165, 196; propaganda and, 47–48, 59; religion and, 31–32, 87, 191n26; symbolism and, 45–46; women's writings on, 30, 32–39, 177–87
La Poncella de Francia, 54
portraits: Catherine of Brandenburg, *90–92,*

91–92; clothes depicted in, 145, *145;* Elizabeth I, 147–48, 154–55n20; Isabel de Valois, *112,* 113; Juana of Austria, 109
power: absolute, 196–202, 203n4; cosovereignty and, 64–70; of diets, 85–87; division of labor and, 49–50; loss of, 167–68; military actions and, 106, 170–71; shared, 43–44, 51–53; symbolism and, 46, 51–54. *See also* authority
Primo de Rivera, Pilar, 57–58
La Princesse de Clèves, 194–202
propaganda, 47–48, 59
Protestantism, 31–32, 38–40, 87, 108, 183–85; Church of England and, 125–26, 129
Pulgar, Fernando del, 51
Puteanus, Erycius, 71

The Queenes Visiting of the Campe at Tilsburie With Her Entertainment There, 182
Querelle de la Rose, 22

Radcliffe, Henry, 128
Rákóczi, George, 93
Reformation, the, 31–32, 38–39
religion: court conflicts over, 108, 119n20; imprisonment and, 37–39; Jesuits and, 107–8; national, 56–57, 108; politics and, 31–32, 87, 191n26; succession and, 125–26; translations of pamphlets from French to English, 174; violence and, 183–85, 192n32; Virgin Mary and, 21–24; writings on, 38–39
Renard, Simon, 128
Richards, E. Jeffrey, 24
Richard III (England), 157
rituals, marriage, 62n33
Rodríguez, Alonso, 113
Roman de la Rose, 22
Rosenfeldt, Deborah, 46
Roser, Isabel, 107
Roussel, Gérard, 31
Rubens, Peter Paul, 75
Rudolf II (Austria), 66
Rueda, Lope de, 113

Sade, Marquis de, 18
Salmon, J. H. M., 174
Salve Deus Rex Judaeorum, 178
Sánchez, Magdalena S., 6
Sánchez Coello, Alonso, 109
Scanlon, Larry, 25
Scudamore, Mary, 152
Sebastián (Portugal), 104, 111, 116, 118n6
The Secret History of Alancon and Queen Elizabeth, 204n10
Serres, Jean de, 174, 179–80
Seymour, Edward, 134, 165–67
Seymour, Jane, 131
Seymour, Thomas, 124–25, 138
Shakespeare, William, 158, 161–64, 175, 182
Shelton, Anne, 152
Sidney, Mary, 175, 187
Sidney, Philip, 174, 176, 184
Sigismund, John, 82
The Six Books of the Republic, 34
Smeaton, Mark, 125
Smith, Thomas, 187
Smuts, R. Malcolm, 146
Somerset, Edward, 125, 129
Speght, Rachel, 178
Spínola, Ambrosio, 72, 74–75
Stafford, Pauline, 9
Staley, Lynn, 25
Stephan III of Bavaria, 14
Stephen V (Hungary), 80
Strassburger, Paul, 82
Stubbs, John, 176, 183–84
Suzuki, Mihoko, 8
A Sweet Nosegay, 175
symbolism: coats of arms and, 44–46, 51–56, 60n6; sovereignty and, 68–70

Talbot, Elizabeth, 150, 156n34
Teresa of Ávila, Saint, 57
Thibault, Marcel, 19
Timme, Thomas, 174, 180
Tragedie of Mariam, 178, 187
Transylvania, Principality of, 81–82, 85–87, 94n7
Treaty of Arras, 13, 17
Treaty of Troyes, 13, 16–17, 20, 159–60
Tudor, Edmund, 157, 159
Tudor, Owen, 158–59, 161, 164–71
Turvey, Roger, 135
Twelfth Night, 175
Tyrwhitt, Robert, 124–25

Utopia, 176, 186

Valdés, Fernando de, 108, 119n20
Valera, Diego de, 50
Vallet de Viriville, Auguste, 19
van der Straaten, Jooris, 109
van Veen, Otto, 69

Vásquez, Gaspar, 113
Velásquez, Jerónimo, 113
violence, religious, 183–85, 192n32
Virgin Mary, 21–24
Visconti, Thaddea, 14
Vitoria, Tomás Luis de, 108
Vives, Juan Luis, 3

Warnicke, Retha, 131–32
Watkins, John, 204n10
Weber, Max, 34
Webster, John, 175
Weissberger, Barbara, 3, 5
Wendy, Thomas, 128
Weston, Richard, 74
White, Micheline, 175
Whitney, Isabella, 175
Whitrowe, Joan, 187
Wiesner-Hanks, Merry, 1
Wilkinson, Maurice, 183
William of Orange, 115
William III (England), 177
Windebank, Thomas, 136
Wingfield, Anthony, 150–51
Wingfield, Elizabeth, 150–51
women rulers, 3, 25–26; absolute power and, 196–202, 203n4; adultery and, 13 17–19; associated with the Virgin Mary, 21–24; authority of, 34, 49, 168–69, 196–99; coats of arms of, 44–46, 51–56, 60n6; coronation cloth and, 142, 144–46; as cosovereigns, 64–66; courts of, 82–83, 90–91, 106, 108–9, 142–44, 147–48; criticism of, 180–84; defense of, 25–26; financial issues and, 82–83, 90–91; gift exchanges by, 142–44, 149–52, 155n29; historical accounts of, 1–3, 157–61, 164–71; imprisonment of, 37–39; interconnectedness across nations, 157–58; jewels worn by, 147–48, 151–52, 153n9; as judges, 50–51; literary portrayals of, 158, 161–71, 177–82, 194–202; as mediators, 15–16, 22–23, 25–26, 74–76; military actions and, 106, 170–71, 182, 191n23; misperceptions about, 20–24; modern scholarship on, 24–26; opposition to, 88–93; propaganda used by, 47–48; relationships with siblings, 123–25, 132–38; religion and, 31–32, 37–39, 56–57, 183–84; resignations of, 93; responsibility to produce heirs, 109–11; secular interests of, 104–6, 108–9, 112–15; self-satisfaction of, 39–41; writings dedicated to, 54–55. *See also* writers, women
writers, women: collaborations with men, 175; letters to their children, 39–40; letters to their spouses, 96n27; on loss of sovereignty, 67–68; political, 30, 32–39, 177–87; published after death, 39–40; readers of, 34–35; on religion, 38–39; self-satisfaction expressed by, 39–41. *See also* d'Albret, Jeanne; Dowriche, Anne; Cary, Elizabeth; Cellier, Elizabeth; Elizabeth Tudor (Elizabeth I England); Fell Fox, Margaret; James, Elinor; Lafayette, Madame de; Lanyer, Aemilia; Navarre, marguerite de; Pizan, Christine de; Sidney, Mary; Speght, Rachel; Whitrowe, Joan
Wyatt's Revolt, 128, 203n3

Yarza Luaces, Joaquín, 45

Zanger, Abby, 46, 55

Contributors

TRACY ADAMS is a senior lecturer in French at the University of Auckland, New Zealand. She is the author of *Violent Passion: Managing Love in the Old French Verse Romance* (2005). Her monograph on Isabeau of Bavaria is forthcoming from Johns Hopkins University Press.

ANNE J. CRUZ is a professor of Spanish and former chair of Modern Languages and Literatures at the University of Miami. She is the author of *Discourses of Poverty: Social Reform and the Picaresque Novel in Early Modern Spain* (1999) and has published extensively on Petrarchism, Cervantes, and gender in early modern Spain. She has edited *Symbolic and Material Circulation Between Spain and England, 1554–1604* (2008) and *Approaches to Teaching* Lazarillo de Tormes *and the Picaresque Tradition* (2008). She is the editor of Hispanisms, a series with the University of Illinois Press.

ÉVA DEÁK recently completed her PhD in the program "History of Central, Southeastern and Eastern Europe" at the Central European University in Budapest, Hungary. Her dissertation, "Expressing Elite Status Through Clothing in Early Modern Europe: The Examples of Gabriel Bethlen and Catherine of Brandenburg," examines representation through clothing in the princely court of Transylvania between 1613 and 1630. She is currently working as a research assistant in the Open Society Archive in Budapest.

MARY C. EKMAN is an associate professor of French at the State University of New York at New Paltz. She holds a PhD in French and a certificate in Women's Studies from the University of Michigan and has published articles on early modern memoirs and French and Francophone women's autobiography of the twentieth century. Current research interests include women's autobiography and first-person fictional narrative, travel writing, and food in early modern French literature.

CATHERINE L. HOWEY is an assistant professor of Women's and Gender History to 1750 at Eastern Kentucky University. She recently received her PhD from Rutgers, The State University of New Jersey, and is currently working on turning her 2007 dissertation, "Busy Bodies: Women, Power, and Politics at the Court of Elizabeth I, 1558–1603," into a book examining the ways Elizabethan court women participated in court politics and helped fashion Elizabeth's monarchical image.

ELIZABETH KETNER is an assistant professor of English at the State University of New York in Plattsburgh. She received her PhD from the University of Minnesota in 2008 and is working to turn her dissertation, "Memory, Monarchy, and Identity on the 'Scepter'd Isle': Constructing Identity Through Historical Fiction in Renaissance England and France," into a book exploring the diverse, ambivalent images of England's and France's monarchal past and the writing of national identity in historical fiction.

CAROLE LEVIN is Willa Cather Professor of History at the University of Nebraska. She is the author of *The Heart and Stomach of a King: Elizabeth I and the Politics of Sex and Power* (1994), *The Reign of Elizabeth I* (2002), *Dreaming the English Renaissance: Politics and Desire in Court and Culture* (2008), and (with John Watkins) *Shakespeare's Foreign Worlds: National and Transnational Identities in the Elizabethan Age* (2009).

SANDRA LOGAN is an associate professor of English at Michigan State University, specializing in early modern historiography, drama, and rhetoric. She is the author of *Text/Events in Early Modern England: Poetics of History* (2007) and articles on Shakespearean drama, science and literature, gender, and national identity. Her current research includes projects on mediation in Shakespearean drama and silent film, and on sovereignty and state violence.

MAGDALENA S. SÁNCHEZ is an associate professor of History at Gettysburg College and the author of *The Empress, the Queen, and the Nun: Women and Power at the Court of Philip III of Spain* (1998). She also contributed an essay entitled "Court Women in the Spain of Velázquez" to the *Cambridge Companion to Diego Velázquez* (2001). She is continuing her research on Isabel Clara Eugenia, particularly her early life at the Spanish court of Philip II.

MIHOKO SUZUKI is a professor of English and the director of the Center for the Humanities at the University of Miami. She is the author, most recently, of *Subordinate Subjects: Gender, the Political Nation, and Literary Form in England, 1588–1688* (2003), and co-editor of *Debating Gender in Early Modern England, 1400–1700* (2002) and *Women's Political Writings, 1610–1725* (4 vols., 2007). Her current projects include volume 3 of the *Palgrave History of British Women's Writing* (1610–1690) and *Antigone's Example*, a study of women and civil war in early modern England and France.

BARBARA F. WEISSBERGER is an associate professor of Spanish, Emerita, at the University of Minnesota. She is the author of *Isabel Rules: Constructing Queenship, Wielding Power* (2004), winner of the 2006 La Corónica International Book Award, and editor of *Queen Isabel I of Castile: Power, Patronage, Persona* (2008). Her research and publications focus on gender ideology in fifteenth-century Castilian literature.

The University of Illinois Press
is a founding member of the
Association of American University Presses.

Composed in 10.5/13 Adobe Minion Pro
with Adobe Minion Pro display
by Celia Shapland
at the University of Illinois Press
Manufactured by Cushing-Malloy, Inc.

University of Illinois Press
1325 South Oak Street
Champaign, IL 61820-6903
www.press.uillinois.edu